SIGNATURE

DISTINCTLY HALLMARK. DISTINCTLY YOU.

INSIDE MESSAGE:

Every size!
Every color!
Every minute of the day!

Happy Birthday

Hallmark Cares
Visit Hallmark.com/ourplanet

MAY REQUIRE EXTRA POSTAGE.

LAD1503 $6.99

7 20473 73689 2

Beyond Patronage

Reconsidering Models of Practice

Martha Bohm

Joyce Hwang

Gabrielle Printz

Beyond Patronage
Reconsidering Models of Practice

Editors
Martha Bohm, Joyce Hwang, Gabrielle Printz

Published by
Actar Publishers
New York, 2015

A publication of
University at Buffalo School of Architecture and Planning (Buffalo)
http://ap.buffalo.edu

Graphic Designer
Joel Brenden

Cover design
Joel Brenden

Distributed by
Actar D
New York
355 Lexington Ave., 8th FL,
NY, NY 10017
T 212-966-2207
F 212-966-2214
www.actar-d.com
eurosales@actar-d.com

Acknowledgements
This publication was made possible, in part, by the University at Buffalo School of Architecture
and Planning and the New York State Council on the Arts, Architecture, Planning and Design
Program, Independent Projects Grant; with Storefront for Art and Architecture as Fiscal
Sponsor; with the support of Governor Andrew Cuomo and the New York State Legislature.

Printed and Bound in China

ISBN 978-1-940291-18-5
A CIP catalogue record for this book is available from the Library of Congress, Washington D.C., USA.

Table of Contents

Preface

Despina Stratigakos

One hundred years ago, the catastrophe on European battlefields
convinced many progressive architects that, when peace returned, their
old ways of practicing would no longer be adequate for a changed
world. In 1919, a group of thirteen German architects and artists
formed the Crystal Chain, a letter exchange that explored in words and
drawings the built shape of a future society. This correspondence,
though utopian in nature, generated ideas that were partly realized in
the radical modernist architecture of the Weimar Republic.

All the members of the Crystal Chain were men. Yet before the First
World War, female architects and clients in Berlin experienced their
own period of intense conversations, in which they imagined a place
that would make room for their changing lives as women began to seek
higher education and careers. The first women to graduate from architecture programs in Germany in this same era enjoyed little of the
patronage that their male colleagues took for granted. Their careers
depended on rethinking conventional practices and creating new forms
of architectural partnerships, often with female clients who sought
help to define new urban spaces where they could feel at home. These
collaborations were both utopian, in imagining a future city built for
gender equality, and pragmatic, addressing immediate physical needs
for shelter.

Although it may be more difficult to pinpoint a single factor that
has necessitated a rethinking of architectural practice today,
few architectural graduates would disagree that such a reformula-
tion is necessary in the face of decades of accumulated changes that
have eroded or shifted older forms of public, corporate, church, and
private patronage. The contributors to this volume are acutely aware
of living in a 'post' world: post-industrial, post-bubble economy,
post-Kyoto Protocol. Like the Crystal Chain architects or the women
builders in Imperial Berlin, they grasp the possibilities of working
experimentally in an altered landscape. Their practices are less
reactive than they are an engine of transformation.

The School of Architecture and Planning at the University at Buffalo,
founded in 1967, began at a time when many young people around the
world, including architects, were similarly questioning the values and
habits they had inherited. That radical spirit guided the creation of
a new type of architecture school in Buffalo and continues to shape
the ethos of its research and teaching today. The Gender Institute at
the University at Buffalo, although a more recent addition to campus,
has become integral to promoting research on gender and women and
providing a forum to disseminate the work and awareness of female
innovators across disciplines. The 2012 Martell "Beyond Patronage"
symposium, organized by Joyce Hwang, Martha Bohm, Shannon Phillips,
and Gabrielle Printz, represented a collaboration between the
Gender Institute and the School of Architecture and Planning around
a common goal: to foster an exchange of ideas among practitioners

redefining contemporary architectural patronage and to highlight the important role that women have had and continue to play in expanding the profession's boundaries. While we recognized that both of these subjects separately merit greater attention in the discourses of architecture, the symposium arose out of the realization that there was a void at their intersection. Although gender itself was not explicitly a theme of the symposium, the presence of a new generation of female practitioners challenging the norms of the profession underscored a forgotten legacy in architecture, where women have typically been considered outsiders and have used this position, out of necessity or choice, to unsettle the status quo.

Extending the symposium's discussions, the essays and interviews gathered here foster creative disruption through an exploration of the dynamics between imagination and practice. Their search unfolds under the guise of three identities: the architect as initiator, detective, and advocate. While each possesses qualities that arguably have long been claimed by progressive designers, more fully stepping into an alternative role sharpens the possibilities of redrawing the lines of conventional architect-patron relationships. Thus the architect as initiator models herself on the entrepreneur, actively seeking out undeveloped markets and investors for experimental built processes and forms. The architect as detective foregrounds her forensic skills to make visible hidden social and environmental conditions, creating previously unforeseen possibilities for design projects. And the architect as advocate reaches out to groups and individuals often neglected by big "A" architecture to identify a new clientele and encourage partnerships with local communities. By repositioning architectural practice in this manner, the book's contributors move beyond traditional modes of patronage to embrace the very real challenges — and opportunities — of the twenty-first century.

School of Architecture and Planning

2012 MARTELL
SYMPOSIUM
BEYOND
PATRONAGE

RECONSIDERING MODELS
OF PRACTICE

10/16/2012

OPENING DISCUSSION: **"Student as Instigator"**
reception to follow / 5:30 PM

GREATBATCH PAVILION
DARWIN MARTIN HOUSE COMPLEX
125 JEWETT PKWY
BUFFALO, NY 14214

(RSVP online)

10/17/2012

Welcome and coffee / 9:00 AM

SESSION I: **"Architect as Initiator"** / 10:00 AM

BREAKOUT SESSION: **"Pro Bono Work"** / 11:45 AM
presented by Buffalo Architecture Foundation

SESSION II: **"Architect as Detective"** / 2:00 PM

SESSION III: **"Architect as Advocate"** / 4:30 PM

Remarks by Lori Brown (Syracuse) / 6:00 PM

105 HARRIMAN HALL
UB SOUTH CAMPUS
3435 MAIN STREET
BUFFALO, NY 14214

All are welcome to a closing reception / 7:30 PM

KLEINHANS MUSIC HALL
3 SYMPHONY CIRCLE
BUFFALO, NY 14201

(RSVP online)

ARCHITECT AS

INITIATOR
LINDA TAALMAN, Taalman Koch Architecture
HANSY BETTER BARRAZA, Studio Luz

DETECTIVE
NATALIE JEREMIJENKO, xDesign Clinic
JULIETTE SPERTUS, Fast Trash
GEORGEEN THEODORE, Interboro Partners

ADVOCATE
LOLA SHEPPARD, Lateral Office
YOLANDE DANIELS, Studio Sumo

Additional Participants / Moderators
DENISE JURON-BORGESE
BHAKTI SHARMA
JOY KUEBLER
KATHY CALLESTO
COURTNEY CREENAN
JOYCE HWANG
MARTHA BOHM
STEPHANIE DAVIDSON
GABRIELLE PRINTZ

#BEYONDPATRONAGE
@BEYONDPATRONAGE
BEYONDPATRONAGE.WORDPRESS.COM

Buffalo University at Buffalo *The State University of New York* UB Gender Institute B/a+p

BEYOND PATRONAGE: RECONSIDERING MODELS OF PRACTICE

Joyce Hwang, Martha Bohm

One could argue that the profession of architecture has traditionally been characterized by patronage. Throughout the twentieth century, wealthy private clients have enabled architects to develop and realize their most significant work. Relationships between Edgar Kaufmann and Frank Lloyd Wright, Pierre Savoye and Le Corbusier, František Müller and Adolf Loos, and Phyllis Lambert and Mies van de Rohe are only a few of the many examples.

Today, the landscape of patronage is shifting. While the role of private clients is still central to the survival of the profession, an increasing number of architects and design practitioners are actively cultivating partnerships with not-for-profits, granting agencies, educational institutions, and other public organizations. At a moment when architects are feeling the urgent effects of sustained economic crises, facing both a surplus of practitioners and a dearth of clients, they are beginning to question the conventional belief that the only viable role for an architect is one that operates as a service-oriented professional in the employ of a moneyed client.

Why move beyond patronage?

Over several decades, the architectural profession has responded to three key challenges embedded in conventional modes of patronage-based practice. Practitioners have arguably begun moving beyond patronage while seeking ways of bringing about architectures which reflect a more progressive set of values and priorities in the realms of ecology, economics, and equity.

First, from the emergence of the environmental movement in the late 60s, to the rise in the 90s of the current sustainability effort, there has been a growing understanding that the natural environment is adversely affected by normative patterns of development. Architecture has several times over developed modes of working where conservation, or indeed even regeneration of the natural environment through the creation of built work, is an objective of design. While sustainable design has entered the mainstream mode of architectural practice, some practitioners have gone further, essentially reconstructing their work around the environment as ultimate 'client.' This reframing broadens the role and purview of the designer to understand and engage consequences and externalities typically unaddressed in her work, and allows the instigation of design for a non-traditional (and non-paying) patron.

A second challenge facing architecture is the powerlessness of the profession against economic fluctuations. Exacerbated by recent decades' celebration of "starchitects" as high-profile members of a design noblesse is the perception of architecture as a luxury good, one for which investment is cut back when belts tighten generally. The recession sparked by the 2008 financial crisis hit the profession hard in the US; as of 2012 several signs pointed to recovery, and architectural unemployment, while higher than typical for recent graduates, had begun to fall (European firms, on the other hand, continued to struggle). While the recent ebb is more extreme than others, the economies of the profession are cyclic, and lean times breed inventiveness.

In our eyes, a last significant challenge to the profession is the glaring inequity between the haves (the profession's typical patrons and clients) and the have-nots — or, put another way, between the wealthiest 1% who can afford architectural services, and the 99% who cannot. Responses to this might be traced back as far as the social programs of early Modernism, or to the global awareness concurrent with the environmental awakening of the '60s. Practitioners have recognized that those who cannot afford their services do still need them, and many more *beyond patronage* practices have arisen since the economic crisis.

Emerging Questions

The emergence and proliferation of these new, dynamic relationships in contemporary architectural practices incite a number of questions: How are these broader relationships between architects and organizations redefining the role of patronage in architecture? How have emerging forms of patronage shaped or enabled design practices, influenced design processes, or instigated agendas of research within the work of architects? Have our current economic, ecological, and political climates provoked architecture to confront its own priorities and assumptions? If so, how are architects rethinking models of practice? How can the practice of architecture be shaped not only through relationships of power, but also through strategies of empowerment?

What are emerging trajectories of reconsidering 'patronage' — and their processes and consequences — in architectural and design practices today?

To explore these questions, we initiated a platform for discussion in 2012: The Martell Symposium — Beyond Patronage: Reconsidering Models of Practice. This was a full-day event, held at the University at Buffalo, State University of New York, to which we invited a number of architects, designers, and scholars to speak about their work. While there were many overlaps in approaches and agendas among the participants, we developed three distinct categories of 'architect-types' to organize the day. These were:

1. Architect as Initiator:

These are architects who enable their practices by restructuring project and business models to initiate new ways of approaching architectural practice. In the symposium, the speakers in this session — Linda Taalman and Hansy Better Barraza — discussed strategies for creative entrepreneurship, ways of initiating exploratory projects alongside conventional business structures, and how innovative collaborations enable new design possibilities.

2. Architect as Detective:

These are architects who deploy strategies for critical observation and research to reveal the unknown. In their work, they visualize the invisible to make the case for instigating projects where opportunities did not previously exist. The speakers in this session — Georgeen Theodore, Juliette Spertus, and Natalie Jeremijenko — discussed how researching hidden conditions can lead to opportunities for further design engagement.

3. Architect as Advocate:

These are architects who critically consider the clients and audiences they serve. They reach out to communities and individuals beyond our conception of the 'typical' client, and discover 'clients' where none were thought to exist. The speakers in this session — Lola Sheppard and Yolande Daniels — discussed projects wherein they attempted to advocate for under-represented 'client bases.'

Lori Brown concluded the symposium by examining the parallels and convergences of this group of speakers, and the potential futures of reconsidering patronage in architectural practices. An underlying current in the symposium addressed issues of gender imbalance in the profession of architecture — very poignantly summarized by Lori's talk

— and how emerging practitioners are grappling with issues of inclusion and exclusion in the field.

This book is, in part, a documentation and reflection of the Beyond Patronage symposium. But it is also a forum for expanding the discussion to invoke new ideas and voices. Through a collection of essays and conversations, our hope is that this volume will tackle two somewhat divergent aims.

First, we want to convey a body of collective knowledge of how one might explore alternative strategies for 'operating' as an architect. What are the salient tactics and methods that designers are pursuing in their practices today? For example, what new forms of connectivity — technological or social — produce innovative modes of collaboration? What are ways of cultivating relationships that allow us to rethink typical hierarchies of those in power and those in service? How does one initiate projects that are not driven by consumer agendas, but instead address interests of "The Other 99%?" What are strategies for transcending the typically exclusive networks of 'advancement' in the field of architecture?

Second, we want to develop an anthology that highlights an inspiring group of designers and thinkers. The contributors to this book drive their practices with intense social, political, and ecological agendas. Yet their sense of purpose does not end with speculation and theory. Rather, they are activists who interrogate the terrain of architectural practice by realizing projects, constructing relationships, and activating communities in the world.

Through this anthology, we expose and initiate new priorities and strategies for architecture as a field of research and practice. Architect as Initiator, Architect as Detective, and Architect as Advocate are categories that serve as frameworks for discussion. But they can also begin to act as provocations in developing an increasingly diverse range of possibilities for how architects construct their roles, responsibilities, and ultimately, identities.

Stephanie Davidson

The current wave of "design entrepreneurship"[1] or "creative capitalism"[2] demonstrates that the kind of skills relevant to architectural design can be successfully expanded into the realms of business and commerce. Whether it is a matter of cobbling together a bare-bones budget to realize a small, one-off project, or developing partnerships and strategies for working at a larger scale, on longer-term projects, architects are—out of necessity and by choice—revising traditional ideas of how architecture is practiced, and more specifically, redefining the relationships between clients and architects.

The Architect-as-Initiator, though not a new model, has become a more prevalent mode of practice for architects working within a context of economic uncertainty and precarious employment. The recession of 2008 disrupted conventional models of professional employment, which largely consisted of architects working in commercial offices. Unlike precedents from the 1990s, when design offices shifted toward representational forms of production, or so-called paper architecture, and away from 'professional' practices because of a lack of concrete opportunities, architects today are proving to be extremely tenacious in their pursuit of building opportunities. Contemporary practitioners are overcoming the limits of a stale market and are using web-based platforms such as YouTube, Vimeo, Facebook, Kickstarter, Twitter, and even Airbnb to generate wide exposure for their ideas. These web-based platforms for exposure have become, for many architects today, new media for both marketing and funding, allowing architects to build what would have most likely remained as ideas on paper only twenty years ago.

In this series of profiles, I describe a variety of Architects-as-Initiators: the Architect-Fundraiser, the Architect-Do-It-Yourselfer, the Architect-Developer, and the Architect-Artist. All of these practitioners demonstrate a heightened level of entrepreneurial engagement, self-reliance, and commitment to see their projects through to realization, characteristics that seem to typify "Gen Flux"[3] architects. These profiles reveal that what is relevant in architecture today is not only the design work itself, but also equally interesting and significant is *how* architects get their jobs done.

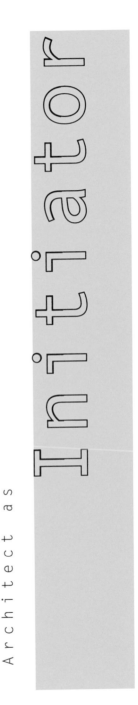

Architect as Initiator

Architect-Fundraiser

This model of practice is extremely optimistic, and relies on a project's presumed popular appeal for its success. Architect-Fundraisers are able to put together proposals that garner donations, often through crowdsourcing, to realize an undertaking. A current example of a practice working on a large, visionary project that uses this model is the Family + PlayLab team (Dong-Ping Wong, Archie Lee Coates, Jeffrey Franklin) with their +POOL project,[4] a fundraising success story for a large-scale public project. The idea of +POOL is simple: it is a public pool in the Hudson River, with views of the iconic New York City skyline. Designed as four pools in one (a Kids' pool, Sports pool, Lap pool and Lounge pool), each can be used independently, combined to form an Olympic-length pool or opened completely into a 9,000 square foot pool for play. Also central to the design of +POOL is water filtration, a tactic to transform the polluted river waters to swimmable blue waters, as shown in the visualizations. More striking than the project itself, however, are the fundraising skills of the design team. Posted on Kickstarter, the project, with 3,175 backers, exceeded its funding goal of $250,000 and raised $273,114 in just 30 days. The designers integrated the fundraising with the design of the pool, offering potential backers nine different ways in which recognition of their support could be incorporated into the realization of the project, depending on the amount of their contribution. For the base pledge of $25, for example, a donor gets her name engraved on a +POOL tile alongside seven other randomly selected names, receives a certificate reserving a spot at the pool, and has her name included as an official backer on the +POOL website. The designers generated hype by stating: "[Your] tile will be there with your name permanently etched into the history of making the world's first water-filtering floating pool."[6] The highest pledge tier of $9,999 or more received no backers, but the second highest, $2,500, received a handful of supporters, and came with a more extensive sponsor recognition package: logo engraving on a tile and free passes to the pool, among other benefits. With most donors contributing between $25 and $200, the appeal of the +POOL as a Kickstarter campaign seems to have been how a large, visionary, public project can be made accessible and affordable to individuals. Also remarkable was the idea that individuals can contribute to realizing a project such as a public pool, which is normally civic in nature and governed by a tight and often closed bidding process, managed by municipal agencies.

Architect-Do-It-Yourselfer

The Do-It-Yourselfer model of practice is characterized by architects who are able to find the means, and have the skills, to realize projects for themselves, by themselves. One might argue that the do-it-yourself ethos has been pervasive in the North American context, rendering the Architect-Do-It-Yourselfer somewhat unremarkable. But there is a big difference between renovating one's own kitchen and initiating an extensive project by oneself. While many architects build their own houses, it is within the current post-recession context that the question of how to build something becomes more difficult to answer. Buffalo, NY artist-architect Dennis Maher is an example of a practitioner whose approach to realizing his work circumvents the need for an external client or a large budget. His mode of production—beginning with an intense process of collecting unwanted objects and urban artifacts, such as used, reclaimed, and repurposed building debris, furniture, and vestiges of domestic environments—is a primary driver in developing his large and on-going project, the Fargo House, both his own residence and what he calls "a center for the urban imagination."[7] Maher bought the then-abandoned, century-old house in 2009 from a local college for $10,000. Since then, he has used the house as the site of perpetual sculptural intervention—cutting through floors, reconfiguring existing building elements, and packing layer upon layer of used, found building materials within the space. Maher's approach to practice has also evolved into a self-sustaining funding system. After purchasing the property, he acquired much of the early seed money for the project by way of a home-equity loan from a local credit union. Because he purchased the house at a below-market price, it immediately had some capital value. This process of obtaining a loan, as straightforward as it may seem, was difficult and complicated due to the 'collaged' nature of the interior. Maher's application required a tour of the house by board members of the financial institution, who tried to discern which elements in the house were permanent and which elements were temporary. Maher explains that, "They wanted to know what was 'wall' and what was 'wall-treatment.' The appraiser's photographs were composed in a very different way from my own and, thus, revealed a different 'value.'"[8] After overcoming that initial hurdle, however, the house became an income generator in two different ways. First, Maher is consistently awarded arts stipends for exhibitions and continued work related to the house. Second, as objects are continually added, shifted and removed from the house, by-products splinter off in the form of smaller-scale sculptural works and collages. The sale of these works offers an additional source of income that, Maher says, "is necessary in order to sustain [the house's] transformations."[9]

Architect-Developer

This model of practice is a highly ambitious and complex one that requires skills and knowledge in real estate, property management, tax credits, development, and design, as well as sustained rootedness in a city. Practitioners working as Architect-Developers pursue projects in which they act as both the designer and developer: buying a property, building or renovating, and then leasing it to tenants. Following the dramatic 2008 financial crash in the United States, the real estate market was flooded with properties, and demand was low. Some real estate "sharks," naturally, took advantage of the housing market crash and picked up multiple properties. In an economically depressed city like Buffalo, cheap housing prices led to the notorious phenomenon of "flipping houses," where buyers (typically contractors or DIY renovators) acquired cheap, derelict houses, renovated them completely, and resold them, making a considerable profit. Similar to flippers, but often with a more altruistic intention to improve properties and revive neighborhoods, some architects jumped into real estate and became quasi-developers, combining ownership and design of residential and commercial properties. The Architect-Developer model has precedents elsewhere in the world, one being the Argentine system of *Fideicomiso*, a term that refers to a system where architects buy land and fund projects using monetary advances provided by future tenants. As a system that emerged after the economic collapse in Argentina in 2001,[10] Fideicomiso is not entirely unlike crowdfunding. In it, contributors have a stake in a project via the architect. In affordable cities such as Buffalo, the relatively low cost of property has enabled architects to buy buildings as investments without the need to pool the money of future users or tenants, but even so, the complexities of property development have propelled architect-developers, even in ultra-affordable cities, to gravitate toward the Fideicomiso model. As a case study, Buffalo-based architect Karl Frizlen has established a practice in which he has already self-funded, built, renovated and rented three multi-unit, mixed-use buildings in the city. His most recent projects, however, tend toward the Fideicomiso model. In his renovation of the locally-known "Horsefeathers Building"—a 25,000 square-foot brick building dating from 1896—Frizlen used the promise of obtaining a certain group of commercial tenants as a way of rousing interest, getting press coverage, and eventually obtaining financial backing. Initially, he experienced difficulty securing a construction loan due to the building's location on the West Side of Buffalo, a neighborhood that is experiencing a slow revival after decades of urban blight. Real estate appraisers were unable to show any local, comparable properties that supported the feasibility of Frizlen's proposal. Banks, as he describes, tend to be generally skeptical about mixed-use schemes. Eventually, Frizlen connected with a former representative of the local Community Preservation Corporation, who understood the tax credit system for buildings of historic value, and had (fortuitously for Frizlen) started to work for a local bank. It was that bank that then organized the loan for Frizlen, the sole developer in the $3.6 million project. Having been a key figure in operating a local foods market in Buffalo for years, Frizlen knew that there was a demand for high-quality local food, and saw the need for a less transient, year-round location for the sale of local goods. He was able to attract people involved in local food production as tenants in the building's commercial space, while also using the basement for a winter market. Like his other properties, the building houses rental units above the commercial space. Frizlen describes the ambitious model of Architect-Developer as a "creative juggling act," in which property management could be a full-time occupation itself.[11] Ultimately, it is a model of practice with high risk, requiring an extremely broad scope of knowledge and experience.

Architect-Artist

The Architect-Artist practice model is characterized by architects who search for grants, stipends, residencies, exhibitions, and sponsorships to fund independently-generated projects. While stipends for these kinds of programs are usually meager and cover only basic subsistence, accommodations, and access to studio space, they enable architects to pursue projects freely and without obligations to the funding bodies. This is a model that my partner, Georg Rafailidis, and I use in our practice. For years, we worked by hopping from one artist-in-residence (AIR) program to another in Europe and North America. Eventually, one of our built projects emerged from this process. Facilitated by an AIR program at Allenheads Contemporary Arts, a small arts facility in Northeast England, we developed Selective Insulation, a temporary construction that explored the potential of temperature to define space. To address the insufficient heating system of the facility itself (an old stone school house built in the 1800s), we defined small areas in the building that needed to be warm during the cold months of the year by designing warm 'pockets' of space within the existing uninsulated enclosure. The installation performed as a small warm room for sedentary or desk-related work, with

15

Above: Drawing of Float Lab, proposed use of Kickstarter funds from 2013 campaign, Family + PlayLab

Right: Rendering of +POOL showing engraved tiles, Family + PlayLab

Right: Fargo House, Room for the Image and Reflected Image, Dennis Maher

Below: Fargo House, street view at time of acquisition, Dennis Maher

Architect as Initiator

Above: Exterior of renovated
Horsefeathers building,
The Frizlen Group

Left: Interior of commercial
ground floor of Horsefeathers
building, The Frizlen Group

Left: Interior view of insulated
space, Davidson Rafailidis

Below: View from exterior of
Old School House building
into insulated space,
Davidson Rafailidis

Stephanie Davidson

its thermal enclosure defined by an insulating layer of double-ply bubblewrap, commonly used to insulate greenhouses. Self-built using modest means, the project demonstrates the extreme level of flexibility and resourcefulness that is required in the Architect-Artist model of practice. For practitioners who are available to travel and work in different locations for a month or two at a time, this practice model is ideal for exploring the seeds of an idea.

Conclusion

In any context, funding is a difficult and often complex subject. Questions of how one acquires funding, and how much is required or warranted, are not typically addressed in architectural discourse. But I argue that examining the logistics of how architects practice—or more specifically, how they pursue work that they find meaningful while making it financially viable—is both revealing and essential in advancing architecture as a field and as a profession. It is clear that in a time of precarious employment, architects have pulled their creative problem-solving skills into realms beyond design. Architects are making their own opportunities and emerging as initiators in various capacities. In terms of funding, they have been able to develop models of practice that no longer hinge entirely on the patronage of a client, but rather, have a financial strategy incorporated into ways of working, designing, and realizing projects. Architects with salespersonly qualities are harnessing the potential of crowdfunding. In terms of resources, Do-It-Yourselfers are working gradually by way of unconventional tactics, such as scavenging and collecting, to accumulate materials and implement methods of production over time. In terms of risk-taking, those who are willing and able to shoulder larger debt are taking on a developer role: investing in real estate, and designing renewed futures for older, often derelict buildings. In terms of planting seeds for future direction, architects are exploring ideas within the loose boundaries of the term "artist" and applying for artist grants, residencies and stipends in order to move speculation into the realm of realization. In this section, we feature two architects, Linda Taalman, partner of Taalman Koch Architects, and Hansy Better Barraza, partner of Studio Luz and co-founder of BR+A+CE, who exemplify the characteristics of Architects-as-Initiators. They are practitioners who take on the challenges of creative fundraising, unconventional resource strategies, and risk-taking investments to establish new opportunities and audiences.

NOTES

1. Jessica Karle Heltzel and Tim Hoover, *Kern and Burn: Conversations with Design Entrepreneurs* (2013), http://www.kernandburnbook.com/

2. Bruce Nussbaum, "Want To Know More About Bruce Nussbaum's Creative Capitalism? Read On," *Fast Company*, October 4, 2011, http://www.fastcodesign.com/1665140/want-to-know-more-about-bruce-nussbaums-creative-capitalism-read-on (Accessed June 6, 2014).

3. Dan Matthews, "Move over Gen X, 'Gen Flux' is here," *Your Better Business*, January 1, 2013, http://www.yourbetterbusiness.co.uk/move-over-gen-x-gen-flux-is-here/ (accessed June 6, 2014).

4. +POOL, http://www.pluspool.org/ (accessed June 6, 2014).

5. Kickstarter, "+POOL, Tile by Tile," https://www.kickstarter.com/projects/694835844/pool-tile-by-tile (accessed June 6, 2014).

6. Ibid.

7. The Fargo House, http://thefargohouse.com/ (accessed June 6, 2014).

8. Dennis Maher (Assembled City Fragments), in discussion with the author, August 2013.

9. Ibid.

10. Vanessa Quirk, "Fideicomiso: When Architects Become Developers (And Everybody Wins)," ArchDaily, April 25, 2013, http://www.archdaily.com/?p=364223 (accessed January 5, 2014).

11. Karl Frizlen (The Frizlen Group), in discussion with the author, August 2013.

PROJECT CREDITS

+POOL, New York, NY, USA, 2013-
Family (Dong-Ping Wong) + PlayLab (Archie Lee Coates, Jeffrey Franklin)

Fargo House, Buffalo, NY, USA, 2009-
Dennis Maher

Horsefeathers Building Renovation, Buffalo, NY, USA, 2013
The Frizlen Group (Karl Frizlen)

Selective Insulation, Hexham, UK, 2009
Davidson Rafailidis (Stephanie Davidson, Georg Rafailidis)

18

Searching for an Authentic Production

Hansy Better Barraza

The word "patron" derives from the Latin word *patronus,*
meaning "advocate," "defender," or "protector." This developed
in ancient Rome into the term "patronage," which describes a very
specific form of relationship between individuals or entities. In the
most traditional sense, monarchies, governments, and religious organizations have been part of the political patronage structure. For
the purposes of this text, I am going to consider the term "patron"
as a powerful social agent that commissions work to serve its agenda
or purpose. Given the traditional relationships I have just defined,
we may consider how the mutual obligations between *patron* and *client*
may be improved in order to serve a larger public good. I believe
that public commissioning entities have an obligation to serve public
interests, but, often in that process, end up promoting the status
quo, and not creating the best value for the communities they intend
to serve. By examining the traditional patronage structure, its
hierarchies, and its influence on the current 'democratic' selection process for designers, I hope to discover and suggest ways to
reform the current system; ultimately enabling more innovation and
increasing access to opportunities for people who wouldn't otherwise
have them.

Mattapan Food & Fitness
Vigorous Youth riders at the
Mattapan MBTA Station

In the award process of public sector projects (despite rhetoric about full transparency in the selections process), a younger, less-experienced designer or smaller design practice has great difficulty winning commissions. Breaking through traditional forms of hierarchy has its challenges as the process favors the status quo: those who have done it before, 'the tried and true' so to speak. Major structures are in place that create barriers to opportunity for emerging design practices. In requests for qualifications and requests for proposals in the United States, designers often are asked to prove tremendous amounts of experience in very narrowly-defined skill categories or hyper-specific building types. This categorization and attempt to quantify one's qualifications may have nothing to do with the complexity of the design or designer's expertise. Further, the designation of entire buildings as a certain 'type' is problematic. Most buildings are complex hybrids, serving various uses and constituencies. The selection process should recognize this. Most architects are skilled problem-solvers, with the ability to synthesize a wide range of programmatic 'types' and offer new ideas for a project's design and realization.

With the exception of some innovative programs that exist, such as the Design and Construction Excellence Program in New York City, there are few initiatives that create opportunities for talented, intelligent, and capable designers to receive a public commission. Here is where the understanding of traditional forms of patronage is helpful to note — there is another way to receive design commissions. If one is born lucky enough to be surrounded by a privileged community with access to a network of 'patrons' that can award private projects, then a designer can gain and exhibit relevant project experience. Expecting designers to rely on the largess of an established patronage system for opportunity, when not all have access to the system, is problematic. It calls to mind Mitt Romney's suggestion to "Borrow money from your parents" when starting out, revealing a naive assumption that all have access to familial wealth as he did."[1]

This attitude — that the public should not bear any investment and therefore risk in the development of innovative design — is the problem with the public system as it stands. If architecture is a reflection of the cultural, social, and political systems that enable it, then the 'public' must be invested in the intellectual infrastructure required to create architecture. After all, public institutions should strive to select projects that transcend 'quick return' market-driven solutions, given that their charge is development and stewardship of the built environment for the long term. Until that mindset permeates, we have to look for alternative models on which to base our arguments and create influence.

I would like to discuss emerging alternatives to the 'waiting for opportunities' game. The design profession is turning to new ways of generating work, including creating it from within through small-scale interventions, urban installations, and programs that re-map or re-activate the city. Independent design firms are conceiving of projects, raising capital, and fully realizing these, using crowd-sourcing, micro-grants, bake sales… using 'whatever means necessary' to get things done. These initiatives are creating eddies, and ultimately may begin to reverse the traditional flow of power and ideas. As patrons of their own work, they have the ability to bring the ethical responsibilities of design to consciousness over that which would otherwise be overshadowed by capital interests.

In our practice, we embrace this new form of patronage, to challenge the status quo of the design process, and rethink how various design ideas are ultimately realized. We search for an authentic production that is meaningful to the culture in which it operates. Throughout the design process, we ask ourselves how technology and social constructions enable us to reshape our relationship to cultural identity and architecture. With examples from two recent self-initiated projects, architecture can operate locally, while engaging in a wider-reaching conversation about power, economy, society, cultural identity, and their inherent instabilities.

In searching for an authentic production of architecture, I would like to offer three guiding principles that inspire our work:

1   *Do not channel technology from developed to developing sectors. Use only appropriate local technology.*

2   *Technology is only meaningful to the culture in which it operates.*

3   *Form is a resultant of shared experiences.*

REVERSE FLOW OF POWER AND IDEAS

Many buildings, technologies, and ideas have already been imposed on developing sectors. In contrast, we are interested in models that successfully reverse the usual flow of power and ideas. In seeking alternative ways in which information is learned and accessed as a means to expand the impact of our discipline, I am reminded of the famous representation of South America by the Uruguayan modernist Joaquín Torres-Garcia, the *Upside-down Map* (1943). It is a provocative map that attempts to reframe the world view of South America as an important continent, placing the South Pole at the top of the Earth. Torres-Garcia wanted to present South America as a "modern school of the south," a place of experimentation, as relevant as places like New York and Paris at the mid-twentieth century.[2] This simple re-orientation instigates a new image of South America pouring its influence onto the north.

There is much that architects can learn from people who have been ignored by mainstream authorities. Take, for example, the way in which the space of information technology and electronic communication is experienced in Latin America. It has a face, so to speak, and creates a place where socialization occurs, regardless of whether it is inside one's home or on the streetscape. The physical space required to purchase and use digital technology is often shared by many users. Internet and telecommunication spaces are social destinations for the community. For example, if you run out of cellular phone minutes, you can buy more from a seller on the street or at the corner store. Need access to the internet or a phone? With purchased minutes, one can reserve a space to sit and use a computer. Spaces to purchase minutes for telephone or internet use are everywhere, informally and formally. Locations of transactions — "This is where we should meet" — are broadcast on tee-shirts, at home, or at retail locations. These telecommunication spaces not only bring people together, but also provide access to technology and knowledge. What

at first may appear to be inconvenient or inefficient may actually be a means to enhance the social bonds of a community.[3] This stands in contrast to a large part of the United States, where the paradigm of individualism has led to personalization of space; shared resources no longer fit into the cultural or collective consciousness. This will become increasingly problematic as resources become more scarce. I find this to be telling of a larger set of conditions. We will have to ask: how can spaces be productive, effective and beautiful when communication exists over a virtual network and in isolation? I find the spatial experience of telecommunication in Latin America to be a valuable lesson. Spaces are meeting points of shared experiences; they are active and lived in by the user — not contemplative and isolated. It is the encounter of the other, a chance to negotiate, to share and exchange, which builds stronger bonds for a community.

In the Mattapan Mobile Farm Stand project, we were interested in the design of a community space that didn't have a fixed location, but created an itinerant meeting point of commercial and educational exchange. Mattapan is one of Boston's most diverse and underserved neighborhoods, with a population that is 90% non-white. It has very high rates of obesity (40%) according to 2010 data from the Boston Public Health Commission Research Office. In collaboration with local health advocacy groups, Mattapan Food & Fitness Coalition (MFFC) and Brookwood Community Farm, BR+A+CE, a 501c3 non-profit organization that my partner, Anthony Piermarini, and I co-founded in 2010, began tackling issues of equity, health, and nutrition through the design of a pedal-powered farm stand. BR+A+CE's role was to initiate the project, find partners, locate project sites in Mattapan, raise funds, coordinate fabrication of the mobile stand, and coordinate all partners to make the project a success.

Left: Rear view of the Mattapan Mobile Farm Stand at Ryan Playground

Above: Mattapan Food & Fitness Coalition Vigorous Youth rider driving across the train tracks at the Mattapan MBTA station

Our idea was simple: if people couldn't get to fresh food, we were going to bring fresh food to them. Mattapan has no full service grocery store. Given that it is a food desert, many residents rely on corner stores and, therefore, purchase unhealthful food. Not everyone has a car or easy access to public transportation, to travel to a typical farmer's market in the city center.

The pedal-powered mobile farm stand was designed to have moving parts for visual impact and functionality. In its most compact form, it transports 500 pounds of produce. Think ice-cream truck or the donkey-push cart meets Transformers. When open, its wings spread to provide shade from the sun. The Mattapan Food and Fitness Coalition and its youth arm, the Vigorous Youth, operate the mobile farm stand. Brookwood Community Farm, a working organic farm, is located a few miles away from Mattapan Square and provides the produce. The stand does business at a local public transit hub, a senior residence, and a popular playground, bringing attention to healthful foods, and promoting cycling as a healthful activity. To have a bigger impact on

Above: Detail view of produce bins

Center: Opening up the Mobile Farm Stand at the Mattapan MBTA parking station

Right: Displaying produce at the Mattapan Mobile Farm Stand at Ryan Playground

the community it serves, Mattapan residents and seniors can purchase produce from the mobile farm stand using SNAP benefits.[4] The idea was simple in its conception: we introduced mobility to increase access, instead of accepting the acquiescence that usually results from lack of access to fixed sites.

The next project co-opts forms of leisure to create casual encounters. During the design phase of the Big Hammock Project, I visited an indigenous community, the Wayuu at Rancheria de La Paz (The Peace), in northern Colombia. There was much of value to be learned from the Wayuu Community, a semi-nomadic indigenous community which resides in the Guajira region of Colombia, bordering Venezuela. They are one of the few indigenous groups that successfully resisted European domination. In the post-colonial period, the Wayuu have been displaced due to civil war and political instability. Many of them have been separated from their clans and have forgotten much

cultural history, artistic tradition, and social structure. Despite this, they have attempted to preserve and maintain their culture and way of life, blending the traditional with the new; they have adapted and transformed to survive. The traditional art of weaving is still practiced today by the Wayuu, and is a form of building construction. Their structures are woven from dried cactus hearts. Structures are nodal, open, and social. Each one is built around an activity, such as eating, sleeping, bathing, or communing. In essence, the buildings are reflections of the way they live. Take, for example, how the Wayuu weave their "chinchorros" (similar to hammocks but made of loose thread): they use the structure of their buildings, such as columns and beams, as looms. The Wayuu inspired me for the Big Hammock project and I borrowed their technology for the design of the loom, which was the structure itself. Once the hammock was woven on the site, the loom bars were removed from the structure and became the spreader bar, independent of the structure.

TECHNOLOGY, MEANING AND CULTURE

TECHNOLOGY: A manner of accomplishing a task esp. using technical processes, methods, or knowledge.

-Merriam Webster's Collegiate Dictionary

Technology is the making, creation of, or usage of tools and techniques to solve problems. We use technology to create solutions. For the design of our Mattapan Mobile Farm Stand, very simple elements were used in non-standard ways to make the farm stand more dynamic and adaptable. Basic fundamental technology was employed, so that the project would be easy to maintain by a community with few resources. We used very simple metal fabrication techniques, common tube steel and sheet metal, interchangeable gas spring hardware, and hinges to make an operable or transforming stand. With limited resources, the mobile farm stand can be maintained by any local bike shop with basic tools.

Human-powered technology is a sustainable alternative to conventional options. For the Wayuu, tools advance in response to community needs, and are often hybridized with the architecture. For example, a structural column and beam may be sized not only for the bearing capacity of the building, but also in accord with the weight, size, technique, and ergonomics of weaving their large textiles. Here it is evident that technology is only meaningful to the culture in which it operates. Martin Heidegger provides a broader context for technology in his discussion of the hammer as a link in a network of interconnected activity, or a "totality of involvements" as he describes it.[5] It is only when something goes wrong — the hammer is broken — that we become aware of the object at work, the broken link. The existence of hammers and doorknobs is only consequential in the social context of wood construction and homes. Like what Heidegger calls "being-in-the-world,"[6] technology is thus always interconnected to its purposefulness. Its role as an instrument is invariably bound to its role in enabling meaningful human activity and engagement in the world.

Similarly, there is a hybridization of structure and the process of making in the Big Hammock. A new piece of urban art and furniture was woven over a four day period on the site of a public green space. The spreader bar and shuttle were tools we had to make to weave the large hammock on site. The suspension system for the hammock was conceived as the loom itself, and designed such that it could be assembled and disassembled using only hand tools. The only heavy machinery commissioned was the delivery truck. The hammock was woven directly on the suspension frame, then released and allowed to swing. The four day process of on-site weaving made people aware not only of the labor invested but also the craft required in weaving. It communicated the potential of the greenway site as a rich public space for leisure. It negotiated the formality, scale, and distance of that space such that people could engage with each other in a neighborly and friendly way. It brought people together so they could strike up conversations. The program was geared toward inclusiveness; it provided a social ground where strangers came together to share their stories and experiences.

CULTURE AND ITS RELATIONSHIP
TO THE PRODUCTION OF ARCHITECTURE

Our cultural experiences and our identity shape how we think about and produce architecture. I'm Colombian, and a descendant of three different races: Black, Indian and White. In the United States, I am Hispanic or, at times when I want to emphasize my gender, I say I am Latina. I live in two worlds, between Colombia and the US, and I'm linked to those places through the web. Linking the global to the local was an opportunity where my culture, identity, ethnicity, and my race could be explored and shared with others through the construction of the hammock. The object itself didn't explicitly speak on issues of race and identity, but provided a space in the city that broke boundaries, avoided classification, and created community through the shared interests of relaxation and conversation.

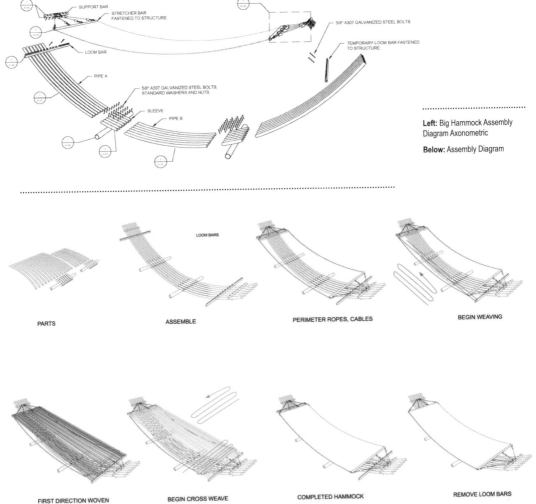

Left: Big Hammock Assembly Diagram Axonometric

Below: Assembly Diagram

PARTS

ASSEMBLE

PERIMETER ROPES, CABLES

BEGIN WEAVING

FIRST DIRECTION WOVEN

BEGIN CROSS WEAVE

COMPLETED HAMMOCK

REMOVE LOOM BARS

The Big Hammock on
Boston's Greenway

How do our culture and shared experiences give identity to the
production of architecture? For the hammock project more specifically, the challenge was to create an object onto which a plurality
of identities could be projected. Color is a critical design element;
depending on its arrangement, it suggests national identity. We
assembled the colors in a loose way, so that people of different
nationalities could find a cultural association with the hammock.
Colombians thought the hammock represented their country, Americans
saw the American flag, but looking closely at the color sequence, it
didn't fit either group. It was in between, reflecting the spaces
that I occupy as a Colombian raised in America.

Shared experiences form common references. The Mattapan Mobile Farm Stand was readily accepted by the community partner because mobile push-carts are still a familiar form of food transportation in the home countries of many of Mattapan's residents. Cultural identity is the result of common experiences, and form can reflect this. Form can be the resultant manifestation, or hybridization, of shared experiences and influences.

The architecture that emerges from a shared experience and exchange has motivated our office to find alternative models of practice from the traditional models, where either extensive prescribed experience or access to private wealth is a prerequisite for a design commission. Ted Landsmark, Past President of the Boston Architectural College, quotes Jim Cramer, in *Practice is Learning Through Experience*, about contemporary challenges within the design fields. What's needed today, he states, is a paradigm shift from valuing objects as an economic investment to "a new moral design capitalism that serves society's interests."[7] I argue that new modes of practice are beginning this shift within the architectural profession.

To serve a diverse society and to do creative work, we've had to take on the roles of initiator, fundraiser, implementer, and at times operator, to see the project through from its concept phase to construction. We inverted the traditional client and architect power relationship by envisioning the client as part of the end user group and architect as initiator of a project, so that we ultimately had creative freedom to find solutions to community needs. The Big Hammock Project and the Mattapan Mobile Farm Stand were crowdsource funded via individual donations on Kickstarter and Indiegogo; funding from the virtual community built physical communal structures. In the spirit of Hannah Arendt, we are again reminded that to 'act' means to 'begin,' and to 'lead' is to 'set something in motion' with the expectation of the unexpected.[8]

NOTES

1. Speaking at Otterbein University in Ohio, in a U.S. presidential campaign stop during April 2012, Romney states: ""We've always encouraged young people: Take a shot, go for it, take a risk, get the education, borrow money if you have to from your parents, start a business." This was cited in multiple news sources including video documentation from MSNBC: The Cycle Staff, "Romney Tells Students to Borrow Money 'from Your Parents'," MSNBC.com, September 6, 2013, http://www.msnbc.com/the-ed-show/romney-tells-students-borrow-money-f, (accessed December 23, 2013).

2. Yasmin Ramirez, "Latino Art Crossing Borders," *NYFA Quarterly*, New York Foundation for the Arts, Summer 2001, http://legacy.nyfa.org/archive_detail_q.asp?type=2&qid=44&fid=1&year=2001&s=Summer (accessed June 24, 2014).

3. To read more on cybercafés as the ultimate 21st century public space, see: James Stewart, "Cafematics: The Cybercafe and the Community in Gurstein," *Community Informatics: Enabling Communities with Information and Communications Technologies*, ed. Michael Gurstein (Hershey, PA: Idea Group Publishing, 2000), 320-338.

4. Supplemental Nutrition Assistance Program is offered by the United States Department of Agriculture to help eligible low-income residents. See: United States Department of Agriculture: Foods and Nutrition Service, "Supplemental Nutrition Assistance Program (SNAP)," http://www.fns.usda.gov/snap/supplemental-nutrition-assistance-program-snap (accessed December 23, 2013).

5. Martin Heidegger, *Being and Time* (New York: Harper and Row, 1962).

6. Ibid.

7. Ted Landsmark, "Practice is Learning Through Experience," *Architect Magazine*, April 28, 2011, http://www.architectmagazine.com//education/a-new-theory-war.aspx?page=2 (accessed February 10, 2014).

8. Hannah Arendt, *The Human Condition*, 2nd ed. (Chicago: The University of Chicago Press, 1998), 177-178.

PROJECT CREDITS

Mattapan Mobile Farm Stand Project, Boston, MA, USA, 2012
BR+A+CE | Building Research + Architecture + Community Exchange, Inc. (Hansy Better Barraza, Anthony Piermarini, Erik Nelson, Mykel Terada, John DiSalvo, Kristen Zeiber, Nick Polansky Eugenia Yu, and Loren Howard)

The Big Hammock Project on the Rose Fitzgerald Kennedy Greenway, Boston, MA, USA, 2010
Studio Luz Architects (Hansy Better Barraza, Anthony J. Piermarini, Andy Wise, Ruth Bohn, Michelle Mizioch, Myla Tak, Chelsea Plumb, Carlos Villamil, Jesen Tanadi, Taijasa Jordan, Allie Surdovel, Antonia Better-Wirz, Ann Woods, Eun Joo Kim, John Carli, Kate Cho, Stefan Di Leo, Phillip Glenn, Christine Tan)

A conversation with

Hansy
BETTER BARRAZA

by

Jon KING &
Micaela BARKER

Jon King, Micaela Barker:

> In addition to working as a practicing architect, you are a
> professor of architecture as well. Do you have any advice for
> students or designers just starting their careers, who have a
> particular interest in how design can address societal issues?
> Are there any particular schools, firms, or methods of estab-
> lishing yourself that you would recommend?

Hansy Better Barraza:

> I would recommend to those interested in doing socially engaged
> work to find a firm that positions itself in its mission state-
> ment as committed to solving societal problems. You can also

search for a firm that does the majority of its work in the public sector. For example, you will only find commissions to design a fire station or a prison from a public agency. Do some research and find firms that are not only working for private developers. Look for designers that share your beliefs and concerns.

I would also recommend to students to work for themselves right after school. Find an interest or topic, find a group of friends who share common values, and offer your creative services to a non-profit group that can benefit from your creative input. Even if the non-profit doesn't have a specific need, I like to think we can always create work. We can seek out things that need improving or innovation.

JK, MB: How do you solicit support from a community and engage their feedback when initiating a community-oriented project? How does the design process change when you are not working with a single client, or when your relationship with the client is less clearly defined?

HBB: There is always a discernible client or stakeholder, even when working on a community project. Whether it is the person who owns the land or the leader of that community group, a representative or stakeholder has input in the design process and finalizes the parameters of the intervention. Each organization has a specific way of dealing with community-based projects.

At BR+A+CE, the non-profit organization that I co-founded, the board collectively decides on a topic. This year, we are focusing on issues of immigration and immigrant communities, for example. Then, we each pitch a design idea that we all vote on. We take that idea to the community that the project will serve, and it is then molded and enhanced by their input.

In terms of soliciting community involvement, we are actually going through this process right now with this project on immigration. We started by looking in the city of Boston to see where there was a high concentration of foreign-born communities, and we identified East Boston as a potential location for a user group. In this case, we ran into a situation where a community was already maintaining a specific public space that had a great cultural history. However, they wanted us to beautify the public space, not raise awareness of its cultural history. This is an example of how it's not always the right fit. We realized our interests and goals were not in alignment, so we went on to find other partnerships. We went to non-profits that work with immigrant groups to establish a more direct relationship with the user group. So the process of identifying the stakeholders of a particular site is really about establishing a close connection to the end user community. For us, this is a result of our own research, but often involves pursuing a few different avenues.

Soliciting community support is often also a result of the same process — locating stakeholders who share our interests, particularly those who hold office or can organize resources for a project. For example, in the Mattapan Mobile Farm Stand, Mayor Menino, the mayor of Boston at the time, had a major interest in food and fitness. The Mattapan Food and Fitness program was already receiving support from the city to run the Mattapan Farmer's

31

Market, one of the smaller markets in the city. The Office of Food Initiatives, whose goal is to increase access to healthy and affordable good in the city, was already offering support to the market. Vivien Morris, who was leading Mattapan Food and Fitness, made a call to City Hall and through her network convinced the Mayor to match all of the crowd-funding we coordinated for the Mobile Farm Stand. So this is a case where identifying stake-holders can reach beyond the site or the user community itself.

JK, MB: You mention on the BR+A+CE website that you are interested in designing spaces that engage social, economic, and cultural issues facing communities around the world. Have you worked on community-based projects where it has been difficult to identify shared cultural factors from which to draw inspiration?

HBB: For the Mattapan Mobile Farm Stand and The Big Hammock project, I think that everyone was able to identify with a mobile food cart and a hammock. These cultural artifacts are global. While the forms might differ slightly across cultures, the identity and function are the same. I believe, for these reasons, we can bring together many people from a wide range of different cultures, based on shared references and experiences.

The topic of immigration will have some interesting challenges in this respect, because it is exactly these cultural differences that we want to celebrate. Still, there is some collective notion of the immigrant experience in America, regardless of where they emigrated from.

I actually put this challenge to our community partner: how can we have an architectural expression of the concept of immigra-tion? It's difficult. How do you abstract a project so that a diverse group of people can identify with this theme? The orga-nization actually came to us with the idea of freedom. In that sense we're identifying a unifying cultural value, not something that articulates the differences among immigrant communities.

We then suggested the archetype of a fence, as a way to consider boundaries. Everyone can relate to a fence, but how can we rethink the fence in service to ideals of freedom and belonging and place — all constituent parts of the immigrant narrative? So the architectural contribution is to put forward a culturally identifiable example. Because the cultural group in this area is constantly changing, in terms of the influx of immigrants, an essential dynamic of cultural difference will always be there. The real challenge is: how do you design a place of belonging for a changing cultural group?

We don't have a program yet, all we're bringing is this interest in recognizing this immigrant narrative. So the design problem is: do you politicize a topic, or do you fulfill a need? What are the support services for this population, and how can we fuse those services with a design-minded project?

JK, MB: In serving these diverse cultural interests, how do you find common ground and maintain a strong sense of architectural expression?

33

HBB: With the community groups, we discuss the role and function of our projects, and try not to bring aesthetics or form into the picture initially. The form and aesthetic is our delivery method. I think, in the two projects that we've done, the aesthetics are stripped down to the essentials. In The Big Hammock, the texture of the rope has an aesthetic value, so there it comes from a material choice. In the Mobile Farm Stand project, we were working with just the skeletal structure of the cart, so we had an opportunity to play with form in the containers that hold the food. We chose to use some old postal containers instead. So the aesthetic interest of the cart was ultimately the produce it was designed to carry, and the fruit completely changed the reading of the postal container. The aesthetics here were derived from material and economy.

We also make an effort to run BR+A+CE as an 'out of the box' design community. When I go to community partners, I tell them, "We are all designers, and you have to imagine what is possible. You're not getting pre-packaged design." Part of our process is to support imagination — not just ours, but theirs. And that's what I mean by "form is a resultant of shared experiences." To be meaningful, it has to come from someone's own memory and imagination. It has to come from these exchanges. At BR+A+CE, we strive to create something that is unique, both to challenge ourselves and to initiate a conversation with the public about the fundamental role of design in shaping a shared and sustainable future.

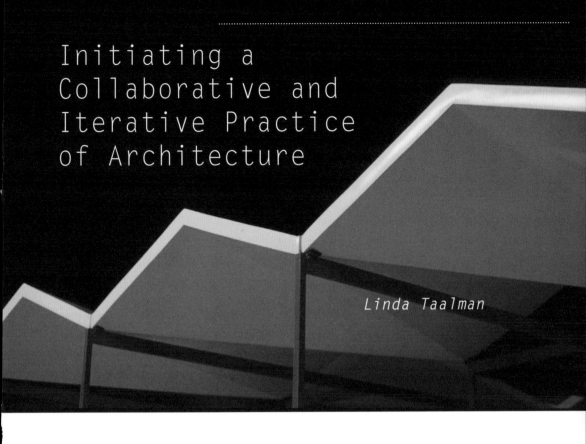

Initiating a Collaborative and Iterative Practice of Architecture

Linda Taalman

Creative Partnership: From Patronage to Collaboration and Speculation

My practice as an architect evolves directly out of an interest in the processes of collaboration and speculation to produce architecture, in lieu of a more traditional process of patronage. I welcome the possibility of collaboration with artists, designers, engineers, and creative clients in the making of each project. The kind of work I am interested in creating is not an architecture of exclusive authorship; it is an open process of design that involves multiple constituents through creative partnership.

Architecture is a medium between people who create it, commission it, and use it. It provides a framework for this exchange, with the architect as the mediator. As such, the architect is engaged in a dynamic conversation, focusing on the processes of designing and making space. By its sheer scale and complexity, architecture requires discussion among many entities in its creation. Given that it must ultimately be a living structure engaged with the larger environment, it is continually being re-imagined by designers, makers, or users.

In my early work with OpenOffice, we invited visual artists to collaborate with us to conceptualize and design a group of houses in the project called Trespassing: Houses x Artists. We welcomed the outside perspective that these artists brought to our design processes, and the project became a multi-year collaboration that redefined our notions of architecture and our role as architects.

This openness to dialog and collaboration, specifically with artists, led to OpenOffice being commissioned to work with Robert Irwin to design the Dia:Beacon museum, an adaptive renovation of a former industrial factory building. The project required collaborating with the museum's director and curator, the living artists of the collection, and a large team of engineers and builders. The goal was to make a seamless experience of art and architecture, combining the existing building with new interventions, and integrating all the building operations needed for a twenty-first century museum. The architecture was so smoothly integrated that many wrote about the project as a museum without an architect.

These early collaborations persuaded me to reconsider the practice of architecture, to be more about developing processes of exchange for creative production than to be a purely creative process unto itself. Rather than expressing a singular design vision, architecture should craft new processes and systems of design, with the potential of engaging in a dynamic dialog with a wider audience.

Initiating Processes

The IT HOUSE evolved from wanting to create a customizable kit of parts that could engage numerous clients and sites, and respond to a wide range of needs while creating a highly efficient building system. The flexibility of the system to adapt to changing needs is as important as the particular combinations of parts. The IT HOUSE is about a flexible design process and flexible architecture using highly specific materials and details, the DNA of a system that can create a variety of building envelopes and typologies. Much like Trespassing: Houses x Artists, we welcome interaction with the system, and seek opportunities to test the limits of its flexibility. Here, the client is the collaborator.

The IT HOUSE project provides a framework for design collaboration in outfitting its skin and interior living environment. In its inception, we established the ambition of creating opportunities for a user to tailor the house design and assembly, including the use of graphic treatments called "outfits," house wrappers of vinyl film created by invited artists and designers. In our first off-grid IT HOUSE, we collaborated with Liam Gillick and Sarah Morris to design the outfit that wrapped along the entrance and west elevation. The graphic outfit creates privacy, defines space, and provides shade from the late afternoon sun, creating dynamic shadows and patterns throughout the house.

The IT HOUSE led us to initiate an architectural project that would unfold as a series of iterations, in a process that simultaneously reinvents the idea of a living environment and acts as a stealth operation to transform the way we construct architecture. The IT HOUSE retools the way we as architects engage the design and construction process, and hacks established distribution networks and material systems to achieve a higher level of design quality and affordability. By taking on the fabrication and manufacture of architectural components as a critical part of our practice, we are redefining our role in architecture's realization: we design and detail the house, produce shop drawings, and direct the manufacture of the building's major components. The components arrive on site and are assembled by the builder, much like an erector set. By taking

Previous: House, Jim Isermann and OpenOffice, image of structure and roof system, installation at the MAK Center for Art and Architecture, 2003.

Opposite: Dia:Beacon, Robert Irwin and OpenOffice, image of Richard Serra gallery, Union of the Torus and the Sphere, 2001. The relationship among art, architecture and viewer is where the museum exists; each one requires the other two parts to construct meaning.

on this risk, we are able to produce buildings that are highly detailed and made of high quality materials, in an efficient manner, at a reasonable cost.

The IT HOUSE is a speculative model for alternative architectural practice, in which the architect plays a highly active role in developing architecture as both a product *and* as a process that the client can directly engage in. By developing a flexible kit of parts, a set of pre-determined and yet re-configurable components, we developed an architectural product that deeply engages the client in a design process that yields highly customizable results. This new hybrid of product and process allows the client to envision the look and feel of the space, and to tweak the design to suit their specific requirements.

Loophole Insights

The ideas for the IT HOUSE developed directly from several conversations in the collaborative project, Trespassing: Houses x Artists; most significantly, the Small Skyscraper developed in collaboration with artist Chris Burden. Starting from a loophole in the Los Angeles County zoning code, Chris Burden sketched an idea for the most extreme building one could build without a building permit. In 1994, when he drew the sketch, the code outlined that small outbuildings measuring no larger than 400 square feet and no taller than 35 feet could be built without a building permit. The Small Skyscraper both adheres to the legal restrictions and pushes the envelope of the code, resulting in a 4-story mini skyscraper of 100 square foot floor plates with 8 foot ceilings. Just as Hugh Ferris' drawings visualized the future of New York City's skyline through his interpretation of its early twentieth century zoning code, the Small Skyscraper sketch shows the potential lurking within the city's desire to control all but the smallest interventions by the public.

The Small Skyscraper is a sculpture as well as a prototype for a hypothetical dwelling, with each floor presenting a framework for flexible use. When we approached Burden in 1999 to develop a speculative project for a house, he proposed developing his concept sketch, but by then the loophole had closed. To develop the house and maintain the agenda of resisting zoning restrictions, we found a different loophole that allowed for unpermitted temporary amusement structures. Keeping the previous dimensional parameters, we proposed to rework Burden's design by developing a kit of parts structure that could be disassembled and reassembled.

The final structure mines both of the codes' loopholes, resulting in a 4-story tower made of prefabricated components, that is entirely bolted together like an erector set. Similar to Burden's sculptures

Above: Off-grid IT HOUSE, Taalman Koch Architecture, 2006, interior view looking north. Off-grid IT house, Pioneertown, CA, 2006. View of kitchen looking north with graphic outfit by Liam Gillick and Sarah Morris. The art and architecture are spatially linked as the art casts shadows through the building.

Opposite: IT STUDIO, IT HOUSE Inc., 2013, Pioneertown, CA, construction photo showing the construction of lightweight framing elements. A small scale prototype for a 120 sf minimal dwelling, built as a kit of parts for on site assembly.

of bridges and towers made from Meccano parts, the Small Skyscraper is as much about an inventory of pieces and a set of instructions, as it is about a final structure or installation. This systematized approach led to a series of building technology experiments, centered on the reworking of the parts to change the whole.

Developing the IT HOUSE as a Holistic System

The structural system developed for the Small Skyscraper became the basis of the IT HOUSE: an open framework that could shape a myriad of configurations and be freely and flexibly enclosed. The development of the IT HOUSE created a new practice of fabricating architecture. This new process for designing and thinking about buildings engages the client with a clearly visualized product creation process. It streamlines the process of building, preventing typical defaults to crisis management. The house itself is an architectural product comprised of a series of components, which, as a whole, strive to maximize spatial experiences, while minimizing impact on the environment. This part-to-whole relationship is critical; the way the building comes together is made apparent by the design of its components. Together, they are a holistic system, embodying an archi-tectural philosophy for making and experiencing space.

Less is less: Lightweight building

The IT HOUSE lands lightly on the landscape by removing many of the complexities and conflicts that often occur when building. Simply put, it weighs less; it is a lightweight building system, primarily made of aluminum, steel and glass. The pieces are small and can be carried by small crews without the use of heavy equipment. It requires minimal foundations. The structure's lightness and simple construction help preserve natural site features, and minimize grading and site impacts. Each building component in the system is designed and engineered to be efficient and high-performing. Minimizing costly and time-consuming on-site labor eliminates much of the unpredictability of home construction. Materials arrive on site prefinished. Conventional materials that require a high degree of finishing and maintenance, such as drywall and tile, are replaced with prefinished solutions.

Just-in-time fabrication

By combining the bolted aluminum frame structural system with several other commercial and industrial off-the-shelf components, such as aluminum-framed commercial storefront glazing, and acoustical struc-tural steel decking, we were able to create a minimal building shell that clipped together rapidly. Rather than setting up a dedicated manufacturing facility, we tapped into existing manufacturers as our sources and fabricators, who deliver parts directly to the job site. This piggyback model enabled us to innovate quickly, and produced a just-in-time fabrication process that made use of existing resources. Just-in-time off-site fabrication minimizes waste; all materials are formed, cut and drilled off site when ordered, allowing waste to be recycled at the source. The IT HOUSE generates zero on-site construc-tion waste.

Top Left: Hugh Ferris (1889-1962). Drawing: Study for Maximum Mass Permitted by the 1916 New York Zoning Law, Stage 1. New York, NY, 1922. Black crayon, stumped; brush and black ink over photostat, varnish on illustration board; 665 x 510 mm. Gift of Mrs. Hugh Ferriss, 1969-137-1. Photo: Ken Pelka.

Bottom Left: Small Skyscraper, Chris Burden and Taalman Koch Architecture, 2004, Installation at Los Angeles Contemporary Exhibitions, installation view in gallery.

Right: Small Skyscraper, Chris Burden and Taalman Koch Architecture, 2012, Public Installation in Los Angeles County, Pasadena, CA, view from plaza.

Closing the gap between design and construction

Typically the architect designs and draws the intent, primarily focused on visible aspects, and construction is left to contractors and fabricators. However, in the case of the IT HOUSE, the design process more closely resembles industrial design or product development, but at the scale of a building. To fabricate the components, we develop our own shop drawings for each element of the building systems, and handle the manufacturing, finishing and delivery to the site. The site is the point of assembly for all components from different manufacturing sources. The parts are made for assembly on-site using simple hand tools; a socket wrench, Allen wrench and hand drill are all that is needed to assemble the primary structure, wall framing and cabinets. The framework of the house's assembled components acts as formwork for the concrete slab, simplifying construction that cannot occur off-site. A small crew follows a

standardized set of instructions to assemble the building with
minimal site disturbance. By making the assembly process so simple,
it is possible for crews to work quickly.

Integrating environmental systems and thinking off the grid

The IT HOUSE is as much about developing alternative models for
environmental control systems as it is about developing alternative
construction practices, materials, and systems. In addition to minimizing weight, stripping unnecessary finishes, and eliminating site
work, the house integrates environmental systems and uses renewable
resources where possible. The heating and cooling systems use radiant

42

IT STUDIO, IT HOUSE Inc., 2013,
Pioneertown, CA, front elevation
showing the lightweight elements
in the rugged landscape, built
over granite rock. The house
should feel as if it landed in the
landscape without altering it.

thermal technology and mini ducts that fit within and maintain the
low profile roof and floor slabs. In the case of the Off-grid IT
HOUSE, we set out to create a self-sufficient structure with a strong
visual and physical connection to the landscape, with a minimal
physical and environmental footprint. The structure maximizes the use
of glass, allowing views from inside to expand out to the horizon.
The remote site necessitated that the house be self-sufficient and
truly off the grid, with no ties to municipal infrastructure. The
strategy for the house is two-fold: stripping back to the essentials
and complete integration, allowing all the systems to be both exposed
and an integral part of the experience.

Plugging in

All of the houses we have built are either off-grid or include grid-
tied systems that produce solar electrical power and/or solar thermal
heating. Taking off-grid solutions to the grid hybridizes a closed

loop model within a broad network;
plugging in local renewable systems
to the larger conventional system
makes the whole system better. Many
of the IT HOUSES are in California,
where there is an abundance of solar
resource. It seems only natural to tap
into that. Solar panels are integrated
with the structural framing of the
house, as the panel mounting racks
use the same aluminum extrusion at a
smaller scale.

The IT HOUSE also plugs into social
networks for exchanging ideas and
materials as the community of the
project grows. Our process of commu-
nicating with potential clients about
our process and product has dramatically shifted through the engagement
of social networks and tools. We have initiated discussions with
clients through tools such as Facebook; some people who started out
"liking" our page or following our posts have ended up engaging us
in their design problems. By blogging about the construction of our
prototype off-grid IT HOUSE, we picked up hundreds of followers,
two of whom have since built their own. The prototype off-grid IT
HOUSE has an audience of design-loving travelers on networks such as
Airbnb, and we have hosted hundreds of guests and potential clients
who have test-driven it. The exposure and exchange made possible by
these networks should not be underestimated; since Airbnb's launch,
the IT HOUSE has been saved to over 8,000 wish lists. The potential
for architecture to be broadcast and experienced is greatly expanded.

Clearlake IT CABIN, IT HOUSE
Inc., 2011, exterior view of house.
The IT CABIN incorporates the
Blue Sky Building System as
a platform and the IT HOUSE
systems for the frame and
enclosure of the house. The
house is our third house built
entirely off the grid. The Clearlake
house incorporated the Blue
Sky Building System (bolted
light-gauge steel framing system)
as a platform to minimize the
use of on site construction work
to simple footings at each point
the structure touches down on
the site. The structure allows
the building to float above the
landscape and the landscape
continues uninterrupted.

Barter and trade and future lifestyles

Through these social networks, there is potential for the collaborative architectural processes that the IT HOUSE establishes to
continue to develop, even after completed construction. The nature
of the IT HOUSE as a system that can be assembled and disassembled
lends itself to the making of temporary or adaptable structures that
can be repurposed and transformed. For example, an IT HOUSE owner
group on Facebook could allow our clients to exchange materials or
ideas. Clients could develop innovative solutions and share them with
the larger community, just as we continue to post our innovations as
we develop the systems. Our client base thus becomes a community of
users who can share ideas on house customization, trade parts, should
they want to expand or remodel their systems, and up-cycle their
components for future IT HOUSE projects, in a kind of architectural
swap meet.

There is yet potential to develop new products that interface with
the building systems of the IT HOUSE. This architectural project can
grow into either smaller or larger scales and still integrate with
the IT HOUSE components and strategies. The interior and exterior
landscapes that are framed by the house can become the site for new
design projects that further reinvent our living environments.

A New Model for Practice and Living

The IT HOUSE is a small project with a big agenda. It aims to change the way we design and collaborate, fabricate components, integrate systems, and construct buildings, with the goal of changing the way we practice architecture and the way we live.

The IT HOUSE is an open source tool kit that allows all collaborators to work together, to achieve a better end product. The project proposes a new kind of practice in which the architect takes an active role in the design and construction interface processes — redesigning how architecture is made. Architects had historically been involved directly in the design and construction of buildings, but in the last century, as building material and system complexity increased, the role of the architect has become one of master coordinator rather than master builder. The distance between a building's design and its realization has become greater. At the same time, the craft of building has decreased overall, even though we may have more sophisticated materials and systems.[1] The IT HOUSE strives to reconnect the process of design with construction and increase craft quality by integrating the fabrication process as a critical part of the design and construction process. Our model of integrated design and fabrication also reconsiders the way we engage our clients in an open process of exchange. This allows them to see the end product clearly from the outset of design, including projected costs and schedules, and also get a high degree of customization to meet specific site and program goals.

As a new model for living, the IT HOUSE proposes an open framework and flexible set of systems, allowing adaptability over time and interaction with its users. It is a dynamic system that mediates relationships with the surrounding environment and expands the ways in which the architect operates and initiates the process of making space. Developed as a flexible building system that can adapt to a range of site and client constraints, the IT HOUSE is conceived as a minimal structure that frames one's relationship to the landscape and experience within it. Strategic sourcing of architectural components helps to make smarter buildings with minimized resource, and to preserve natural landscapes through a reconsideration of all systems in the building project in a holistic process. The consideration of the building extends from the intimate interior of objects that make our domestic environment of everyday life, and out to the exterior landscape, establishing a relationship with nature and larger ecosystems. The IT HOUSE mediates between these two realms, and allows the inhabitant to exist in a constant dialog with them.

Opposite: Off-grid IT HOUSE, Taalman Koch Architecture, 2006.

The Off-grid IT HOUSE enables occupation of remote sites such as this high desert in California. The house is 100% solar powered. The solar panels are integrated into the building design and also provide shade for the courtyards.

Below: Off-grid IT HOUSE, Airbnb, since 2010.

Airbnb empowers one's ability to experience private domestic architecture by opening up sharing to a global audience. Airbnb renters can stay at the house and experience the space as a temporary inhabitant.

Next Page: Santa Cruz IT HOUSE, IT HOUSE Inc., 2013.

The IT House framing elements are bolted on site, the frame is used to establish a precise formwork that regulates the on site construction work and the other assembled components for enclosure of the space.

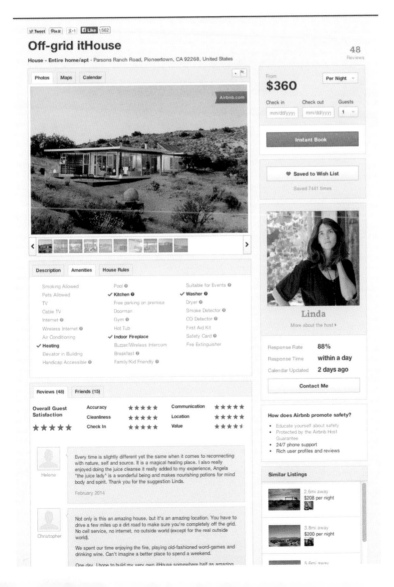

NOTE

1. Stephen Kieran and James Timberlake, *Refabricating Architecture: How Manufacturing Methods are Poised to Transform Building Construction* (New York: McGraw Hill Professional, 2003). Kieran and Timberlake clearly outline the problem of how the building industries have increased in complexity and removed authority from the hands of architects, making ever more complex building problems with more and more parts.

PROJECT CREDITS

Isermann House, Trespassing Houses x Artists, Installation at the MAK Center for Art and Architecture, Los Angeles, CA, USA, 2003
Jim Isermann and OpenOffice (Linda Taalman, Alan Koch)

Dia:Beacon, Beacon, NY, USA, 2001
Robert Irwin and OpenOffice (Linda Taalman, Alan Koch, Lyn Rice, Galia Solomonoff, Jay Hindmarsh, Astrid Lipka)

Off-grid IT HOUSE, Pioneertown, CA, USA, 2006
Taalman Koch Architecture (Linda Taalman and Alan Koch, graphic outfit by Sarah Morris and Liam Gillick)

IT STUDIO, Pioneertown, CA, USA, 2013
IT HOUSE Inc. (Linda Taalman, Laura Steele, Dave Bailey)

Study for Maximum Mass Permitted by the 1916 New York Zoning Law, Stage 1. New York, NY, 1922.
Hugh Ferris, (1889-1962).

Small Skyscraper, Installation at Los Angeles Contemporary Exhibitions, Los Angeles, CA, 2004
Chris Burden and Taalman Koch Architecture (Linda Taalman, Alan Koch)

Small Skyscraper, Public Installation in Los Angeles County, Pasadena, CA, USA, 2012
Chris Burden and Taalman Koch Architecture (Linda Taalman, Laura Steele, Wallace Fang)

Santa Cruz IT HOUSE, Santa Cruz, CA, USA, 2013
IT HOUSE Inc. (Linda Taalman, Alan Koch, Alex Webb, Laura Steele)

Clearlake IT CABIN, Clearlake, CA, USA, 2011 (derived from Off-grid IT HOUSE, 2006, Taalman Koch Architecture)
IT HOUSE Inc. (Linda Taalman, Alan Koch, Ryan Whitacre, Dave Bailey)

A conversation with

Linda
TAALMAN

by
Joseph SWERDLIN

///

Joseph Swerdlin:

> Winding back to the lecture that you gave, you described your
> career path through a progression of events, moving from collabo-
> ration with artists, to designing houses, to the fabrication and
> installation of the Small Skyscraper with artist Chris Burden, and
> now to the design of the IT Houses. What is it about your design
> process that has enabled you to make continuous discoveries and
> forge new development as you move from project to project?

Linda Taalman:

> Looking back over all these different projects that seem not to
> be very similar — that is, they are very visually different, they
> feel different, the processes are different — the one thing that I
> realized was consistent was the idea of a kind of open framework,
> the idea that architecture could be a framework or scaffold that
> allows things to interact with each other. That framework could be
> two people who are collaborating, to allow different ideas to be
> grafted onto the structure. It could be a user and an owner, in an
> exchange through the structure. And it could be, in a museum situ-
> ation, an artist with a viewer. The architecture exists among all
> these different dialogs.

> One of the things I'm really interested in is the idea of an open
> framework that is adaptable or able to be changed by the partici-
> pants. So, the participant might be the person who I'm collab-
> orating with. It might be the person who's the end user. It

might be the people who come to interact with it. This framework remains, to some degree, changeable or programmable. When you look across scales, it doesn't really matter what scale it is. That can happen at every scale.

JS: So, looking more specifically at your collaborations with artists, how did you first engage the artists for the *Houses x Artists* project? And what did that collaboration look like?

LT: In the beginning we didn't have clients and we didn't have projects, and we wanted just to start working. But we didn't want to be working in a vacuum or just to develop a language independently, which is a 'paper architecture' model one could follow. The idea of *Trespassing: Houses x Artists* was to allow other people into the process, because architecture is — by its very nature — a collaborative discipline involving lots of people. And the idea was that by inviting these artists to work in a new way, to bring their ideas that they used in their own work to our field, they would essentially make us have to think about what we were doing, as architects, differently.

In this collaboration everyone is outside of their own comfort zone, but producing something with the tools that they know or the processes that they know or ideas that they know.

And, amazingly, a lot of the artists we invited said "yes" to our invitation and were very open to see and discuss this idea. It wasn't an open call but a personal invitation. We thought, in the beginning, that we would have a very straightforward process

and that we would use the tools of architecture, the standard
drawings, the standard processes, and model making, to create
a way of seeing the differences between each collaboration. And
we anticipated producing, in the end, the same kind of working
drawings and a model for every single project.

But what we realized in working with these ten different people
is that every artist works in a unique way and we had to make a
completely different model of production for each collaboration.
So, some of the processes were passing drawings back and forth,
ending up in a set of plans and sections and elevations. Others
don't draw and so it was more of a conversation that went on for
a very long time that maybe even looped in all kinds of crazy
ways and then ended up becoming something else—would it become
a video or would it become a kind of installation in a room? We
really allowed the conversations to develop what the project would
become. So, it unraveled as we were going.

JS: That's really fascinating, how you have to react and change the
process in every way. So, was there anything that you could really
predict in that sequence, in that interaction?

LT: I think the process was good in terms of a learning experience. I
have to work with different kinds of people all the time. Some of
these are clients, some of these are project teams, and some of
these are people that I'm collaborating with creatively. And you
really have to customize the process. Every project is unique.

If we're getting building permits for a project, we're going to
follow certain standards. And we have certain things set up to do
that. But the design process is often an undefined and extended
process. I think in every project the design process requires some
level of customization.

There are times I can work with collaborators for only an hour
before they get exhausted. They just can't handle it. Others might
be able to go on for six hours. Some can read drawings and some
can't, etc.

JS: When you spoke about the IT House you described it as developing an architectural product rather than the service. And I'm
wondering, as the IT House becomes a refined product, a set of prefabricated parts, how do you remain engaged with clients so that
the product does not become something that you don't want, for
example, an awkwardly cobbled-together selection of catalog parts?

LT: Well, I want to be open to having both kinds of interaction,
because if I can create a product that is simple enough for people
to do it themselves, there's an advantage to that. I would like to
make a super simple product that allows people to have 'one-click'
architecture, and just get it delivered to their doorstep without
even interacting with us.

I see the IT House as a product that has so much range, we can do
anything with it. One of the ideas is to find ways to make it a
more accessible kind of architecture; to make it more accessible

for people to build it themselves or to design it themselves.
Or if you want to, we'll work with you to make something super
special out of those same materials.

For us what's interesting about that is it's a kind of extended
building technology research project where we're just, in every
iteration, refining the details or adding a new detail or tweaking
the details. Now we're working with a client who has a site
in upstate New York, in the Rhinebeck area. We have to create
completely new details, because it has to be a four-season house.
And that's pretty interesting, to take what we've been doing and
now say, "Okay. How do we do this in this new climate?"

JS: What have you been finding as a result of that?

LT: Well, there's a lot of weatherizing that we have to do. There's
probably a reduction in the amount of glass. But I mean with that
building we're actually going for a high sustainable building
envelope as well. So, it's not just to make it work. It's also
to make it as close as possible to a net zero building. So, we're
working with an energy consultant to help us do that. A lot of
making the house perform in this climate is choosing the right
equipment and using the right building insulation and those kinds
of things.

JS: That's great. Going back to the idea of collaboration in your
work, in your description of the Dia:Beacon you spoke about your
project merging seamlessly with the existing building, in a way
that it becomes hidden. And maybe in a similar manner, the high
amount of collaboration in a lot of your work begins to blur the
hand of the architect. And so, what is your view of authorship of
your work?

LT: I don't know. It's not the most important thing, I would say.
It's more about making things. And sometimes those things that you
make—your authorship is invisible, especially when you make things
that are about being open to other people, or experiencing other
things through; or when you are making buildings that are about
blending with the landscape, so the architecture disappears.

I was joking with someone that I should write a book called *On
Being Invisible*, because I'm actually really interested in that
idea. But it's been very problematic to collaborate with so many
people, and even to be in collaboration with another architect,
because the general public and the media really don't know what
to do with that, and they want an author. There's a strong need
to point to one person who is responsible, or who did this or who
made this, either for blame or for praise.

Everybody wants to point to one person, and it's not one person.
I mean, there are people who are working in my office and they're
as much the authors. But the public and the media want to have
stories that have one person. I'm not so interested in it, but
to some degree you have to play this game. Maybe you could form
an organization with no author whatsoever. I mean, you could be a
collective.

Dia: Beacon, Robert Irwin and Open Office. Image of The Equal Area Series, Walter de Maria.

JS: That's one way of kind of blurring the boundaries.

LT: More and more people are working in teams, in groups, and that
           makes sense in terms of architecture. So, in general, I think the
           world is still set up in a singular author way. But I think, if
           you look at the long-term, what does it really matter?

JS: I have another question about the development of the IT House
           and the trajectory of your career. Do you see that the IT House
           project is branching into other projects, or do you see the IT
           House being at the focus of your practice right now?

LT: Well, it's about 50 percent of what we do — maybe more in terms of
           inquiries. But I feel like it could expand into other domains. It
           could be taken and adapted for other programs—schools, classrooms,
           or even to do things—temporary structures, relief structures. I'm
           very interested in exploring how it could be expanded to be part
           of more public realms. Or it could be housing, at bigger scales
           or smaller scales. The idea of doing this very, very small scale
           project is that it could happen at a larger volume. So, the IT
           House averages at 1,200 square feet, and we've done 10 of them
           now. But if we design something that's 120 square feet, maybe
           we could do 100 of them. Or if we make it bigger maybe we could
           do two of them. I'm interested in scaling in both directions and
           shifting to other programs.

           The larger project, of course, is not just the IT House; we have
           a general philosophy about developing building systems as opposed
           to, let's say, fixed designs in which those building systems aren't
           just the IT House systems we've already been playing with. There
           are other systems that we want to explore, other materials. And
           then those could get plugged into lots of different things. I'm
           interested in the general approach to how you might engage in
           making buildings or developing systems.

           I think if you make a good system it can actually work very well,
           even if it's misused. I'm interested in that as well, that we
           might develop a system and then someone might use it in a way we
           didn't expect.

JS: Right, the error that can occur. Could speak about the idea of the
           error, how might that be included in the system? And how, if you
           have seen any misuse, could those develop further?

LT: Well, I don't think we've opened it up enough to other people to be
           able to do it on their own yet, but I've certainly seen a lot of
           people making their own details, which I'm very charmed by.

           It is a bit of a collective design process. A lot of the people who
           we've worked with have their own very strong design inclinations,
           but they may not be designers. Some of them are designers. Some of
           them are frustrated architects. Some of them are people who went
           to architecture school and dropped out and decided to do something
           else, and now this is their way to get back into it. Or they've been
           engaged in making things, but in a different kind of making.

So we've had the opportunity with all the IT Houses to work with people who have, in one way or another, some creative input on their own projects. But I do think it would be interesting to open it up, and to have it be more open source, and allow people to work with it, and then say, "Wow! What can people do with this?"

JS: Yeah, just open up to the field of people who could really re-imagine what it could be used for and how it could be implemented.

LT: I think, when you have a big group of people working on something collectively, there's bound to be ideas that you never thought of before. That goes back to the question of authorship. There's the idea historically of the architect as a kind of master, and educator, and the one who's making all the decisions. Everything is under their control, and they can envision all the way down to where the furniture should be placed, and they bolt it down to the floor. In several of Mies' houses, he actually had the furniture bolted to the floor, and you couldn't rearrange it, allowing no interaction with the person who's actually using it. And I think that's why something like the Farnsworth House became so stifling, because you can't change it. From the very beginning it's a fixed entity, but the opposite would be to allow your process to be contaminated by all kinds of outside forces.

But I am still interested in making beautiful things. There's always that desire. In the process we use when we make the houses there is actually a higher degree of control than we would have on a normal house because we're actually deciding without the builders how it's going to be put together. These are where all the holes go. These are all the parts, and you can't substitute the parts. We're going to send you all the parts. You can't make up your own methods for doing it. We're actually going to send you a manual and then you simply put it together.

So, it sort of goes both ways, because, in order to allow it to be so precise and flexible as a system, we actually have to control it much more.

JS: That's an interesting balance between maintaining control and opening up, giving freedom to the builder.

LT: Well, there's been a lot of research over the last 100 years to create a truly universal system that is highly precise, but, at the same time, adaptable. So, Konrad Wachsmann's Universal System or even Buckminster Fuller and his Dymaxion house or his domes: these are all attempts at making systems that can be, in fact, flexible, but that are precise.

I'm interested in things that already exist in the world like scaffolding, as an example. They are just simple kits of parts, but you can do anything with them.

53 |

Martha Bohm

Architect as Detective

The closest many of us will ever come to detective work is that of popular writing and film. The clever detective is a familiar and beloved trope, a character that can forge connections between disparate snippets of imperfect information, and then see clearly what others cannot perceive. Part everyman and part superhero, this character observes and engages with the same world, day to day, as the rest of the hoi polloi, yet manages to extract meaning and narratives which evade most. From fragments of clues collected, curated even, and interpreted through a careful and particular way of thinking, the detective draws conclusions and creates new understandings. Not typically a self-serving character, the detective works on behalf of another. In classic private detective lore (think Sherlock Holmes, Mike Hammer, or Guy Noir) the private detective has a patron—an individual client, often well-to-do, in need of investigative services. In this book that examines territory outside the bounds of patronage, it must be noted that in our many popular contemporary crime dramas (take *Law & Order*, *NCIS* or *CSI* as examples) detectives work for public law enforcement on behalf of society as a whole. Arguably the landscape of patronage has shifted in the fictional detective world as well over the last one hundred and fifty years, since Edgar Allan Poe first sketched its literary form.[1]

The work which follows in this chapter shows that the essential skills of architects and detectives have much in common, and that the comparison productively defines the contours of one of several non-traditional approaches to architecture. I argue that both good detective work and good architectural work include observation, documentation, and synthesis. Identification of these core elements in new modes of work allows the profession as we know it to broaden its scope and enrich its identity without reinventing it, recognizing emerging practices as being fundamentally of the same stuff as conventional practice, yet moving beyond its typical extents.

Observation of What is Invisible to the Untrained Eye

Detectives are renowned for keen powers of observation. Sherlock Holmes, for one, can distinguish among hundreds of types of tobacco ash, a subtlety lost on even the most inveterate smoker.[2] While less recognized by popular culture, but by no means less characteristic of her profession, an architect's principal skills also include careful examination and discernment. The architect must study what has been called an "essay of clues" before beginning any design consideration.[3] These clues spring from a host of contexts: the physical (surrounding buildings, infrastructure, climate, and soils), the legal (building codes, standards, and various other regulations), the social (local economies, construction practices and management approaches), and the cultural (aesthetics, history, and semiotics), to name a few. The ability to recognize at the outset this host of forces influencing a project is a necessary component of a design process.

Documentation of Evidence

Whether via notepad and pencil, photograph, or corkboard collage of clippings, photos, and scrawled notes, a detective methodically records evidence found during the investigation. Documentation helps connect the miscellany; identifying the specific cigar ash at the scene of a crime is meaningless, unless it is also observed and recorded that the suspect smokes Cohibas. In film and television the documentation is conveniently visual; often the graphic device of colored string links photos of key characters to bits of evidence, and helps the inexpert audience member keep pace with the on-screen whiz as new discoveries are made. Here the architect also exercises a core strength, as visual documentation, diagramming, and graphic exploration of spatial contexts, constraints, and opportunities are central to and generative of architectural work.

Synthesis of Disparate Elements into a Meaningful Whole

The climactic moment of detective work is the construction of a narrative with explanatory power sufficient to solve the crime. This quintessential synthesis is powerful for both the elements of surprise and anticipation: simultaneously "SHE can't be the murderer!" and "That makes TOTAL sense!" While Holmes is famous for his deductive reasoning, teasing out a conclusion inductively, through observation of patterns, figures widely in detective work, particularly in contemporary fiction capitalizing on current data collection techniques.[4] Here once again the core of architecture finds a parallel, whereby design weaves constraint, opportunity and invention together into meaning. Successful architecture does not simply solve the problem of housing program for a specific user, but brings something new to this pragmatism, and contributes to a larger body of cultural work. The best design work feels both surprising and fresh while concurrently seeming like nothing else could be in its place.

Architects as Detectives

The reductive simplicity of the triad of observation, documentation, and synthesis is not intended to exclude work that is "not architecture," but rather to frame the work of architects broadly and abstractly, to bring more under the umbrella of architectural practice. It is for their similar set of skills and approaches that we can consider architects and detectives as working in similar craft. The parallels to detective work are these: detectives and architects are keen observers, make rigorous and enlightening documentation, and synthesize a culmination of their work to create meaning.

However, we have chosen to characterize as detective work this thread of novel architectural practices, not architectural practice as a whole. While it is situated firmly within core architectural skills, detective work represents another new model of practice. The work in this section of this book is a recasting of conventional architectural practice in two ways. First, it places greater priority on close observation and creative documentation. This may conventionally be seen simply as a part of an architect's due diligence, or a visual prelude to the "real" work of architecture, that of conceiving and representing new built work. Second, the work presented here shifts the medium of synthesis from necessarily being a built work, to possibly being some other creative output. The work of detective practitioners shows that these are products uniquely suited to architectural processes and skills which fall outside the domain of conventional deliverables.

Observation and Documentation: The Power of the Image

Architects excel at visualizing that which does not yet exist, and consequently has never been seen. Driven by a need to communicate fundamentally nonverbal ideas, architects have facility with a range of two- and three-dimensional techniques for translating ideas from mental concept to palpable reality. Harnessing this skill brings architects some of their greatest power as detectives. Rather than plans and renderings of a new design, graphic skills are used to create maps of spatial context and patterns, charts of sociopolitical influences, collages of historical traces, or diagrams of ecological flows, all to bring

This "blue marble" image of earth as seen by the Apollo 17 crew on December 7, 1972 is familiar today. Its initial publication marked, and may indeed have triggered, the beginning of a shift in our conceptualization of the fragility of our planet.

these hidden forces into the open. This process is a creative one—the architect creates both new drawings and new understanding. Rather than visualizing what has not been seen yet, this is showing what is there (and may have been seen) but is not yet understood. Close observation and rigorous documentation are not simply mimetic acts, but more akin to excavation or translation.

Juhani Pallasmaa writes, albeit critically, about the primacy of vision as a means of experiencing and understanding the world, noting that, "Since the Greeks, philosophical writings of all times have abounded with ocular metaphors to the point that knowledge has become analogous with clear vision."[5]

He quotes Susan Sontag's writing on the role of photographed images in perception, as a "mentality which looks at the world as a set of potential photographs."[6] Architectural detective projects look at the world as a series of potential diagrams, maps, installations, or exhibitions.

In its best incarnation, the carefully crafted image wields great power. The creation of an image may, in itself, precipitate reframing and reconsideration of the subject and its context. As argued persuasively by Denis Cosgrove, the first publication of the Earthrise photo, taken by astronauts on Apollo 8 in 1968, and the "blue marble" image of the earth, taken by astronauts aboard the Apollo 17 spacecraft in 1972, caused significant shifts in "geographic imagination." Seeing the earth whole, not to mention in well-framed, crisp, and balanced images, forced a reconceptualization not only of the planet, but of ourselves as its stewards. As American poet Archibald MacLeish wrote then in the *New York Times,* "To see the earth as it truly is, small and blue and beautiful in that eternal silence in which it floats, is to see ourselves as riders on the earth together, brothers on that bright loveliness in the eternal cold—brothers who know now that they are truly brothers."[7] MacLeish evinced the modern belief in the power of photography to capture reality as it is. Writing more recently, Bruno Latour recognizes that, 40 years on, an unintended outcome of the Apollo missions was a refocusing of our social attention on the fragility of our own planet, not on the ongoing conquest of others.[8] This photographic observation and documentation by the astronauts-as-detectives arguably found synthesis over the subsequent decades in growing environmental awareness and engagement. Architects are not alone in their ability to create meaningful visual material. However, this skill, typically developed in the profession as a means to another end, is an instrument of meaningful creation on its own. Powerful visual material is not simply a means by which something else is made, but an end in itself.

Creative Synthesis Is Not Necessarily a Building

Architectural practitioners pride themselves, rightfully, on being makers. Design is an act of creation, of bringing into being something which did not exist. Architectural design directly produces drawings, renderings, models, and other means of representation of physical form, and indirectly produces built work as a consequence. Architecture has distinguished itself as a creative and productive field, but perhaps its identity as such has constrained an ability to see other kinds of work as within the profession. The relentless pursuit of built production allows too-casual a dismissal of work which does not result in wholly new objects. Pejoratively dismissed as "paper architecture" (or even "dead projects"), unbuilt work is easily disregarded or devalued in comparison with built work. In the same vein, analysis and investigative work leading to a design is framed as an auxiliary "pre-design," a necessary preamble to more substantive phases of design and construction.

Analysis cannot be entirely segregated from design and creative acts. A visually compelling curation allows the architect-detective to better understand relationships and patterns within a set of information. While correlations exist absent the designer's hand, the organization and presentation of them is not a neutral act, but requires measured judgment

and sound intuition. More to the point, it requires the designer to take a position vis-a-vis the information, and is an act of design. New things are created: unique understandings, novel conclusions, and an original graphic artifact. That these creations do not, and largely cannot, take physical form is irrelevant.

Architectural detective work sets itself apart by not producing anything like a building (or even drawings for one), but rather by creating a synthetic and meaningful whole in the shape of an exhibit, map, curated collection, performance, or other type of work. While stemming from the same basic processes as building design, this model of practice is distinct, and a valid departure from conventional notions of architectural practice.

Contemporary Architectural Detectives

While perhaps not self-identifying as such, many contemporary practitioners create work as detectives. The two selected projects below show how acts of uncovering and visual explanation provide meaning.

Million Dollar Blocks

The Spatial Information Design Lab (SIDL), directed by Laura Kurgan, at the Columbia University Graduate School of Architecture, Planning and Preservation, focuses on the visualization of information about the contemporary built environment. The work involves not only spatial data, but narrative and imagery organized into compelling visual presentations.

Since 2005, the SIDL has engaged in numerous efforts marrying data with maps, notably The Million Dollar Blocks, a work which investigated the geography of incarceration. These new data mappings focus on the locations of prisoners' residences, rather than on crime "hot spots." An emerging pattern showed that a disproportionate number of incarcerated people come from a very few neighborhoods, often at exceptionally high concentrations. In certain of these areas, the state spends over a million dollars each year to imprison the residents of a single city block—the so-called "million dollar blocks." Further graphic examination of the data shows that while many incarcerated people return home, more than half are readmitted to prison within three years; there is thus a cyclic spatial flow of people between prisons (often in rural areas) and home (typically in dense urban areas). This project argues that, despite their physical location hundreds of miles away, prisons are in some ways the most significant elements of infrastructure to these neighborhoods.

The data gathering, or "observation", for this project is massive. Vast tables of statistical data had

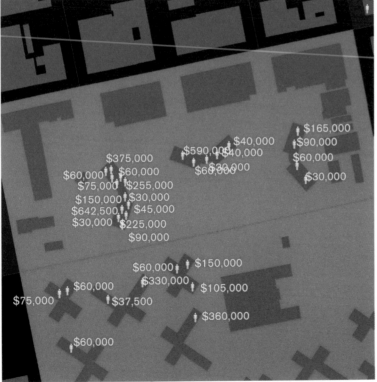

$165,000
$40,000
$90,000
$590,000 $40,000
$60,000
$375,000
$60,000 $60,000 $68,000 $30,000
$75,000 $255,000 $30,000
$150,000 $30,000
$642,500 $45,000
$30,000 $225,000
$90,000

$60,000 $150,000
$60,000 $330,000
$75,000 $105,000
$37,500
$360,000

$60,000

Top: A map from the Million Dollar Blocks project shows total 2003 prison expenditures for residents of each census block in Brooklyn, NY.

Bottom: Another Million Dollar Blocks map highlights two census blocks in Brownsville, Brooklyn, NY. Here 31 men were imprisoned in 2003, yielding a total expenditure for these two blocks of $4.4million.

Martha Bohm

2006-7-10 16:30

2006-7-10 20:15

2006-7-11 0:15

2006-7-9 16:30

2006-7-9 23:0

2006-7-10 9:15

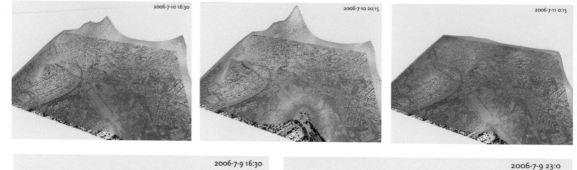

to be examined on both the criminal justice system and the city. Data geolocation correlates spatial significance, and documents emerging phenomena in an accessible way. According to the lab's founders, "Putting data on a map can open new spaces for action, and new options for intervention, as the often-unseen shapes and forms of life in the city becomes visible. Design, here, is less like a tool and more like a language, a practice that shapes the outcomes and understandings of the things we do. It is not simply an aesthetic prejudice. The ways in which we present ideas and information can sometimes be even more important than the material itself."[9] Synthesis here comes from aggregation and compilation of maps, which demonstrate that there are multiple phenomena at play: the same blocks tend to feature overlapping concentrations of returned inmates, poor people, and people of color. Mapping this data also reveals the questionable environmental conditions defining several of the blocks under study. This work cannot help but raise questions and suggest more thought on the allocation of infrastructural resources in cities.

Real Time Rome

Another university-based architectural research lab provides examples of detective work. The SENSEable City Lab, a research group at MIT, headed by architect Carlo Ratti, capitalizes on the recent ubiquity of handheld electronics to develop new modes of observing and documenting the built environment. As their web portfolio notes, "the way we describe and understand cities is being radically transformed."[10] The tools of data gathering have shifted—smart phones, auto GPS systems, GIS software—but the fundamental architectural detective work remains the same.

The project Real Time Rome, first presented at the 2006 Venice Biennale, collected cellphone tracking information, and data from sensors in Rome's taxis and buses. From this, the team developed graphics showing, in real time, the ebb and flow of city life.[11] While the city is experienced variably by pedestrian and driver individually, aggregate movements of people, traffic and transit reveal relationships between various urban elements which, at best, could be only partially glimpsed from within the flux. The maps describe how the city's diurnal patterns take shape without the gauzy film of subjective first-hand impression. They show how distribution of vehicles relates to densities of people, and how various groups inhabit the city.

Here is observation by prosthesis: the city is "seen" simultaneously and continuously, many thousands of times, by sensors deployed in a comprehensive network. The documentation of this project contributes another entry to the rich legacy of Roman cartography, memorializing our age of ubiquitous sensing through maps which Nolli could never have fathomed, and prefiguring the kind of spatial information served up by our ever-smarter phones. The synthesis of work through the exhibition at the Biennale is indeed the creation of something new: dynamic visualizations of the city which allow us not only to intimately know its present, but also speculate on its future. We see the city we know so well, yet with fresh eyes.

These examples and the projects discussed at greater length in this chapter evidence that the work of seeing, showing, and tying together is not simply a precursor to, but is in itself, a creative architectural end. That said, detective work *can* subsequently be further leveraged, often for architectural activism or design. By highlighting unseen or marginalized groups, as in the Million Dollar Blocks, it can easily be a springboard to the architect acting as advocate. The pursuit of specific questions can arise from explorations of the investigator, as in Real Time Rome, where the architect as initiator enables new work. Also, as in more conventional practice models, it can contribute to thoughtful production of built work.

The Liberation of Detective Work

The work emerging from today's architectural detectives is generated using the same skills and processes as conventional architectural production. It takes different shapes and forms, and thus can be too easily marginalized as something other or something incomplete. However, we can and should recognize that broadening our conception of architectural practice to include this mode of working plays directly to core strengths of the profession, and enriches its contributions to society and culture. An expanded understanding of the architect's work is liberating, in part *because* architectural detective practice does not necessarily yield new built work. There are at least three key dimensions to this freedom. First, detective work is undertaken without the expense of site and material acquisition, and hence does not engender the same models of patronage as the design and construction of most built works. Detective work thereby allows for a greater breadth of clients who can afford to

Left: Images from the Real Time Rome project show the citywide movement of people and traffic following Italy's victory in the final match of the 2006 World Cup. The game was July 9 from 8 to 10pm, afterward, people started celebrating around the Circo Massimo. Celebrations the following day can be seen from the dataset.

engage architects, many of whom otherwise have too small or unusual a voice for architects to hear. The post-patronage practice of detective work liberates the architect to be able to work freely, on issues of social, cultural and ecological relevance, without need to cultivate conventional sponsorship. Second, as sensitive built environment experts, architects are uniquely qualified to uncover truths about our current buildings, neighborhoods, and cities. Constraining validation of architectural talents to production of new work forestalls the insight and discovery to be gained through study of the existing. Third, detective skills may allow newly minted architecture graduates to add to meaningful social discourse ahead of their contribution through built work.

The practitioners in this chapter take on detective work with gusto. Georgeen Theodore, in her work with Interboro Partners, uses rigorous analysis, coupled with innovative graphics, to uncover and convey site specific spatial understandings. Juliette Spertus observes and documents the urban phenomenon of a unique infrastructure. The curation of this information reveals not only the existence of this hidden and quirky system, but also makes manifest the range of sociopolitical constructions which govern a city's spatial decision making. Natalie Jeremijenko describes a range of techniques for making our relationship to our ecology evident, and through her work plays matchmaker between the observer and various specific elements of the natural environment. The work of this trio of architects-as-detectives is simultaneously familiar and novel, allowing us to recognize it as architecture, yet rethink how it is made.

NOTES

1. Many have written extensively on the history of the fictional detective. A good historical overview was put together for an exhibit 1973 at the Lilly Library at Indiana University, documented online at http://www.indiana.edu/~liblilly/etexts/detective/, accessed June 6, 2014. Crime novelist Mark Billingham has discussed the evolution of the fictional detective on his website http://www.markbillingham.com/detective.html, accessed June 6, 2014.

2. Sherlock Holmes not only could distinguish among over 140 varieties of tobacco ash, but his character wrote a monograph on the subject in *The Sign of the Four*. For more discussion, see the essay "140 Different Varieties" by Holmes enthusiast John Hall here: http://www.artintheblood.com/misc/tobacco.htm , accessed June 10, 2014.

3. William McDonough uses this term in the architectural work of his firm, William McDonough + Partners.

4. HBO's TV series *The Wire* is consummate example, whereby the name of the series refers to data collection through various modes of electronic surveillance, whereupon analysis for patterns is a significant plot device for apprehending targets.

5. Juhani Pallasmaa, *The Eyes of the Skin: Architecture and the Senses*, (Chichester, England: Wiley Academic 2005), 15.

6. Susan Sontag, as quoted in Pallasmaa, *The Eyes of the Skin*, 30 .

7. New York Times, December 25, 1968 as quoted in "Contested Global Visions" by Denis Cosgrove

8. Bruno Latour. "40 Years Later", in *Ecological Urbanism*, ed. Mohsen Mostafavi and Gareth Doherty. (Baden, Switzerland: Lars Müller Publishers, 2011), 137. Latour writes, "Could I have imagined, forty years ago, that the Apollo missions were not leading toward outer space, but, on the contrary, would soon backfire and lead our attention to inner space? I mean the space of the Blue Planet that astronauts were filming with such rapt precision.... So much for the macho imagination of space adventure: Forward! Forward! Back to Earth, rather. And to discover what? That the Earth is about as fragile as this tinly model of the Earth that was called a space station. Billions of dollars spent by NASA to give some weight to a sheer metaphor: the Blue Planet as a spaceship—and a makeshift one at that."

9. From the SIDL website: http://www.spatialinformationdesignlab.org/about.php?id=13, accessed July 2, 2014.

10. From the MIT SENSEable City Lab website : http://senseable.mit.edu/, accessed July 2, 2014.

11. http://senseable.mit.edu/realtimerome/, accessed July 2, 2014.

PROJECT CREDITS

Million Dollar Blocks, 2006 Images: Spatial Information Design Lab. (Laura Kurgan and Eric Cadora: Project Directors. David Reinfurt, Sarah Williams; Research Associates)

Real Time Rome, 2006-7 MIT SENSEable City Lab (Carlo Ratti, Andres Sevtsuk, Burak Arikan, Assaf Biderman, Francesco Calabrese, Filippo Dal Fiore, Saba Ghole, Daniel Gutierrez, Sonya Huang, Sriram Krishnan, Justin Moe ,Francisca Rojas, Najeeb Marc Tarazi)

62

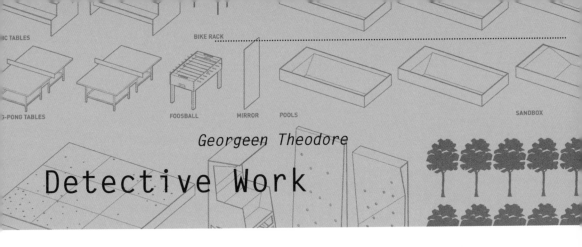

IC TABLES BIKE RACK ....

3-PONG TABLES   FOOSBALL MIRROR POOLS   SANDBOX

Georgeen Theodore

Detective Work

Architecture is changing, and as *Beyond Patronage* suggests, architectural practices that go beyond the traditional patron-led model are gaining importance. An increasing number of practices are exploring new models of architectural project development, partially in response to the decreasing number of traditional commissions for small firms, and partially motivated by the desire to formulate their own project briefs. These alternative models — where work is self-initiated or engages non-traditional patrons — upend conventional understandings of project basics, such as the identity of client or owner, program, and financing. I would put Interboro Partners, the office I co-founded and lead with Tobias Armborst and Daniel D'Oca, squarely in the "beyond patronage" camp. In our work, we have challenged traditional definitions of the client, thought expansively of what the architectural project and program is, and explored alternative means of financing.

Most of our projects begin not with a phone call from a prospective client, but with our unsolicited interest in a specific place, like a dead mall, a shrinking city, or a neighborhood. Turning this interest in a place into a design project first requires that we get to know the place very well, and we therefore begin our work by asking questions: *What is going on here? How do people here see their neighborhood? Who are the actors?* And: *Is there a need for architecture?*

These questions initiate the work, define its scope, and identify its "clients." We call it "detective work," and it's a critical phase in our process that allows us to practice *beyond patronage*. By visualizing the results of this investigative process, we reveal an understanding about a place, how it works, how it doesn't, if there is any need for architecture, and, if so, what we could do. Our detective work — looking around for clues, interviewing a wide range of witnesses, and trying to suspend judgment for as long as possible while we embrace the seeming infinity of conflicting, partial views — gives us the material to define the project itself. Based on this approach, our projects have taken up a number of strategies, which range from advocating for a particularly worthwhile spatial practice (emphasizing the ways in which people already use space), to developing plans that strengthen the specifics of a site, to improving the physical environment by making it more inclusive and open to potential actors and activities. Working in this way has allowed us to think more expansively about what architecture is, what it can do, and what our role as architects is.

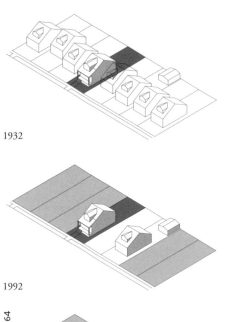

1932

1992

1999

1992

2002

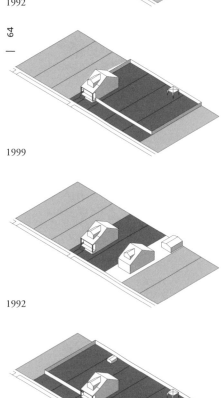

Improve Your Lot!

"Blotting" happens when a homeowner takes, buys, or borrows one or more empty adjacent lots. We observed this practice in Detroit, where widespread disinvestment and depopulation of the city had resulted in thousands of vacant parcels of land. We saw this as an epilogue to the familiar narrative of abandonment: people acting out of self-interest to take on the problem of the shrinking city.

Garden blots, trampoline blots, satellite dish blots, above-ground pool blots, semi-circular driveway blots, carport blots: These are examples of how "blotters" are changing the genetic code of the city. By conjoining multiple lots into a single larger parcel, they produce opportunities for new living configurations, differing significantly from the historical housing stock of the original parcels.

Blotting, as small, distributed land investments, constitutes a bottom-up form of incremental urban redevelopment that doesn't rely on the mega-project. It's a re-platting of the city that suits the immediate needs of its constituents.

We located our role as architects in ghostwriting; that is, advocating for these practices and rendering them visible, by starting blotsblog.org, by organizing public symposia, by telling the stories of these people and their properties.

The Garden Blot

The Anderanin's Garden Blot is a six-lot blot whose growth reflects the incremental way in which many blots are assembled. Initially, Jean Anderanin owned a single-family bungalow sited on one 30'x104' lot. By the early 1990s, numerous vacant, city-owned parcels surrounded the Anderanin home, and in 1992, Jean acquired the two next to the Anderanin home. In 1999 and 2002, Jean's son Michael purchased three additional lots, expanding the family's property to six contiguous parcels.

The result is an expansive, suburban-scaled property. Enclosed by a wooden fence, the six contiguous parcels are reconfigured as a large, walled garden of 180'x 104'. The fence does not entirely enclose the house, but intersects it roughly at the back of the front porch. The elevated front porch projects out of the enclosed area, and provides both a view over the fence back into the enclosed garden and a clear, long view down the street. The Anderanin's house is now at the intersection of two very different types of private open space: a large private garden and the semi-private porch that connects to (and to a degree controls) the street.

Photos of Detroit "blots"

In the Meantime, Life with Landbanking

Focusing on a presumed "Dead Mall," our investigation of the Dutchess County Mall in Fishkill, New York revealed that the seemingly abandoned place was actually full of life.

The isolated Dutchess Dry Cleaners is one of the few remaining businesses at the mall. It doubles as an Atlantic-City-bound bus stop.

A hotdog vendor anticipates the truckers for whom the mall has become an informal rest stop.

A flea market moves in each weekend.

Jay noticed that after the mall was abandoned, truckers started pulling off of I-84 to rest in the mall's parking lot.

Opposite: Stills from the video "An Autobiography of the Dutchess Mall"

but let's take a closer look:

If I was dead, would I still be served by the Dutchess County Loop Bus?

Or the Short Line Bus to and from Atlantic City?

If I was dead, who would be here long enough to need these?

It appears also that I am a temporary home for certain things.

The Dutchess Mall is not dead.

On this Autumn Sunday, The Dutchess Mall is the least dead place in Dutchess County.

GREEK-AMERICAN FOOD
GYRO · SOUVLAKI

FLEA MARKET
OUTDOOR MARKET EVERY SUNDAY

Here we see how businesses or public spaces can emerge from the absence of density—where the remaining elements of public space and its endogenous cultures have to merge to survive.

Based on these informal occupations of the "dead mall," we proposed ways of recolonizing the space, rather than re-planning it.

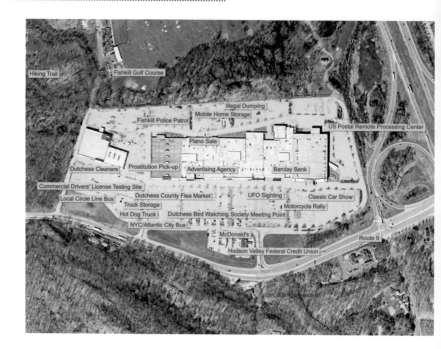

Hiking Trail
Fishkill Golf Course
Illegal Dumping
Mobile Home Storage
Fishkill Police Patrol
US Postal Remote Processing Center
Piano Sale
Dutchess Cleaners
Prostitution Pick-up
Advertising Agency
Barclay Bank
Commercial Drivers' License Testing Site
Dutchess County Flea Market
UFO Sighting
Classic Car Show
Local Circle Line Bus
Motorcycle Rally
Truck Storage
Hot Dog Truck
Dutchess Bird Watching Society Meeting Point
NYC/Atlantic City Bus
McDonald's
Route 9
Hudson Valley Federal Credit Union
Van Wyck Expressway

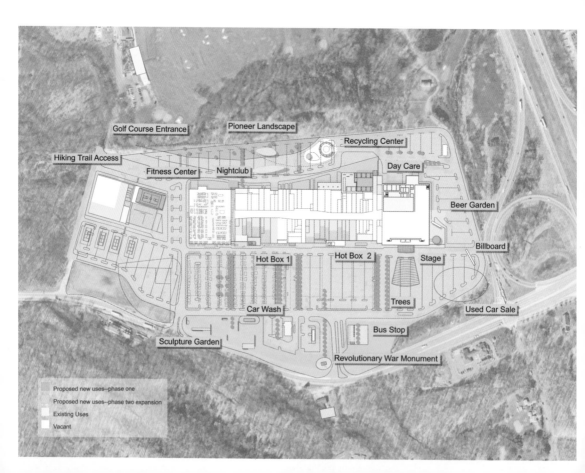

Golf Course Entrance
Pioneer Landscape
Recycling Center
Hiking Trail Access
Fitness Center
Nightclub
Day Care
Beer Garden
Billboard
Hot Box 1
Hot Box 2
Stage
Car Wash
Trees
Used Car Sale
Sculpture Garden
Bus Stop
Revolutionary War Monument

Proposed new uses--phase one
Proposed new uses--phase two expansion
Existing Uses
Vacant

The question about temporary projects is: what happens to all the stuff once the installation comes down? We wondered if we could build something that could be put to good use after MoMA PS1 was done with it. So we asked businesses and organizations in the surrounding Long Island City neighborhood if there was something they needed, that we could design or buy, that we could give them after the installation ended.

The MoMA PS1 courtyard was then converted into a kind of storage space for the period of Warm Up (June to September), where these items of both temporary and eventual, permanent use were held.

TREE

To create Holding Pattern, we asked MoMA PS1's neighbors the following question:
Is there something you need that we could design, use in the courtyard during the summer, and then donate when Holding Pattern is deinstalled in the fall?

↳ A lot of MoMA PS1's neighbors needed trees. The eighty-four trees in Holding Pattern were donated by New York Restoration Project. As part of MillionTreesNYC, New York Restoration Project will plant the trees on the properties of the neighbors who asked for them.

RED OAKS, 8 TREES, EACH APPROXIMATELY 1" IN CALIPER, INSTALLED WITH MULCH AND STRAW, GIFT OF THE NEW YORK RESTORATION PROJECT AND UNIBELL/CENTERSERV.

PURPLE LEAF PLUMS, 40 TREES, EACH APPROXIMATELY 1" IN CALIPER, INSTALLED WITH MULCH AND STRAW, GIFT OF THE NEW YORK RESTORATION PROJECT AND ORIBAR/LAKEBRESARV.

CHESS TABLE

To create Holding Pattern, we asked MoMA PS1's neighbors the following question:
Is there something you need that we could design, use in the courtyard during the summer, and then donate when Holding Pattern is deinstalled in the fall?

↳ Three of MoMA PS1's neighbors wanted a chess table. The three chess tables in Holding Pattern will be donated to the neighbors who asked for them.

PED PLASTICORE, PIX MINIMUM, ABOUT, PLYWOOD, 3 UNITS, 33 X/X' X/X'

ROCK-CLIMBING WALL

To create Holding Pattern, we asked MoMA PS1's neighbors the following question:
Is there something you need that we could design, use in the courtyard during the summer, and then donate when Holding Pattern is deinstalled in the fall?

↳ Long Island City Kids wanted a rock-climbing wall for their gymnasium. The rock-climbing wall in Holding Pattern will be donated to them.

POLYURETHANE ON MARINE-GRADE PLYWOOD, 1 UNIT, 15/X2' X/X' - 15'

PING PONG TABLE

To create Holding Pattern, we asked MoMA PS1's neighbors the following question:
Is there something you need that we could design, use in the courtyard during the summer, and then donate when Holding Pattern is deinstalled in the fall?

↳ Two of MoMA PS1's neighbors needed a ping pong table! The two ping pong tables in Holding Pattern will be donated to Checker Management Corporation and Information Technology High School.

ALUMINUM, 1 UNIT, 108'X60'X30'

FOOSBALL TABLE

To create Holding Pattern, we asked MoMA PS1's neighbors the following question:
Is there something you need that we could design, use in the courtyard during the summer, and then donate when Holding Pattern is deinstalled in the fall?

↳ Jacob A. Riis Neighborhood Settlement House needed a foosball table for their new recreation room. The foosball table in Holding Pattern will be donated to them.

BAKED PVC CABINET AND LEGS, 1 UNIT, 37'X30'X56'

What's Good for Long Island City is Good for MoMA PS1

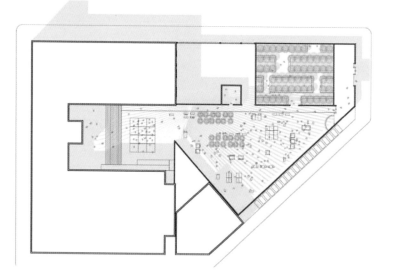

Trees, requested by teamsters and cab drivers and many of the PS1 neighbors, were planted in temporary beds, each tree tagged with its ultimate location.

Mirrors earmarked for the Long Island City School of Ballet were mounted on the concrete walls in minimalist fashion where they became the summer selfie locale for Warm Up hipsters.

The pre-allocated Ping-Pong tables, foosball tables, rock-climbing walls and chess tables were set up in the courtyard to make what Barry Bergdoll has called the "public rec room."

Under the shade of a light-weight canopy, the installation created a space of encounter for several different publics: the Warm-Up crowd, the museum goer, and people from the neighborhood—otherwise insulated from the institution—who could go and visit their stuff.

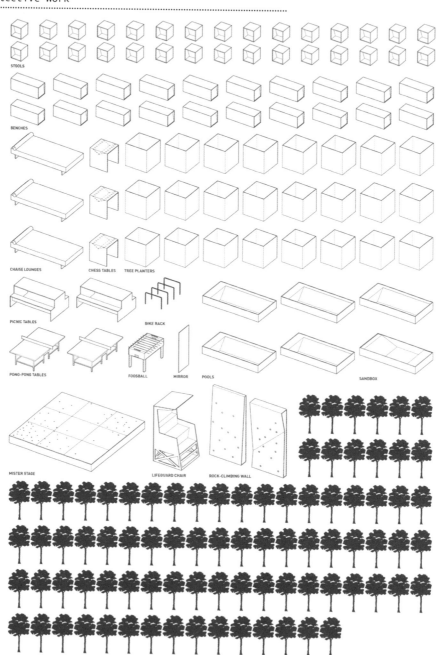

STOOLS

BENCHES

CHAISE LOUNGES   CHESS TABLES   TREE PLANTERS

PICNIC TABLES   BIKE RACK

PONG-PONG TABLES   FOOSBALL   MIRROR   POOLS   SANDBOX

MISTER STAGE   LIFEGUARD CHAIR   ROCK-CLIMBING WALL

TREES

Project Credits

Improve Your Lot!, Archplus "Shrinking Cities" International Ideas competition, 2006-
Interboro Partners (Tobias Armborst, Daniel D'Oca, Georgeen Theodore, Christine Williams), in collaboration with CUP

In the Meantime, Life with Landbanking, LA Forum for Architecture's "Dead Malls" Competition, 2002
Interboro Partners (Tobias Armborst, Daniel D'Oca, Georgeen Theodore, Christine Williams)

Holding Pattern at MoMA PS1, MoMA PS1 Young Architects Program, New York, NY, 2011
Interboro Partners (Principals: Tobias Armborst, Daniel D'Oca, Georgeen Theodore; Project Manager: Rebecca Beyer Winik, Kathleen Cahill
Andrew Coslow, Jenessa Frey, Lesser Gonzalez, Trevor Lamb), with Buro Happold (Structural Engineering), New York Restoration Project, Thumb (Graphic Design)

Build It In:

Making the Case for Garbage
Collection in Urban Design

Juliette Spertus

73

FAST TRASH

Garbage, piled up in waist-high mounds on sidewalks, is a defining
feature of New York City's public space, yet in architecture and
urban planning, the staging, collection, and transport of these flows
is nowhere: not in architectural renderings, not in urban design
briefs, not in environmental impact statements. Except, it turns
out, on Roosevelt Island, a sliver of land in the East River between
Manhattan and Queens, where residential waste has been collected
underground via pneumatic tubes since the island was developed
as a "new town in town" by the New York State Urban Development
Corporation (UDC) in 1975. The UDC (1968-1975) was a housing and
community renewal agency with broad powers and a mandate for social
and architectural innovation. The UDC had integrated waste handling
into the built environment. I wondered why New York State had chosen
this alternative strategy. Was Roosevelt Island's AVAC (short for
automatic vacuum collection) still running thirty-five years later?
Could this alternative approach offer lessons for the design of
public space and urban infrastructure in general? What follows is the
story of how, as a designer with no previous experience, I advocated
for garbage collection as an urban design and planning issue and
went from digging around for explanations with images and stories to
making policy recommendations with tables and charts.

I visited the island and learned that the system is still running, and that administrators and residents like it. Indeed, they tend to forget about it except on rare occasions when service is interrupted and black bags begin piling up on the sidewalks (as they do in every other New York City neighborhood). This mile-long tube network is owned by Roosevelt Island Operating Corporation (RIOC), the public benefit corporation that manages the Island for New York State, and operated by New York City Department of Sanitation. One striking feature of the system is that it operates in isolation. The stationary engineers, high pressure plant tenders, machinists, oilers, and electricians who worked with AVAC didn't have time to explore whether other pneumatic systems existed let alone what could be learned from them. There are no other government-run pneumatic collection systems in the U.S. and it appears that the handful of other systems built in the 1970s were also managed without the benefit of information sharing on operations, repairs, or upgrades. Technicians come up with their own solutions, in house. The benefits of pneumatic collection are self-evident: reduced congestion, noise, odors, rats, and improved public health and public space. Sanitation departments have the relentless tasks of moving the waste the city never stops producing and keeping things clean under all conditions, yet they are not expected to address larger public interests. So, there is no inherent incentive from the waste handling side to change course. Meanwhile, the scale and complexity of solid waste systems — behind all of those collection trucks lies a regional-scale industrial processing and freight transport network with its own logics of efficiency — discourage urban planners and designers from proposing meaningful improvements.

Other technical services such as public transportation or storm water management have been integrated into design proposals and master plans. Perhaps the absence of waste management in design can be understood as a ramification of its intangibility just as operations and maintenance, so critical to the life of a new building, are often considered distinct from the architectural project completed by the architect. When it is considered, maintenance is often undermined by poor communication between designers and building managers, inadequate funding, or a combination of the two. Talking about garbage actually makes people nervous.

Others had already discovered Roosevelt Island's quirky garbage collection. But to me, the challenge—and the opportunity—was to use AVAC to reveal the material flows as a feature of the built environment that could be discussed, invested in, and improved upon with pride just like a bridge, a subway station, or a public park.

The fortieth anniversary of the Philip Johnson and John Burgee master plan for Roosevelt Island (1969) became my excuse to celebrate AVAC and collaborate with RIOC. This collaboration allowed me access to the system and to RIOC's informal archive, which turned out to be critical. I engaged the design firm Project Projects and together we generated a conceptual framework for an exhibition that would both give form to an invisible system, and create a spectacle that would be appealing and authoritative enough to attract a broad audience. Jack McGrath, an artist, archivist, and musician gearing up for a graduate degree in Landscape Architecture answered a call for interns. He was initially attracted by the steam punk aura of tube networks but became an integral part of all aspects of the project. I also had the opportunity to work with Jack Conviser, a licensed architect and urban designer who was between jobs and, like me, thought garbage was important. My approach was to generate as much new content as possible in a variety of media, taking advantage of the resources and talents available, and see what worked best. Developing original content was important because until then most of the material on pneumatic collection was published in obscure 1970s engineering journals and technical reports or based on developer or manufacturer press releases. No in-depth independent source of information on pneumatic collection existed. Without this kind of information how can anyone take tubes seriously? The goals were to create a critical, open-ended experience and invite visitors to draw conclusions from the diverse material, along the lines of the thematic architecture exhibitions at the Canadian Centre for Architecture in Montreal or the Museum of the City of New York, and to avoid the appearance of a trade show booth.

Fast Trash exhibition postcard using photo of the AVAC facility

The exhibition opened on April 22, 2010 as part of RIOC's roster of Earth Day programming and closed on May 24 to make room for the community-run Roosevelt Island Visual Arts Association (RIVAA)'s annual members art show, "The Island of Art". It took some negotiating, including detailed presentations at membership meetings, promises to staff RIVAA's gallery during the show and restore it afterward, and convincing Island artists that an exhibition about garbage would not tarnish their image. We characterized the exhibition as part infrastructure portrait, part urban history, and produced it as a site-specific installation. We installed sections of old pneumatic pipe in front of the gallery (they were so popular as seats that one gallery member wondered if they could be left permanently) with a 2-minute video loop of garbage swirling around inside the system whose tubes run six feet under the building. From inside, visitors looked past the exhibits at a stretch of Main Street essentially unchanged since the development was built in 1975.

We identified different ways of telling the story, each alluding to the wider implications of the hyper-specific subject, and these became sections of the show. "How Did Roosevelt Island Get a Pneumatic Garbage Collection System?" juxtaposed the history of the Island's development as a residential community with the garbage crisis in New York City. "Pneumatic Transport" described New York's own pneumatic network for first-class mail delivery (1897-1953) with maps and photographs of that system, and the installation of a 4-inch diameter Plexiglas tube, through which visitors could send canisters criss-crossing and looping around inside the gallery. The tube was donated by Lamson Airtubes, the manufacturer of both the tubes in New York's old mail system and, until recently, the central branch of the New York Public Library. (Most of their current clients are hospitals and warehouses.) "Vacuum Collection" presented the history of pneumatic networks for waste through the 1970s to explain where the notion came from (built-in vacuum cleaner systems) and how Roosevelt Island's engineers could have known about the technology. "Sanitation" presented Roosevelt Island's experiment in the context of conventional truck-based collection in New York City and case

Above: Installation photo, history of Roosevelt Island development with view of Main Street beyond

Right: View of Fast Trash exhibit from Street with section of AVAC tube and reflection of Jose Luis Sert façade

studies of pneumatic systems in other countries. For this we created maps of tube networks against the street grid, in the spirit of the identically-scaled streetscape comparisons in Jacobs' *Great Streets* (1995). In "Operations" photographer Kate Milford portrayed each of the nine Department of Sanitation employees at work inside the AVAC facility. Early in my research I contacted Envac, the original Swedish manufacturer, for information. By chance, the communications director happened to be on vacation with his children in New York and so we met. Perhaps as a result of this meeting and the novelty of the suggestion, the firm later agreed to sponsor the exhibit. They provided access to information and allowed us to retain control of the content. I did accept their suggestion to include what they called their "Counter Proposal," a set of schematic plans describing the design of a typical modern system and including the cost, roughly, to replace the current equipment with a modern facility. We included their drawings as they were, without additional graphic treatment, as we had manufacturer brochures and diagrams from earlier periods. "What If There Were No Roads?" and "Breaking It Down" presented drawings and interpretive materials created by Roosevelt Island Middle School students during a workshop organized by the Center for Urban Pedagogy (CUP), a Brooklyn-based urban policy education organization and fiscal sponsor for the exhibit. With a 14-minute documentary by filmmaker Greg Whitmore projected along a back wall, visitors first heard the voices and then saw the faces of engineers and residents as they described the experience of running the AVAC system or using it to take out the trash.

To encourage visitors to the relatively obscure location (most non-resident visitors had never been to the Island) during the exhibition's short one-month run, I developed a series of walking tours and events in collaboration with Urban Omnibus (the Architectural

League of New York's online publication), the Roosevelt Island and
Astoria historical societies, CUP, Habitatmap (an environmental
advocacy group), and The Public School (an autodidactic education
organization). I also organized an evening-long "Fast Trash" symposium in Manhattan hosted by NYU's Wagner School of Public Service,
co-sponsored by RIOC and Envac. The event brought together public
officials from Barcelona, Stockholm, and Montreal; an urban designer
from Toronto; and a housing expert from London to discuss their
experiences with pneumatic collection with counterparts from New York
City. In 2011 we launched fasttrash.org, an online version of the
physical exhibition, also designed by Project Projects, with additional archival materials and media from the show.

COST BENEFIT ANALYSIS

When I began organizing Fast Trash I saw my role as a curator
generating cultural programming to advance urban design by exploring
alternative urban infrastructures. I imagined that if the exhibit
was very successful it might be picked up by a museum. What actually
happened was even better. CUP invited Benjamin Miller, a former
director of policy planning for the Department of Sanitation and
author of *Fat of the Land* (2000), a history of garbage in New York
City, to give a talk in the gallery. Miller also studies the last-
mile problem for inbound freight in New York as a senior research
associate at CUNY's University Transportation Research Center (UTRC).
So, tube networks for garbage were as exciting to him as a "first-
mile" transportation alternative as they were for me with respect to
public space. Miller used his talk to suggest a bold next step: apply
Roosevelt Island's strategy to Manhattan, the city's densest, most
congested area where the volumes of trash are highest.

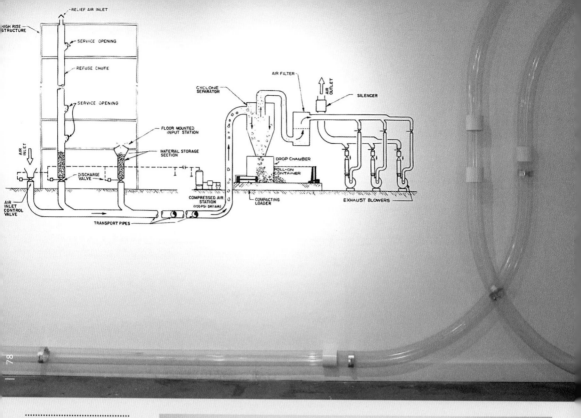

Top: Installation photo, Operations Diagram (1970) by engineering firm Gibbs and Hill with functioning Lamson Airtubes pipe

Right: Installation photo, One-to-one comparison of Stockholm and Barcelona networks

Bottom: Installation photo, CUP operations diagram and city comparisons

Opposite: Walking tour organized with the New York Architectural League's Urban Omnibus entering the Fast Trash exhibit

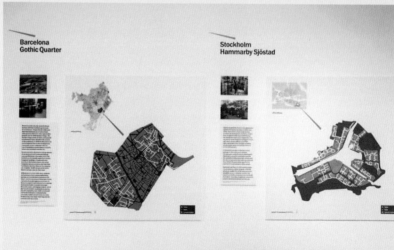

Barcelona
Gothic Quarter

Stockholm
Hammarby Sjöstad

Miller explained that beyond the obvious operations benefits, pneumatic collection could also help New York City adopt policies that
would significantly reduce the amount of waste it sends to landfills.
Because the Fresh Kills Landfill closed in 2001, New York City's
waste must be sent to landfills as far as Virginia at huge cost.
The City has struggled to improve its 15% diversion rate[1] (Seattle
recycles about twice as much). The Department of Sanitation qualifies
its relatively low rate by explaining that it is very difficult to
adopt policies such as source-separation of organic wastes, a third
of the waste stream, because storage and handling of organic wastes
in multifamily buildings is particularly hard.[2] A pneumatic system
addresses this because once waste enters the system it is sealed in
from the inlet point to the container at the other end. No storage or
handling areas are needed. Also challenging is implementing "save-as-
you-throw" (SAYT) programs in which residents are charged on a unit
basis for the waste they produce, with special bags or rates based on
bin size, offering an effective economic incentive to reduce waste
in cities and suburbs comprised mostly of single-family homes. In New
York City a reduction of 12%, almost doubling the current diversion
rate, would be expected. The problem in dense cities like New York
is figuring out ways to make individual efforts count. For example,
New York was the last major city to charge residents for water use
because of the impracticability of retrofitting buildings with water
meters for individual apartments. Pneumatic collection networks can
incorporate accountability with card readers installed on inlet doors
to identify users and measure how much they are throwing in.

Two months after the exhibit closed—with Envac as the industrial
partner and letters of support from the Mayor's Office of Long-term
Planning and Sustainability, the Department of Sanitation, RIOC,
and various other city agencies—Miller, Professor Camille Kamga of
UTRC, and I applied for and won two New York State Energy Research
and Development Authority (NYSERDA) grants: one to explore upgrading
and expanding Roosevelt Island's system to save energy and reduce
emissions and another for a feasibility study to explore the costs
and benefits of a pilot system to collect waste in Manhattan using
existing transportation infrastructure. The grant timeframes were
originally 12 and 18 months, respectively, with cost-sharing by
UTRC and in-kind contribution from Envac. They were completed in
July 2013, three years after we began the application process. The
entire team consisted of Miller and myself as project managers,
Kamga as principal investigator and two UTRC research assistants:
Lisa Douglass, a cultural anthropologist, and Brian Ross, an urban
planner.

The mere fact that an independent exhibit could lead to a serious
study supported by the Mayor's office and led by one of the city's
foremost garbage and transportation experts, with the potential to
influence the future of the system on Roosevelt Island and perhaps
across the City, was extremely satisfying. What we were trying to
achieve with these studies, however, was much more ambitious: demonstrate technical and financial feasibility of the strategy and, if we
were successful, convince land owners, private carters, developers,
and city agencies; raise around 10 million dollars; and then apply
for a second round of NYSERDA funding to develop detailed plans for a
pilot project in Manhattan. Understanding that a concept as radical
as tubes for trash would require more than positive study results, we
took every opportunity to brief key politicians, agency executives,
private carters, environmentalists, developers, and other experts, to

Opposite:: Network map
of Roosevelt Island

bring them into the project as informal advisors and supporters of our advocacy campaign for the serious consideration of tubes.

The Roosevelt Island work was fairly straightforward: figure out how many tons of waste the current facility is handling; how many tons it could handle and from what sources; and how much it costs to run (how much electricity it is using, how many hours of labor). With this data we developed three scenarios ranging from simply replacing the equipment to expanding the system to incorporate residential recyclables as well as all of the refuse and recyclables from businesses and litter bins along Main Street. We then compared Envac's projected installation and operating costs and electricity requirements for these scenarios with two benchmarks: the costs and energy use of the current system, and a hypothetical scenario in which the AVAC facility is shut down and all waste is collected conventionally by truck.[3]

The purpose of the study was to provide RIOC with recommendations based on a cost-benefit analysis and to evaluate the environmental impact (fuel use, greenhouse gas emissions [GHG] and truck trips). As expected, we found that the current 40-year-old system is incredibly costly to operate and maintain, and a replacement facility would pay for itself in several years. A new system would also use much less energy and produce fewer GHG emissions but not less than truck-based collection. This finding was initially surprising until we thought about the shift of storage and staging from individual buildings to a single neighborhood collection point. The pneumatic system is 'run' five times a day, or more for multiple waste streams, instead of several times a week. Efficiency is highly contextual: the relatively small volume of waste and dense collection route on Roosevelt Island actually make conventional truck pick-up efficient, from a collection perspective. GHG emissions were calculated based on official New York City energy production data, but emissions could be reduced if the almost all-electric system were to run on renewable energy sources. We found that, excluding the initial capital investment, the operating and maintenance cost of a modern facility is less than conventional curbside collection. When the facility construction cost is included, all pneumatic scenarios are more expensive.

The arguments for upgrading and expanding pneumatic collection on Roosevelt Island are: quality-of-life benefits of fewer trucks, dumpsters, and bags; a transition away from fossil fuels; and opportunities for progressive waste management. Fewer trucks mean more room on Roosevelt Island's single two-lane road for buses and deliveries, better air quality, less noise, and less pavement wear. Eliminating staging and set-out leaves more space on the sidewalk for bike racks and benches, cafe tables and flowers, with fewer rats and

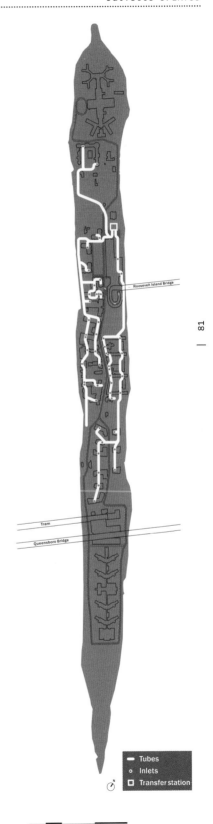

Roosevelt Island Bridge

Tram

Queensboro Bridge

— Tubes
○ Inlets
□ Transfer station

0   500 ft   1000 ft   1500 ft

81

20" Tube

Above: View of High Line from street with proposed tube location

Opposite: High Line/Chelsea Market Pneumatic Network: (1) Trunk line/inlets for High Line Park refuse; (2) Chelsea Market inlets for refuse, paper and organics; (3) Terminal; (4) Hudson Yards

odors. We argued that leveraging the Island's pneumatic system to pilot waste reduction strategies (source separated food waste and unit-based pricing) will help reduce the impacts of long-haul transport and disposal. Roosevelt Island could even leverage its unique situation to help the City test strategies before they are deployed in other neighborhoods whether or not they are using tubes.

We began the Manhattan study working with the Metropolitan Transportation Authority (MTA) to explore the feasibility of a pilot project to retrofit subway tunnels with pneumatic tubes to collect waste from subway platforms as well as from the streets and buildings above. We were interested in the Number 7 Line extension that runs from Times Square, down 11th Avenue to the new Hudson Yards development, over the rail yards on Manhattan's Far West Side. Not only would it be easy to locate a 5,000 SF terminal under the concrete deck, but waste could be loaded on rail cars, eliminating trucks entirely. Also the Hudson Yards developer had just announced, independently, plans to incorporate pneumatic collection on the 26-acre site. A year later, as we were preparing to collect data, the MTA suddenly declined to participate.

We then approached Friends of the High Line (FOHL) about the possibility of strapping a tube to their elevated-rail-line park. The High Line seemed perfect: a high visibility location adjoining the Hudson Yards, a commitment to design and innovation, a nimble, well-run organization. Perhaps most exciting of all, the High Line was built to carry freight in and out of the Chelsea manufacturing district and our tube would put freight (solid waste from the Chelsea Market or another high-volume producer) back on the High Line where material flows could "gurgle like a brook," as Miller likes to say, alongside park visitors, while eliminating idling trucks from the highly congested neighborhood. With approval from FOHL we began searching for terminal sites, analyzing Chelsea Market's waste and producing preliminary designs. Before we were able to go any further, FOHL withdrew from the study, explaining that though they were still enthusiastic about the idea, the demands of their current building program would not allow them to continue hosting our study at that time.

We returned to the MTA with preliminary results from Roosevelt Island and the High Line. This time we were able to present the study directly to one of the Authority's highest-ranking officials, who was a civil engineer. He instantly understood the concept and suggested that we pursue a pilot on a four-block stretch of 2nd Avenue from 92nd to 96th Street on the Upper East Side. Safety and quality-of-life concerns generated by the MTA's seven-year bedrock tunneling project in the mostly residential neighborhood had already led the City to create a high-level taskforce to manage, among other issues, truck access for garbage collection. The street would be open for the next three years while the MTA completed the first phase of the Second Avenue Subway. Our tube could hang under the street with other

utilities and a temporary terminal could be located within one of the construction staging areas. We expanded the scope to include the Housing Authority's Washington Houses and the Metropolitan Hospital campus and were beginning to explore a financing strategy when the MTA again declined to participate further. We were not given a reason but it could not have helped that, in an attempt to solve its waste management problems, the MTA had recently begun removing litter bins from subway platforms, asking riders to take their trash with them out to the street.

ONWARD AND DOWNWARD

Our studies suggest that retrofit-ting Manhattan with pneumatic tubes for garbage, as radical as it sounds, is perfectly reasonable. For the same kinds of context-specific reasons that made the cost-benefit results on Roosevelt Island mixed, we found that for both Manhattan sites pneumatic collection would be more energy-effi-cient and produce fewer GHG emissions than conventional collection.[4] Without continued participation of the host institutions we were unable to develop a pilot directly from the feasibility study but publication of the study results and discussion around them may inspire interest from the original hosts or others.

Despite the rising cost of long-haul transport and disposal in New York City, the environmental impacts and costs of waste are not recognized in planning documents.[5] Although policies are begin-ning to change, there is little economic incentive for developers to take steps to support waste prevention strategies, let alone build pneumatic networks. Currently, the only responsibility that property owners have with respect to waste is to provide the capacity to store waste for up to three days.[6] The size of the garbage room is not defined and no official coefficient of waste per resident or per square foot by occupancy is provided. In effect, devel-opers are encouraged to provide as little space as possible. Signaling recognition of the space required to support recycling efforts, a recent local law will mandate the size of recycling rooms in new construction but the space required to stage material on the curb will

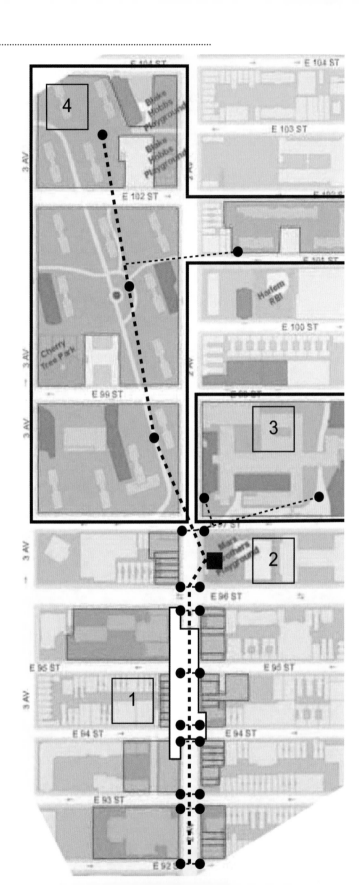

still be ignored. Piles of garbage bags awaiting collection take up room and reduce the value of the space around them (not to mention breeding rats, etc.). The Planning Department could offer bonuses to developers who, by connecting to a pneumatic tube network, free up sidewalk space, just as floor area bonuses are exchanged for publicly accessible plazas in Midtown.

In cities like Toronto, with a save-as-you-throw system and source-separation of organic wastes already in place, spatial requirements are tuned to support waste reduction. Guidelines specify that the location of bins and chutes for diversion (recycling) must be as convenient as those for refuse disposal. They allocate twice as much floor area for recyclables and organics storage as for waste.[7] New York could make similar requirements, or encourage developers to provide additional chutes for recyclables and organics by excluding the space occupied by garbage chutes from floor-area calculations. In large buildings, loading docks are typically used for both incoming deliveries and outgoing refuse. If the building's compactor or waste storage room is in the basement (as is often the case) wastes must be transported to the loading dock for pick-up. In addition to the inefficiency of these maneuvers, in New York City the private carters that collect commercial waste are required to come at night to minimize congestion, thus blocking loading docks when other off-hours-delivery programs could use them.[8]

Of course, more dramatic steps could be taken. In Barcelona, in 2002, pneumatic collection systems were built in the historic city center as part of a large restoration program. A Montreal system was installed in its cultural district in 2010 and a network under the Holy Mosque in Mecca that will collect waste from a million pilgrims is currently under construction. In New York, costly renovations of public space occur all the time: Washington Square Park was renovated several years ago, Times Square will be entirely resurfaced in the next couple of years, Brooklyn's waterfront is being redeveloped for recreation, the Queens' waterfront was rezoned for residential use. Cornell University is building a two-million square foot applied engineering and technology campus on Roosevelt Island that offers a prime opportunity to incorporate progressive waste management into the campus and, by extension, the curriculum. These re-zonings and renovations could be accompanied, at relatively marginal cost, by an integrated urban infrastructure program in which services such as fiber optic cables, district heating and cooling, and pneumatic collection, are incorporated.

The Manhattan pilot, if one is built, could be the first phase in a progression from the current truck-based status quo to a hybrid system of trucks and built-in collection infrastructure, not unlike that of Barcelona. Once opportunistic installations establish pneumatic collection as a practicable and desirable alternative to truck-based collection, a City-wide master plan could identify neighborhoods where pneumatic collection would be most advantageous and set design standards for developing pneumatic networks in these areas. A compelling feature of tube-based collection is that it is inherently modular: networks typically have a radius of a mile or so and, unlike conventional transfer stations that process hundreds or thousands of tons per day, pneumatic terminals can economically handle volumes under 20 tons. Terminals are clean because waste is always sealed within the system. They can be located under parks and in residential neighborhoods. Eventually the City could require

Opposite: Second Avenue Pneumatic Network:
(1) Second Avenue trunk line and street-level inlets (subway station shown in white, subway-level components not shown),
(2) Terminal, (3) Hospital,
(4) NYCHA Washington Houses

Following page: Study Locations in Manhattan

(1) High Line Chelsea Market
(2) Second Avenue Subway
(3) Roosevelt Island

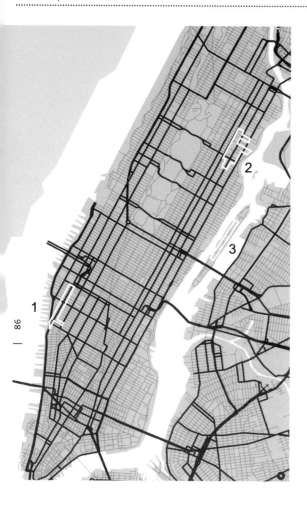

developers to hook up to a pneumatic collection network just as they do water and sewer mains today.

Fast Trash opened a conversation that, in turn, engendered a serious apples-to-apples comparison of pneumatic and conventional systems. These studies may help shape the future of Roosevelt Island and may even inspire someone to replace idling trucks with the gentle murmur of carrot peelings shooting north on the High Line in a Plexiglas tube. There are no shovels in the ground yet, but I am convinced that following the impulse to understand urban conditions and to imagine improvements will eventually spur projects inconceivable within the conventional boundaries of discipline and audience.

NOTES

1. New York City Dept. of Sanitation, "Target Waste Reduction", April 6, 2012, http:// www.nyc.gov/html/dsny/html/emerging_technology/new_emerging_convtech_DSNY.shtml (accessed July 15, 2013).

2. New York City Dept. of Sanitation, "Recycling in context: A Comprehensive Analysis of Recycling in Major U.S. Cities," August 2001, http://www.nyc.gov/html/nycwasteless/ html/ resources/reports_recycling_in_context.shtml (accessed February 12, 2014). See also: plaNYC, "About plaNYC," 2014, http://www.nyc.gov/html/planyc2030/html/about/ about.shtml (accessed February 14, 2014).

3. For details see study report: Camille Kamga et al., "Eliminating Trucks on Roosevelt Island for the Collection of Wastes," University Transportation Research Center, Region 2, 2013, http://www.utrc2.org/sites/default/files/pubs/pneumatic-waste-roosevelt-island-report-Final.pdf (accessed February 12, 2014), 27.

4. For details see study report: Camille Kamga et al., "A Study of the Feasibility of Pneumatic Transport of Municipal Solid Waste and Recyclables in Manhattan Using Existing Transportation Infrastructure," University Transportation Research Center, Region 2, 2013, http://www.utrc2.org/sites/default/files/pubs/pneumatic-waste-manhattan-report-Final_0.pdf (accessed February 12, 2014).

5. See: Citizen's Budget Committee, "Taxes in: Garbage out: The Need for Better Solid Waste Disposal Policies in New York City," May 2012, http://www.cbcny.org/sites/default/ files/ REPORT_SolidWaste_053312012.pdfhttp://www.cbcny.org/sites/default/files/REPORT_SolidWaste_053312012.pdf (accessed July 27, 2012).

6. New York City Rent Guidelines Board, "New York City Housing Maintenance Code," Subchapter 2: Maintenance, Services, and Utilities, Article 5: Collection of Wastes, Sec. 27-2021 Receptacles for waste matter, http://www.housingnyc.com/html/resources/hmc/sub2/art5.html# 27-2021 (accessed July 27, 2012).

7. "The storage room must be large enough to accommodate the following: 2 square metres for every 5 units for the garbage stream, 2 square metres for every 4 units for the recycling stream (including bulky items and electronic waste) and 2 square metres for every 4 units for the organics stream." City Of Toronto, "Requirements For Garbage, Recycling And Organics Collection Services For New Developments And Redevelopments," http://www.toronto.ca/garbage/pdf/requirements_all.pdf (accessed July 27, 2012), 14,16.

8. New York City Dept. of Transportation, "Off-Hour Delivery Program," 2013, http://www.nyc.gov/html/dot/html/motorist/offhoursdelivery.shtml (accessed July 27, 2012).

PROJECT CREDITS

Fast Trash, Exhibition on Roosevelt Island, New York, NY, USA, 2010.
Juliette Spertus (organizer), Project Projects, Jack McGrath, Jack Conviser, Gregory Whitmore, Kate Milford

A conversation with

Juliette SPERTUS
&
Georgeen THEODORE

by
Robert YOOS

//

Robert Yoos:

I would like to start by taking a look at your methodologies of research and practice. Juliette, with your project, you
started with a self-driven idea to investigate garbage collection in New York City. And Georgeen, you took on the idea of the
MoMA PS1 competition and used it as a platform to interject other
ideas stemming from your research. Both of these projects have
reached out to larger audiences, through self-driven methods. I
am wondering: how can architects introduce their own research into
more typical scenarios like RFPs, and typical interactions with
clients? Where do you see potential in interjecting research in
the profession of architecture, and in the field?

Juliette Spertus:

I observed that there were elements of the built environment —
such as garbage — that are very present and have a very large
spatial impact, yet are not inscribed within the typical urban
design brief. Before you can have a design brief there must be
a perception that something can be designed. Urban systems have
their own centuries-old histories. One city's infrastructure
differs from the next thanks to political structures, geography,
cultural expectations, rules, and funding structures. The people
entrusted with day-to-day operations — the ones who truly understand
their city's particular system — tend to be most invested in
keeping things the way they are: "That's the way that it's

always been done, so it's just the way that it is done." To risk politically complex, potentially costly experiments with vital services, decision makers must perceive the cost — in financial, environmental, or public health terms — of the status quo to be intolerably high and the benefits of change all but guaranteed.

What is great about Roosevelt Island is that you have something in the city that has already been operating for about 35 years, so it becomes possible to compare two *existing* strategies for handling trash in the same city. Roosevelt Island's system wasn't widely known and those who knew that it existed considered it unique to Roosevelt Island. Coming back to the idea of an exhibit, if you can reveal the system, it can become an alternative. And suddenly people say, "Why aren't we looking at this?" So, then you have, "Why aren't we looking at this?" counterbalancing, "Well, we always do it this way, so we don't need to look at it."

Georgeen Theodore:

Thinking about research and how it fits in the working process and how the market works, you could say that it's an interesting time for us working in the discipline, because we can be much more opportunistic about identifying certain roles where we can bring value into the process. I think that at the outset you just have to really have something to believe in. It's not just about fitting architecture in with a developer's sensibility, but you actually have to want to advocate for a particular thing, first, before you can even say, "This is how I want it to fit in to whatever system." I think with your work, Juliette, it's very clear what you're advocating for. You created a moment in which you could actually insert your agenda into this context and I think that that's really great. That's a way we can work right now. In our case, at Interboro, when we won PS1 we actually used that competition as a way to pursue questions we're really interested in, for example, "What is the nature of the temporary project?"

This is something that we do with all our clients, whether they are a museum or an institution, or working for the city. We always try to tuck in other things that we want to do within a partic- ular context. I think it points to a role where the architect is, in a way, like a matchmaker, where you can figure out how you can advance your agenda, and also fulfill the needs of the client.

That's where I know we're going with our office, but I see it in other people's practices as well.

I think that it's also the time in which we're working, when the economic conditions are very different than they were five years ago. One of the things that we've found in our work with developers is that the same formulas that worked 5 years ago don't work in the same way that they did before. So, there are opportunities when you can create value, in your own terms, even if you're trying to take on the agenda of the developer in terms of increasing real estate value. I think that there are moments when architects can bring value to the process by visualizing conditions and looking at the larger systems that work, and then identifying moments when design or other kinds of actions can make a more profound impact.

Just to give a concrete example, let's say in the past, when a developer acquired a property, they could just make a couple of improvements and quickly create value. I think that the market has changed; there are atypical conditions, like a dead mall or other condition that doesn't fit into a simple category. Those are opportunities when an architect can bring value to the development process. You have to look at those situations creatively, where you can't just follow standard formulas. Again, it's about taking on an adaptive role and identifying unexpected opportunities. As conditions change, I think being able to adapt and see opportunities in that context is an interesting way to work.

RY: Talking about the points that you brought up – how essential is it to involve the city government? In your lecture, Juliette, you mentioned there could be a possibility where developers could be eligible for a higher FAR if a pneumatic tube system is installed within the building. Can you describe what experiences you've had with the city government and how they respond to these kinds of ideas?

JS: As researchers we did not control land or have access to our own financing. Retrofitting a neighborhood requires collaboration of multiple city agencies. Individuals within various agencies were encouraging, writing letters of support, making introductions and organizing briefings, providing straightforward data, but investing

in the actual project was more difficult. A public housing admin-
istrator said he wanted the system for Christmas, it would save
him millions in operations, but it was not up to him. We'd have
to convince his superiors. At the planning department we heard
someone say that they would wait to see what private developers
would do.

We like to think of the High Line as a model. You have something that was started by private citizens who wanted to preserve
an abandoned piece of infrastructure and transform it into a
park. They used photographs of the abandoned viaduct's landscape
and architects' visions for the park to build a constituency.
Eventually the city had to come around and decide to take that on
as a park. There are other independent initiatives like that. We
are trying to do something similar, raising awareness and building
a constituency so that the City can get behind the change.

RY: What I find interesting, though, is the controversy behind the
High Line in terms of gentrification. It starts off as a strategy
for retrofitting infrastructure, and then it increases the cost
of living and real estate value in its surrounding areas and
completely transforms the community. Arguably, it is displacing
the local population. So, Georgeen, I think that your design for
the MoMA PS1 - how the furniture and the other elements are regis-
tered to the community - and Juliette - how the pneumatic tube
service is a sustainable way of retrofitting that benefits a certain
area - are perhaps more sensitive approaches toward urban renewal.

GT: In many of our projects, we decide that we want to advocate for a
particular group. So, for example, in Holding Pattern, the museum
was our client, and so we were obviously working for them and
supporting their agenda. But we also felt that there was room to
advocate and to incorporate other groups into the process, and
bring value to them and to the client as well. So, instead of just
recognizing MoMA as our single client, we made many other institutions and individuals in the neighborhood our clients, and tried
to bring value to them.

The notion of rewriting the city's genetic code applies also to
our project in Detroit, Improve Your Lot. In that context, we saw
that there was already something happening in Detroit. Individual
homeowners were purchasing or appropriating land adjacent to their
homes and we saw value in that, but nobody else had named or visualized it, or saw it as productive. We thought, "Oh, you know,
this actually is something productive and through our work we can
support that particular group."

You have to make choices. In our case, we are very decisive about
saying, "this is the particular group that we want to support."
We think, in particular cases, there are certain groups that are
being underserved. We recognize that they're important and could
be supported through our work. So, we choose to do that.

RY: Speaking of the Improve Your Lot Project and the fact that it is
actually a user-driven phenomenon, you discussed in the lecture
that you were developing mechanisms to better enable this kind of
bottom-up process. Could you describe these more in-depth?

GT: We started the project quite some time ago. The mechanisms that I referred to were ones that helped identify a particular group of interest. The first part of advocating for a group is just to know who the group is. In that case, no one had really identified that. They hadn't identified themselves as a group per se, and if they're not identified as a group then you can't support them properly. So one of the first things that we did was to name the phenomenon – "blots" – and we were able to consequently refer to that group as "the blotters." In this project, we would say that our work was developing instructive visualizations of the process by which people made blots, to clarify the process for potential "blotters." Going back to what Juliette was talking about, through visualization we were advocating for a group of practices.

Other mechanisms that we designed included a website. Even though making a blot seems kind of simple, it is actually not. It's bureaucratically kind of complicated. There are lots of people out there who know how to do it, but they're just doing their things and nobody else knows what they're doing and how they did it. So we thought we could help form a website that would allow people to showcase their practices and exchange ideas.

Maybe this is not what you would consider to be the typical architect's work, but we considered that to be our project. Another thing we did was to organize and facilitate workshops where people could actually come together and see potentially related efforts. For example, there might be one group that's advocating for land banks and there's another group who are turning parks into gardens. The idea was to get a lot of the groups who are working on similar phenomena to come together with residents and stakeholders.

What was really gratifying about the first workshop was that people who attended made comments like, "Oh, yeah, you know there is one of those down the block from me," or "I always wanted to do that with a lot and that occurred to me, but I didn't know how." So, in a sense, they really validated our work, because increasing public knowledge was part of our ambition.

RY: I'm interested in discussing the idea of not necessarily designing a 'clear' picture, but rather designing environments or processes for advocacy. It's a way of looking beyond the scope of what traditional practices do. What are some tactics that you might suggest, in advising architects who are interested in undertaking projects such as yours? How can one design a local event or place that reaches out to a larger, global public?

JS: When I first started that project, I had a typical idea of an exhibit at the Center for Architecture gallery in Manhattan, or at the Storefront for Art and Architecture. That would have been great, as those are wonderful places, but appealing to totally different institutions made Fast Trash much richer and more effective. So, being very open and taking advantage of what you have to work with is important.

The other thing I'm increasingly aware of is the role of a specific place in curating exhibitions. It's become clear to me that the

location and place shape two scales of knowledge; they enable
visitors to take in the exhibit and also experience the place the
exhibit is describing.

It was important to me that the exhibit connected Roosevelt Island
to other places in the world, to put the island into perspective as one of the world's pneumatic collection neighborhoods. At
the time, it was also the 40th Anniversary of Roosevelt Island,
which is itself almost as forgotten as its pneumatic tube. It
was so important in urban planning in 1969 when it was built and
designed, and it's so under-acknowledged now. A two million square
foot engineering campus is under construction, so things are
changing, but the island had basically been on the shelf for forty
years. Bringing it into a larger context is also a way of saying,
"Look at this system that also exists in New York, on Roosevelt
Island."

GT: In my presentation I spoke about the importance of looking at a
place with an open mind. In all of our work we look at places very
closely and really try to understand the local dynamics. One of
the things that we're always doing is trying to zoom out and look
more expansively at even how the site is defined. So, let's say,
for example, with Holding Pattern, we started out with the site
of a courtyard, but then we really made the site the entire Long
Island City. Or say, in the case of Lent Space, we had one parcel,
but then we tried to think about the neighborhood. With our more
recent project in the Venice Biennale, where we had the courtyard
of the U.S. Pavilion as a site, we made the project about engaging
the whole city.

I think in all of those cases, we were looking at larger systems
of material flows and different systems of organization. In New
York City there was a long-established project of planting a
million trees, and so we tapped into that in order to acquire 85
trees, temporarily, for the Holding Pattern project. In Common
Place, the Venice Biennale project, we were able to borrow the
stands that the city of Venice uses to construct their sidewalks
during the high waters, and that became a substructure for our
courtyard installation.

So, on the one hand you could say, well, that's just really smart,
because you are not wasting materials. You are just taking advantage of material flows and using things more efficiently. But on
the other hand, you could say that, by doing so, you're actually
tying the project to the actors who are part of those other
systems. By making your project an extra link to them, you are
then hopefully making it a value to those other groups. So I think
that's another way of thinking about the question of greater value
for a broader group of people.

One of the strategies that we're employing is thinking more
largely about how the site is connected to other systems. Then
we somehow leverage or tap into those systems, making the project
tied not only to our original client, but also tied to more
people.

I think there are certain schools of thought in the discipline
of architecture that have really narrowed the practice to something very formal, and I think that has a tendency to isolate the
practice just to those conditions that people control. Rather than
turn your back on the messiness that's happening out there, if you

embrace it instead, then architecture can really be more integrated, connected to, and valuable to people and entities that are beyond the boundaries of the discipline.

RY: I have one more question. As women in the field of architecture, were there specific challenges that you faced when trying to access these larger audiences? Has that been a limiting factor at all in any of your work, in pushing forward with research?

GT: When you have a firm where there are multiple partners — let's say in my own practice — it is a way of already moving away from the 'man at the helm' model. There are many emerging practices that are different than the traditional ones. They're more collaborative, but also there are some that are working much like we are, which is to say that their practices are much more self-generated and independent. That way of working gives us a lot of flexibility. So, I haven't felt hindered at all in my recent work. But that's not to say that things are okay, because they're not.

JS: But thinking about these management issues can push people to consider other ways of doing things, to be able to have a family. I began working independently because I did not know how to incorporate this kind of work into my role as an architectural designer employed by a small firm. In retrospect, it is probably more practical to invest in finding ways to build research and outreach into the services of professional practice as Georgeen describes than to try to invent a practice based on this way of working. To do this as an employee, you need the same kind of confidence that is required to negotiate salary or advocate for family-friendly work policies and flexibility where they don't exist.

GT: Going back to some of the threads of the earlier conversation, there are different forms of practice that are emerging that vary quite significantly from traditional corporate models. I think that they present opportunities for people to take advantage of these new models in ways that suit their lives. I would say that the kind of firm that I have with my partners — and the projects we tackle — is inherently more flexible than, say, the traditional architectural office where you're sitting at your desk from 8:30 in the morning until 6:30 or 7:30 or 8:30 in the evening every day.

These new models are not going to correct the inequities that are inherent in the larger structures of the discipline — there is still much more work to be done there — but the emergence of these new models of practice can be quite empowering, because in the process of developing or designing one's own practice you can make it work with your own set of circumstances. That kind of flexibility can be liberating and empowering.

94

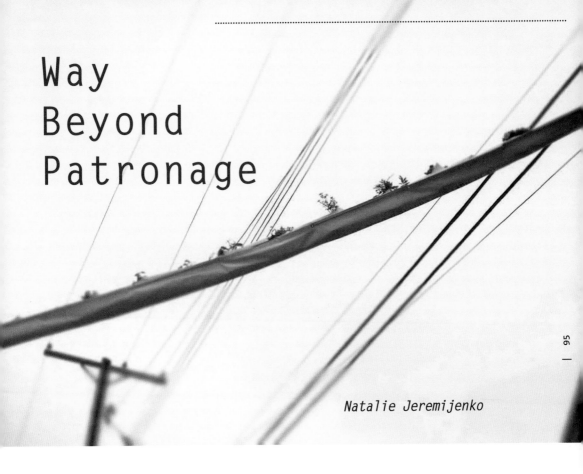

Way
Beyond
Patronage

Natalie Jeremijenko

I've set up my practice, the Environmental Health Clinic at NYU, to reframe the definition of health in a way that is not as we typically understand it, as internal, biological, atomized, genetically predisposed and pharmaceutical. Instead, we regard health as something that is external and shared. It's in the air quality, in the food systems we suckle on, and in the water quality we all enjoy. This kind of reframing aligns with the tradition of institutional critique of conceptual art practiced in the 20th century, of reimagining those durable institutions that choreograph how we interact and what we do.

The Environmental Health Clinic is a university health clinic where people who come in are not patients, but "impatients," because they are too impatient to wait for legislative change to address environmental health issues. They come with their environmental health concerns, as opposed to their medical concerns, and they walk out with prescriptions not for pharmaceuticals, but for things they can do to measurably improve local environmental health.

Dr. Phillip Landrigan's work at the Children's Environmental Health Clinic at Mount Sinai Hospital demonstrates the impact that the environment has on human health. Landrigan writes about the wide array of chronic diseases that pediatricians treat in children. Asthma, he concludes, is the "leading cause of emergency room visits, hospitalizations and school absenteeism." Developmental disorders such as ADHD, dyslexia, and autism have increased dramatically in the last 15 years and "now [affect] one child in 88." Other common chronic

Butterfly Bridge

illnesses that he names include: birth defects, primary brain cancer, childhood leukemia, childhood obesity, and lead poisoning.[1] What's common about these diseases? The environment is implicated. This is not the "germ theory" of health that our medicos are trained in. It's a *redefinition* of health as external and shared. The good news about that is, as opposed to your genetic predispositions, you can act on it. You can change it. You can do something about it.

Our work at the Environmental Health Clinic acts as both a form of detecting environmental ailments, as well as a campaign for increasing proactive awareness of environmental health issues. This kind of work necessarily contends with issues of agency, both in how humans can act constructively for our collective wellbeing and in how we regard the agency of nonhuman organisms as they are implicated in our environmental health. As such, the projects discussed here operate as public experiments in which the discovery and remediation of environmental health issues is itself a collective and participatory pursuit.

1. Animals as Indicators: Conversing with Nonhuman Actors

To become more closely attuned with our environment, I would advocate that we keep talking to our nonhumans. Historically, we have used canaries as bioindicators. So, how might we deepen our conversations with the birds? Perch is a project I did with Phil Taylor that extends communication technologies to birds, specifically the pigeons flying around the Massachusetts Museum of Contemporary Art (MASS MoCA) and the Sculpture Court at the Whitney Museum of American Art, where the project was installed. It brings birds into the smart phone era. When a bird lands on its choice of electronic perches, it triggers a sound file that says something like this:

> *Here's what you need to do. Go down there and buy some of those health food bars, the ones you call bird food, and bring it here and scatter it around. There's a good person.*

In the Whitney Sculpture Court, we set up six of these perches; each one of them had a different 'argument.' My favorite was the one about copyright dues for cell phone ringtones and other melodic resources. But the one that the birds actually decided on, in their experiment on people (what best elicited cooperative behavior from their human subjects), was, by a factor of about eight to one, this particular argument:

> *Tick, tick, tick. That's the sound of genetic mutations of the avian flu becoming a deadly human flu. Do you know what slows it down? Healthy subpopulations of birds, increasing biodiversity generally. It is in your interest that I'm happy, healthy, well fed. Hence, you could share some of your nutritional resources instead of monopolizing them. That is, share your lunch.*

It's a humorous biology lecture from pigeons, but it helps us to understand that our interrelationship with nonhuman organisms actually impacts our health and wellbeing.

Amphibious Architecture is an interactive installation developed in collaboration with David Benjamin and Soo-in Yang (The Living) and commissioned by the Architectural League of New York for the exhibition Toward a Sentient City, organized by Mark Shepard. It is made up of a series of illuminated buoys that float on the East River and the Bronx River. The top layer of lights is always on and shifts from a warm red color to a cool blue-green color when dissolved oxygen is high. As fish swim underneath the array, their movement triggers underwater sensors that then light up the second layer of lights, displaying the presence of fish at low-resolution. So, of course, the first question people ask is, "Well, are there fish in the East River?" And, through this project, we can see that there are.

The idea of Amphibious Architecture is to change the view of these bodies of water from pretty reflective services — the view of which increases our real estate value — to teeming habitats with which we are interacting. Not only can you see that the fish are there, but you can also text the fish, and they text you back.

On the sites of the waterfront installation were business cards of the organisms in the river, with their 'contact details,' so you could text the herring or the tomcod, and they texted you back.[2] At one point, over 700 people were receiving daily updates from the beaver, the most popular organism by far. If you texted "Yo beaver," which was the contact for Jose the beaver, in the East River, he rudely said, "There's no beavers in the East River." He was kind of a sleazy character; the first beaver in over 200 years to settle in New York City, and like two million other desperate single males, if

Left: Amphibious Architecture

Bottom: Organism business cards

Director of Cellulose Cycling & Watershed Mgmt.

(aka the first beaver in NYC in 200 years)

Jose E. Serrano

the Beaver
Castor canadensis

Text "YoBeaver" to 41411
Bronx River Arts Center
1087 E Tremont Ave, Bronx, NY

amphibiousarchitecture.net

Director of Resettlement & Real Estate Asset Development

Gail Nathan
Alewife Herring
Pomolobus pseudoharengus

Txt "BronxRiver" to 41411
to reach my YoY Residence:
Bronx River Arts Center
1087 E Tremont Ave, Bronx, NY

Txt "HolaAlewife" to 41411
To reach my Adult Residence:
Rutger's Slip
Pier 35, New York, NY

you texted him, he was always inviting you to come over for a cross-species adventure, or to come and see his lodge. It was a distinct move away from the pervasive "do-not-disturb" approach to urban environmentalism, but invited curiosity about and engagement with these otherwise invisible organisms.

2. Eating (with) Animals: Food for Environmental Health

Of course, when you set up a relationship between humans and nonhumans, there's always another unsolicited interaction that takes place. In zoos and parks, for example, people have a tendency to throw things at the animals. That's why you always see "do not feed the animal" signs. But if we leave chewing gum, cigarette butts, and Doritos on the ground, why not feed the animals? This question counters the prevailing wisdom that human food is good enough for humans, but not good enough for animals—that we'll interfere with their lives and make them dependent on us. We don't think about that sentiment as we drive along the freeway that cuts off migration routes on the way to Yellowstone National Park, limiting their nutritional resources. We don't think about how we already interfere with their ecologies as human interventions impact the entire global climate.

Yes, we're interfering with the animals. The question is: can we make that productive? Can we make that beneficial? In response, **The Lures Project** is something we developed that delivers nutritionally appropriate food to fish, that humans can also enjoy. It's cross-species food.

The hook is that there is no hook; it's a gin and tonic encased in a gellan-cast commercial fishing lure. I don't know if the fish like the gin and tonic, but they like the gellan, a polysaccharide often used as a culinary thickening agent. You can imagine a busload of kids when they come up to the Amphibious Architecture installation offering this nutritionally appropriate food and augmenting populations of fish whose food sources have been limited by the hard surfaces and edges that we put along our waterfronts in our 'waterfront regeneration' projects. But we've also introduced a medical-grade chelating agent in the lure, similar to the drug that you would be prescribed to take if you had mercury poisoning. When ingested by the fish (or humans), it binds to the bio-accumulated heavy metals and PCBs and passes out in a less reactive form as a salt, where it settles into the silt and is effectively removed from bioavailability. So, it works like a targeted drug delivery model in contemporary medicine, but we're doing it at an ecological scale. Instead of dredging the Hudson, and re-suspending all of that contaminant and toxic sludge, and shipping it off to Texas,[3] where it remains toxic sludge, we can understand a way to locally remediate and repopulate these ecologies, and take advantage of our own agency.

The Lures Project has helped launch the **Cross(x)Species Adventure Club,** which is a molecular gastronomy supper club initiated with Mihir Desai and Emilie Baltz, that meets to enjoy all sorts of delicious cross-species edibles. The charge of the Cross(x)Species Adventure Club is to explore food and food systems that are not only nutritionally yummy for humans and nonhumans, but also reduce the negative damage of our food systems, such as food miles, pesticides, or petrochemical fertilizers. It could be argued that, already, we very effectively manipulate land use with our tongues and taste buds; so, we're driven to build on this reality and experiment with ways to more poignantly connect our food with our environment. How can we eat productively, to actually improve environmental health and increase biodiversity?

I have one word (no, not 'plastics'): wetlands—the technology of the 21st century, albeit wet and slimy. Wetlands are the most critical ecosystem for sequestering CO_2 , for breaking down industrial contaminants. The wetland is a nursery for marine organisms to capture lost nutrients from terrestrial systems and to protect our aquatic ecosystems. Wetlands are also relevant to our food ecosystems. For example, one of the products we've developed for the Cross(x)Species Adventure Club is the **nanoWaterBuffalo Icecream**, a product that has both gastronomical and ecological implications.

Of course, the Romans (and anyone who likes buffalo ricotta) had figured out that water buffalo milk has higher protein and higher fat than cow's milk, and it's creamier and much more delicious. To enhance this quality, we introduced the "nano" part of the equation, which is a liquid nitrogen process that we use to make the ice cream. It produces nano-sized ice crystals to emphasize the luxuriant creaminess of the water buffalo milk.

We proposed our product to Ben and Jerry's Ice Cream: a water buffalo nitrogen ice cream line as a way to create demand for water buffalo, which in turn would require wetland grazing. This projected demand for wetlands reverses the impact of dairy farmers in Vermont who spray their grazing fields with manure that washes into the aquatic ecosystem with every rain event. By incentivizing the construction and stewardship of wetlands, we can improve the environmental performance of these dairy-farming areas while increasing their productivity as well.

This is one of the delicious explorations of the Cross(x)Species Adventure Club, which, of course, as a supper club, must run as a kind of underground operation. So we make these edible invitations that ask you to read them, scan them, and then ingest them. This premise has allowed us to explore materials and forms that are much more ephemeral. In general, these edible projects demonstrate ways in which we can proactively manipulate food systems with our taste buds. It just requires some adventurous eating.

3. Locating Agency: Experiments in Civic Action

All of these projects are really concerned with addressing what I call "the crisis of agency": what to do in the face of shared, uncertain environmental threat, and how that agency can be exercised institutionally, individually and collectively. To illustrate this point, students have said to me something to the effect of: "I'm an environmentalist. I print on both sides of the paper. I ride my bike. I don't eat meat. I turn off the lights. So, shouldn't I just commit suicide? Then my footprint will be even smaller. I'll eat even less meat. I'll use less gas." Obviously, this logic is flawed. We need to shift from this way of thinking about what we *can't* do — the preservationist, conservationist legacy of environmentalism — to what we *can* do, and how our actions can be made productive for our environmental health.

The Civic Action Projects

I was one of four artists invited to develop urban plans for Long
Island City, who took an extensive look at energy systems, waste
systems, manufacturing, and other things, in an exhibition called
Civic Action: A Vision for Long Island City. The first part of this
exhibition took place at the Noguchi Museum, and the second part
involved the implementation of some of these projects at Socrates
Sculpture Park as experiments in structuring public participation.
With Socrates as a both a site and object of experimentation, we were
able to test ways of enabling proactive engagement with environmental
health issues.

As part of this project, the Clinic developed the **eXercise program,**
in which we devised personal training regimes to help you build up
your deltoids or lose weight. It's personal training not only for
your own health, but in order to improve environmental health. So, in
this case, you or a small team of people could join a program around
Long Island City in which you get a series of exercises that all have
positive health benefits for you, and also measurable environmental
health benefits.

Hula-hooping, for example, is really good core body conditioning
for building up that six-pack. Our hula-hoops were adapted with
wildflower seeds from northeastern wildflowers that spread perennial
resources for critical pollinators in the area. It came with a map,
so you can understand the dependent organisms and where your activity
might have the most impact. Obviously, you would be much more likely
to go back next Saturday and do your routine again because you want
to see the effect you've had, the extent to which your actions have
improved the landscape. So, this weaves in an understanding of how we
might adapt our infrastructure to recognize that there are non-humans
amongst us, and they have critical roles to play.

Moth Cinema was another project installed at Socrates. We hung a
silver screen in the park and illuminated it after nightfall every
night. The light that was cast over the garden attracted moths to
it. The garden was planted with nectar plants and other host plants
for these organisms, encouraging the moths to play out their nightly
dramas, their love triangles, their adventures. This nocturnal
activity was projected in dramatic shadows onto the Moth Cinema
screen. We had the first recorded lunar moths inhabiting Socrates
Sculpture Park that summer, the first in New York City in over 40
years. They might have been planted there, but they lived happily
ever after.

One of the characteristics of urban ecosystems is their tremendous biodiversity. The United Nations Environment Programme (UNEP)
conducted a study several years ago on the biodiversity around
Paris. Through a big citizen data collection event, they assessed
biodiversity in metropolitan Paris and the surrounding rural farming
areas to see the difference. We've known this for a long time, but it
was striking to see much more biodiversity in terms of species and
population numbers in metropolitan Paris as opposed to the rural,
agricultural communities around the city. Yet, despite the proliferation of biodiversity in cities, urban ecosystems are characterized
by fragmented habitats with genetically isolated and therefore
frail populations. As designers, we can address the shortcomings of
habitat connectivity. **Butterfly Bridge** is a project that connects
those patches of habitat. The project actually wasn't included in

 **CLINIC** the environmental
health clinic+lab

✖ Project: Moth Cinema
Concept: Concept diagrams
Supervised: Natalie Jeremijenko
Drawings: Fran Gallardo

Screen + Vegetal Moth + Black Light Illumination = **Moth ✖ Cinema**
Provisions Time Lapse Motion

Moth Cinema

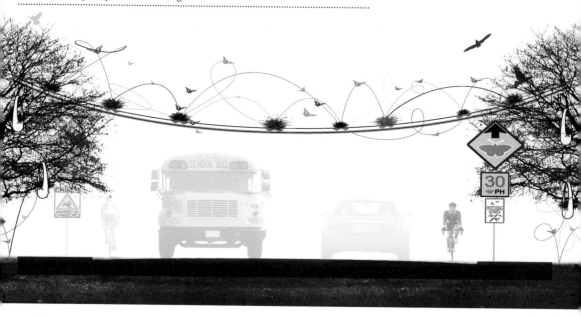

....

Top: Butterfly Bridge

Above: logo, Cross
Species Crossing

....

Opposite: Salamander
Super Highway

the show at Socrates, but it was installed earlier in Washington, DC. The bridge is planted with butterfly-attracting plants, and is then strung from one habitat to the next so the butterflies attracted to the plants bounce across the road safely to the other plants without being smeared on your windscreen. This renewed flow of genes increases the resilience of the population as well.

The Salamander Super Highway similarly connected patches of habitat. In this project, a collaboration with Alexander Felson, we designed a micro-speed bump that provided safe passage for salamanders across the road. There's a passive infrared sensor inside the salamander superhighway that triggers a tweet from the salamander: "Hi, honey, I'm coming home." As a speed-bump, it also reminds the occupants in the car passing above that we are not alone, but share the world with other species.

Salamanders are a critical part of maintaining the world's ecological health. The sheer quantity of salamanders and other amphibians in terms of biomass is twice the amount of all vertebrate animals in the world, which makes them a significant source of important energy transfer. Additionally, salamanders as a species have the monopoly on limb regeneration technology. They can lose their tails, and grow another perfectly good one in a matter of months. At the Cross(x)Species Adventure Club, we actually served salamander edible tail cocktails. It wasn't so popular even among our adventurous eaters, but it was an interesting exploration of how the process of de-tailing salamanders, in a way, parallels the process of milking a cow.

This page: Biochar

Opposite: Tree Office

Biochar is a public experiment in waste-to-energy processes. In a place like Australia, a very fragile old continent with swathes of degraded agricultural land, biochar is actually really exciting. Typically, you burn cellulosic waste and you produce a syngas, which is fuel, but here, through pyrolysis, a low-temperature, low-oxygen fire, we produced biochar. When you work biochar into soil, it significantly increases biodiversity and biomass production up to 40 percent. It also sequesters carbon for, potentially, thousands of years.

For this project, I asked people to come to Socrates with the cellulosic waste that is their junk mail, and we burned it in our Biochar Barbeque. We played some salsa music, ate some salsa, and then people could take home some biochar. At Socrates, we also incorporated biochar into a cross-shaped section of soil, so you could clearly see the effect that it has.

This project starts to explore how we might address local waste-to-energy production; that is, developing local waste handling strategies, instead of delegating it to large city agencies that subcontract to private contractors. The existing process of garbage collection is dizzyingly complex, just considering how much energy goes into dealing with junk mail. Through experiments like these, we can find productive ways to handle waste.

Tree-Office, another project at Socrates Sculpture Park, perhaps best demonstrates the idea of "beyond patronage." It started with a decree: I declared that the trees in Long Island City own themselves and the land they stand on.

This follows an interesting precedent in Athens, Georgia. In 1832, William Jackson decided that he liked the tree that he grew up with, and he willed it to itself. Unfortunately, that tree died. So in 1946 the Junior Ladies Garden Club in Athens took an acorn from the original tree and planted it in the same plot. Heritability laws were tested, and the tree now owns itself.[4]

The tree that owns itself, or at least a version of it, was rebuilt in Socrates Sculpture Park. It's nice to think about how organisms might own themselves, but we took this further and asked: if the tree owns property (itself), how might it be able to exercise that ownership, perhaps in a potentially profitable way? In this case,

Flightpath Toronto

we established a tree office: a rentable co-working space with high speed internet and locally generated power from a micro-hydro-turbine that we built on a mezzanine. It was the best office space in New York City, with stretching views of Manhattan and a delightful context in the park. But it gave the tree financial opportunities. You paid your desk fees to the tree. For the aerial yoga classes we scheduled underneath it, you paid your fees to the tree. The tree was your landlord. That makes sense in a way.

And of course, the tree invested the profits in its own interests, including biocharmentation of the soil around it, companion planting and actually sending its offspring off to college (a couple of the saplings were taken to Cornell and planted there and other places). Exploring how we might generate revenue for nonhumans so that they can invest in their own interest challenges our perception of trees as only fulfilling an environmental service. The value of a New York City tree is said to be between $100 and $400 over its entire lifespan. These are very low-paid service workers, who perform all sorts of duties: air quality improvement, storm water retention, and carbon sequestration are some examples. Yet, we lack imagination in figuring out how we can allow them to generate revenue, to access their own agency.

In terms of our own crisis of agency, transportation is probably the area where we feel most disempowered. Recently, I've been exploring how we might reimagine our flight systems. **FlightPath Toronto** is a project I did with Usman Haque, and it involved flying hundreds of people through downtown Toronto over Nathan Philips Square, past City Hall. It looks at how we get beyond the bike lane, if you will, in terms of reimagining urban mobility. The installation put you through flight school, after which you got your autopilot license, which of course you signed yourself.

Grandmothers, I have to say, were our most enthusiastic flyers, but many people happily flew through and around and had a good old time. I would call this a spectacle to create a shared public memory of a possible future. What's come out of this spectacle is a group of kids participating in a zipline-to-school initiative. Roughly seventy percent of traffic fatalities in Toronto are pedestrians,[5] and those rates are similarly high in New York City.[6] Their argument is it's not safe to walk, so we have to zipline to school.

We also brought the idea of public ziplining to New York City. In UP_2_U, our project for Civic Action at the Noguchi Museum, we compiled a preliminary cost-benefit analysis for zipline transportation in Long Island City in conspiracy with Otis Elevator Company. Long Island City is in a face-off with Manhattan, which has arguably the most charismatic skyline in the world, a big asset to the community. The problem with Manhattan, though, is that you can see its skyline from nowhere. One of the reasons for initiating this project was to prevent the development of high-rise luxury housing blocking that view from Long Island City. To start this project, we developed an upgraded Otis elevator, by taking the Gen-2 elevators (which are already 75 percent more efficient) and extending them 30 percent higher than the surrounding buildings to produce the stretching view of Manhattan, finally realizing that asset. Then, we installed ziplines from these extended elevators to other transportation access points.

This method of transportation has tremendous potential to improve Long Island City's environmental health. In the Tomcat Bakery, for instance, 76 diesel trucks every morning deliver fresh artisanal bread all over New York City (7,000 deliveries a day), and along with it, plumes of diesel fumes to Long Island City residents. So, in this case, we used the elevators three blocks down to the water from Tomcat Bakery, and erected a zipline from there to distribute goods to access points for water-based transportation, which is much more efficient. Consequently, the raison d'être of New York City is made available. An added benefit is that these extended elevators, through fire code engineering, can be reclaimed to passively circulate air through the building, allowing us to radically improve the environmental performance of these urban manufacturing facilities.

These are of some of the experiments in the Civic Action Project, all of which investigate ways we might restructure participation to reimagine what's possible. How might we enlist public experimentation to test how well biochar works, for instance? How can we use our tongues to hack our food systems? How do we locate our own agency and the agency of nonhuman organisms to improve our collective health? What will work to create shared public memory of a possible future?

NOTES

1. Children's Environmental Health Center of the Icahn School of Medicine at Mount Sinai, "New York State's Children and the Environment," December, 2013, http://www.mountsinai.org/static_files/MSMC/Files/Patient%20Care/Children/Childrens%20Environmental%20Health%20Center/NYS-Children-Environment.pdf (accessed June 10, 2014).

2. We used TextMarks technology. This was pre-Twitter.

3. James C. McKinley Jr. "Heading to Texas, Hudson's Toxic Mud Stirs Town." New York Times. May 30, 2009. http://www.nytimes.com/2009/05/31/science/earth/31waste.html?_r=0 (accessed June 12, 2014).

4. E. Merton Coulter. The Toombs Oak, the Tree that Owned Itself, and Other Chapters of Georgia. Athens, GA: University of Georgia Press, 2010.

5. David Hains. "Toronto's Bad Year for Traffic Deaths." Torontoist. January 16, 2014. http://torontoist.com/2014/01/torontos-bad-year-for-traffic-fatalities/ (accessed June 13, 2014).

6. "The New York City Pedestrian Safety Study & Action Plan." New York City Department of Transportation. August 2010. http://www.nyc.gov/html/dot/html/pedestrians/pedsafetyreport.shtml (accessed June 13, 2014).

PROJECT CREDITS

Amphibious Architecture, Installation for Toward a Sentient City, New York, NY 2009
The Living (David Benjamin, Deborah Richards, Kevin Wei, Soo-In Yang), Environmental Health Clinic (Natalie Jeremijenko, Amelia Black, Abha Kataria, Zenon Tech-Czarny, Chris Woebken), with advisors Jonathan Laventhol and Mark Bain

The Lures Project
Environmental Health Clinic / Natalie Jeremijenko, with Mihir Desai

Cross(x) Species Adventure Club, Project: **nanoWaterBuffalo Icecream**
Environmental Health Clinic / Natalie Jeremijenko, with Mihir Desai and Emilie Baltz

Civic Action Projects, in Civic Action: A Vision for Long Island City at the Noguchi Museum and Socrates Sculpture Park, New York, NY, USA, 2012
Projects: **UP_2_U; eXercise program, Hula-hooping; Moth Cinema; Biochar; Butterfly Bridge** (originally installed in Washington D.C.); **Salamander Super Highway; Tree-Office**
Environmental Health Clinic / Natalie Jeremijenko, with Nina Rappaport, Edward Peck, Fran Gallardo, David Fletcher, Angel Borrego, PWP Landscape Architecture, Alexander Felson, Falstudio (Guvenc Topcuoglu), Francisco J. Waltersdorfer, Associated Fabrication

FlightPath Toronto, Toronto, Ontario, Canada, 2011
Usman Haque and Natalie Jerimijenko

A conversation with

Natalie
JEREMIJENKO
&
Georgeen
THEODORE
&
Juliette SPERTUS

Moderated by

Martha BOHM

///

Martha Bohm:

   To start this conversation, would you talk about locating
   the point of action, when and how you realized that there was
   a particularly salient time to jump from investigation into
   action, or from visualization into action? It's a different
   thing to visualize the world and to act in the world. Can you
   reflect on some of your projects and talk about how you shifted
   from the detective role into the active role of making - or
   creating something?

Juliette Spertus:

   For me, it's very difficult, especially if you take pleasure
   in trying to understand the built environment. It's easy to
   continue digging, but the faster you're able to make that a

participatory process, the more you get out of it. It's only
when you make something public that, suddenly, people come
forward. The same is true with information. Once you start
telling a story publicly, then other people come in with parts
of the story that you wouldn't have otherwise had.

Georgeen Theodore:

I would like to respectfully disagree with the division
between visualizing and acting. If we're going to think
more expansively about the role of the architect, then,
what is action? Making a drawing or visualizing something;
isn't that an action? For example, in the NORCs [Naturally
Occurring Retirement Communities] in New York project,
we took on a journalistic role to make visible that this
thing was happening; that somehow through a combination of
different forces, towers in the park were becoming retirement
communities.

I wouldn't say that I have to take that project to a specific
action because I think all of that was an action. I think that
architects and designers have specific skills that have to do
with visualizing and representing spatial complexity. We're
uniquely experienced in taking on that role in contemporary
culture. I don't know if you were provoking us or not, but I
wouldn't make that division between the two.

MB: To frame the question another way, if we think about the "good
detective work" that you mentioned — the idea of looking with
many eyes and trying to maintain neutrality in the investigation, with multiple points of view at once — when does that
perspective shift to taking a position, staking your claim,
and saying, "This is how I then respond to that information"?

GT: Yeah, I mean that's such a hard thing because none of this is
a science, but I do think that in working in this investigative mode you still have to sort of pick sides. I do believe
that it's not neutral. We're trained as designers and architects to look at something like a dead mall or, say, a tower
in the park. We look at these everyday spaces and judge them
in aesthetic or formal terms. The process will be absolutely
enriched if we try not to be influenced by those judgments at
the beginning.

Natalie Jerimijenko:

I'd have to agree. Georgeen, you were talking about a lack
of credibility. As an artist, you enjoy no credibility. No
one believes you. No one trusts you. It's an interesting
lack of credibility because you're only ever as persuasive
as your representations. People generally don't cite artists
on critical issues. For example, you never hear, "Artists say
there's going to be global warming." So, as an artist, you're
forced into a position of having to find forms of persuasion in
order to seem credible.

I can talk about zip lining as a viable means of transportation and even do a cost-benefit analysis. These are forms of persuasion that one needs, but also people who have flown on the zip line suddenly realize how much more feasible it is by virtue of having explored and experienced it themselves. They can see and understand high throughput, high reliability, low maintenance, radically low cost, no emissions, and fast mobility. That would seem otherwise without the material demonstration, without the public experiments, without these other ways to demonstrate and explore complexity. I find that having to use diverse representational tactics — that involve not just drawing, but learning by putting something out there — is what actually develops your understanding.

There's not really a difference between acting and drawing or representing these forms. The strategy of using participatory public experiments includes particular ways of representing that make sense to me. I've learned more from this than doing solitary experiments in my lab.

JS: One thing that I thought was very interesting about our three presentations is the idea of the circulation of material, and that, in the work I'm doing, the 'client' is the garbage. In the same way, the material in the MOMA PS1 project was a kind of client. Georgeen, you were thinking about the furniture you designed, where it was moving to, and what its life was going to be. Just like the tree that owns itself, in Natalie's case. She considers how it can have its own life in which it's not just an object, but an entity. Maybe in response to the question of patronage, we are thinking about the materials in our world that we are used to navigating around, but not necessarily thinking in terms of their paths. In these projects, the three of us have talked about similar paths.

MB: I'm curious if there are questions percolating from the audience at this point.

Jordan Geiger:

Actually, I wanted to pick up on what you just said, Juliette - the notion that you do have 'clients,' — or stakeholders — and they are trees, birds, trash and other nonhuman actors. To me, that resonated with some thoughts I was having about the word 'detective.' A detective conjures for me first a process of detection, which is invested in both sensing and manifesting or making visible, which speaks to this dialogue between action and representation that you've all been talking about. But it also conjures the persona of the detective, who is someone who has a client or a patron of sorts. And, in this case, you can reframe the act of detection in terms of a different set of clients.

Parallel to that, Juliette pointed to the notion of starting with nothing and having no institutional association, whereas, in different ways, both Georgeen and Natalie have some institutional associations that, at times, have played a role in the work. I wonder if you would all speak to that.

NJ: I think it's really hard to be an actor, to figure out how to make these institutions work for us. In effect, the university is my patron, but it doesn't really work for me. So, we've invented an institution inside of the university: the Environmental Health Clinic.

I come out of the interventionist art practice, which is totally disheartening. Maybe you dig up some asphalt and create a new park, and then they come and tarmac over it straight away. The idea of the intervention doesn't work. It doesn't sustain. And so you have to make some unholy hybridization of alliances that are completely unpredictable. The sorts of alliances that Juliette and Georgeen have made may be the genius of what they are doing. I'm struck by the weird mélange of taxi drivers and MoMA and NORCs and City College of New York and Cornell. Georgeen, you're probably the only person conspiring between those institutions. These are weird ways in which we are making these institutions useful. Really, the challenge we have is how to use and abuse them.

GT: But I also think it's a multi-pronged condition. On the one hand, it is about looking for opportunities within the institutions, but at the same time, one of the main challenges that we have today in the American landscape is a kind of spatial segregation. We are increasingly segregated in space based on interest, race, income, or whatever it may be. We're very supportive of this kind of institutional fusing Natalie is talking about — where you might bring together transportation and waste, or trees and office workers, or, for us, MoMA and all the other community groups that we worked with. We were very adamant about opening up the city by bringing those groups together.

It's not just about creating opportunities, but also about cracking open these different systems and fusing them together to make a more open society. It sounds almost naïve, but we really were thinking about making new institutional and organizational relationships in order to bring these different groups together.

Joyce Hwang

To be an advocate—to defend the cause of another or to support the interests of another—is a form of practice that we tend to associate with the realms of politics, law, and social activism. Debates surrounding human rights, civil rights, women's rights, disability rights, and even animal rights might be the issues that first come to mind when reflecting upon notions of advocacy, but how might an architect operate as an advocate? How might we consider an architectural project as a form of advocacy?

Pro Bono Practices

Perhaps a first tendency in identifying moments of social activism in architecture might be to think of examples of volunteerism. Within recent decades, not-for-profit organizations have played a tremendous role in urging architects to engage with communities in need. The field of architecture itself has seen the emergence of several key organizations in this capacity. Architecture for Humanity, for example, was founded in 1999 to provide opportunities for architects to participate in socially-relevant design projects, competitions, and workshops, including efforts from addressing disaster-relief housing and basic services for those living in poverty to soccer fields and community centers.[1] The organization's mode of practice is to solicit volunteer work by architects. As AfH describes, "By tapping a network of more than 50,000 professionals willing to lend time and expertise to help those who would not otherwise be able to afford their services, we bring design, construction, and devel-opment services where they are most critically needed."[2] Another well-known organization, the 1% Pro Bono Design Program of Public Architecture,[3] operates simi-larly. Founded in 2002, Public Architecture, "challenges architecture and design firms nationwide to pledge a minimum of 1% of their time to pro bono service"[4] and connects these firms with nonprofit organizations that request assistance. Today, we see an increasing number of organizational models that support pro bono prac-tices alongside profit-driven businesses. The Open Hand Studio,[5] for example, is a pro bono arm of Cannon Design, a large multinational firm.[6] Through models such as these, the ability for an architect to work as an advocate

| 113

Architect as

through socially-minded projects is increasing, due to the sheer quantity of avenues that exist. Looking at the collective track record of such organizations, it is clear that they fill a tremendous gap between architects and the disadvantaged communities which do not typically have access to professional design services.

Yet, volunteerism—as a proposed framework of practicing social advocacy in architecture—implores us to challenge its most fundamental assumptions. Is it sustainable—or even ethical—to rely on the altruism of pro bono services, particularly in times of economic decline? In order for an architect to have *extra* time for pro bono services, one would typically need to be gainfully enough employed in some other capacity. The amount of time that an architect can afford to spend on socially-motivated projects is therefore relatively minimal, compared to the total amount of time that is spent on profit-generating efforts.[7] So, in instances when the practice of advocacy is pursued as a kind of 'side job,' is the architect really afforded the time and space to explore design through multiple iterations or tests? Or, does the quality of design suffer, reflecting the limited time that one is able to spend on the project? While it is true that this model of practice has produced a number of well-considered projects, the emphasis in this case remains that architecture as a form of social advocacy is presented as a menu of "service offerings" for 'solvable' problems.[8] Here, I am *not* critiquing architecture's goal to solve problems, as this is in fact one of our profession's unique abilities and responsibilities. One cannot undervalue the importance of problem-solving, particularly for communities in need. Small, incremental tasks of assistance—from weatherizing a home to renovating a space to be accessible for the disabled and elderly—certainly contribute immensely to enhancing our inhabitable environment. Rather, I am asking: how can we, as architects, expand the practice of advocacy to cultivate further aims and ambitions, in addition to problem-solving?

As architects, we understand the value of aesthetics in defining culture and in drawing public interest to a place or a cause. Yet, it is the rule, rather than the exception, that well-designed buildings and environments are luxuries, more readily available to moneyed clients. Meanwhile, for those without the same financial means, architecture is often relegated to a more limited role. So, while pro bono activity is indeed an admirable form of 'doing good,' I believe that it is urgently imperative, for the sake of advancing architecture's impact on society, to explore how these and other frameworks of advocacy-based practices can more robustly sustain innovative, experimental, and groundbreaking design in the long term, and in the larger economic landscape.

Toward New Frameworks for Practice

How does one pursue advocacy in architecture? How does one cultivate a productive balance between seemingly conflicting priorities, such as social justice and aesthetics, or problem-solving and problematizing? Looking beyond the short-term goals of volunteerism, architects and organizations are starting to develop long-term strategies to undertake socially-charged work. To consider the notion of architects as 'advocates,' we can begin by examining several fundamental frameworks for practice.

1. Collaborate with Community Organizations

This is a familiar model of collaboration between architects and not-for-profit organizations, and has been infamously energized by Teddy Cruz, now an emblematic figure in the world of activism and architecture. Recognized for his collaborative efforts with Casa Familiar, a community development agency which serves border communities between the United States and Mexico, Cruz and his collaborators have worked with this model to initiate a number of provocative social projects, including a proposal for senior housing and childcare. Today we find a number of designers who, inspired by this model, actively seek alliances with community-based organizations to initiate projects that address social and ecological issues that are left largely unaddressed by market forces. In some cases, these advocacy-based projects are even developed against the grain of officially-sanctioned directives. For example, in Makoko, a waterfront settlement in Lagos, Nigeria, the government has deemed that some of its inhabited areas are dangerous due to the persistent threat of flooding and high waters, and has forced residents of Makoko to relocate. According to *The Economist*, "The entire district may soon be gone. The government is eager to reclaim what has become prime waterfront land. It is only half-fair to depict it as heartless and greedy. Built on a swamp, Lagos is fighting for survival. Ceaseless migration is strangling it."[9] After speaking with Makoko residents, architect Kunlé Adeyemi pinpointed a specific infrastructural problem—that the local school is constantly flooded—and initiated a different kind of response. With help from the community, and with sponsorship from the Heinrich Böll Foundation and the United Nations, he developed a "floating school" that could resist the environmental challenges faced by the settlement. Designed to serve 100 schoolchildren, the structure is a three-story A-frame building with classrooms, a play area, a rainwater collection system, and composting toilets—all buoyed by a layer of plastic flotation barrels.[10] Yet, even with a modest budget, the project does more than satisfy community needs.

**MAKOKO
TECHNOLOGY**
+
**FLOTATION
TECHNOLOGY**
=
**NEW
SOLUTION**

Increase in
sea level

Top Left: Vision for Lagos Water
Communities, rendering by NLÉ.

Top Right: Makoko Floating
School, platform prototype.

Left: Proposed Technology for
Makoko, diagram by NLÉ.

Bottom: Makoko Floating School

Joyce Hwang

Above, Right: Elevator B, winning project of the University at Buffalo Hive City Competition, installed at Silo City

Bottom: Painted Topography at Silo City, by Holes of Matter

Opposite: 2XmT at Silo City, by Chris Romano and Nick Bruscia

Architect as Advocate

Within the landscape of Makoko, it stands as a beacon of resilience and hope. As an architectural artifact, it is striking, and brings public attention to the social and political turmoil in Lagos. For a global audience, Adeyemi hopes that this project is a "seed to cultivate a new type of urbanism on water in African cities,"[11] to catalyze others to rethink ways of building to address climate change and flooding.

2. Form an Organization-within-an-Institution

Another model of advocacy-based practice is to form an institutional program within a university or a school of architecture. This kind of partnership takes advantage of the influence and resources of universities, and gives architects, faculty, and students of architecture the opportunity to realize projects that are spurred by research interests or other meaningful drivers. The Yale Building Project, an early example conceived of in the 1960s by Charles Moore, organizes first-year graduate students to design and construct a building for underserved 'clients' in local communities.[12] Auburn University's Rural Studio, founded by Samuel Mockbee and D.K. Ruth in 1993, is another pioneering example of an organization within an academic institution.[13] Over the decades, design-build programs have been taking shape in many schools of architecture in the United States. In 2012, a report issued by the Association of Collegiate Schools of Architecture (ACSA) noted that among the 123 NAAB accredited schools of architecture, there are approximately 100 design-build programs.[14] Cited by *Architect Magazine* as a school that excels in design-build,[15] University of Kansas' Studio 804, led by Dan Rockhill, has formed its own 501c3.[16] URBANbuild at Tulane University was initiated in 2005, in response to the socio-economic and environmental landscape of New Orleans after Hurricane Katrina.[17] Many schools also offer various design-build courses external to an organized institutional program.

At the University at Buffalo, the Department of Architecture has honed a design-build ethos through its course offerings and multiple faculty initiatives. Most recently, collaborations between faculty members, students, and local manufacturers—such as Rigidized Metals—have yielded the realization of several projects on a formerly abandoned industrial site in Buffalo. In 2012, the Department's Ecological Practices Research Group organized a competition, "Hive City," for students to design and build an urban bee habitat, a process which yielded the fabrication of "Elevator B," a 22-ft tall tower for bees. Later that year, Sergio López-Piñeiro devised a project to reactivate an unused flour warehouse through a simple tactic of painting the building's columns to suggest an interior topography, transforming a derelict space to one that can be occupied by the public. In 2013, Christopher Romano and Nicholas Bruscia, together with several students, designed and constructed a monumental folded stainless steel wall, 2XmT, to define a gateway to the site as well as to demonstrate the structural potential of textured stainless steel sheet material.

While design-build processes do not always translate neatly to advocacy-based practices, it is worth mentioning that the notion of 'design-build' has been, in many cases, synonymous with an activist ethos in architecture. Certainly, the 'do-it-yourself' mentality breeds a great sense of empowerment. The practice of 'tactical urbanism'—initiating small, incremental, often D-I-Y operations in a city to generate more widespread urban consequences—is becoming increasingly championed by forward-thinking designers and urbanists.[18]

3. Amend Traditional Practice Structures

The third model for advocacy-based practice works within a more traditional framework of architectural design. In this model, architects acquire commissions in standard ways—for example, by working with developers or engaging in competitions. Within these conventional project structures, they interject strategies that promote wellness for the project's inhabitants or community. A poignant example is Frédéric Druot, Anne Lacaton, and Jean-Philippe Vassal's transformation of Tour Bois-le-Prêtre, a project to renovate an existing social housing structure, in which the architects developed and choreographed a construction phasing plan that allowed the tower's residents to remain in their residences while construction occurred. The task of easing the residents' sense of disruption and discomfort was a tremendous feat—already an indicator of architects acting as social advocates. Eschewing the perceived conflict between formal and social concerns, the architects put forward aesthetics and space as cultural values. They introduced a sense of openness, lightness and dignity to each residence, with full height glass windows and balconies throughout the project's façade.

Critical Factors Beyond Practice Typologies

The frameworks I just described are, in a sense, easily digestible. They categorize advocacy-based practices in an already-familiar way. One could stop here and suggest that it is possible to simply adopt a particular 'practice typology' in order to pursue socially-engaged work. I would like to propose, however, that subscribing to emerging practice models is not enough. The circumstances of projects and their architects reveal a number of other factors that are critical to the development of architecture as advocacy. In their pursuit of advocacy, architects must ultimately confront often difficult and complex questions that address issues of Time, Labor, Urgency, Risk, and Empathy.

1. Time and Labor

Factors of time and labor cost—not only in terms of construction, but also in design—often render 'architectural services' cost-prohibitive to many individuals and communities. This reality is typically met with the answer of 'community engagement' as a means of enabling a project's realization. Current discourses surrounding socially-driven architecture have already recognized a number of practices that directly involve community members in fabricating and constructing projects.[19] In Gando, Burkina Faso, for example, architect Diébédo Francis Kéré designed a primary school using unbaked mud bricks, a readily available material from the region, and developed a construction process in which community members were trained to use a machine to compress bricks, then assemble them on-site.[20] Along similar lines, architects Anna Heringer and Eike Roswag followed a comparable process in building the METI-Handmade School in Rudrapur, Bangladesh, in which the architects developed construction techniques that drew upon local building materials and traditions, and trained resident unskilled laborers to build using these techniques. Further, the intellectual labor—the research and design process—was accomplished while Heringer was a student of architecture, as the project was her master's thesis.[21]

It could be argued that time scales may be of less importance to those who are able to produce a steady stream of income through more traditional profit-driven practices. However, time scales are incredibly significant for architects who work through fundraising and grant-writing. The prospect of winning a grant for 10 consecutive years, for example, is more daunting than that of winning grants for two years in a row.

2. Urgency and Risk

Another highly critical factor that distinguishes advocacy-based architecture is the often high degree of urgency and a correlated high level of risk. In extremely urgent scenarios, such as post-disaster relief—a project typology that is frequently embraced by not-for-profit organizations—design practices necessarily thrust themselves to work at breakneck speeds. In situations of extreme urgency, typical standards and codes are often put on hold momentarily. One understands, of course, that a shelter for temporary relief does not need to fulfill every standard that is required for long term housing.

There are many worthwhile architectural explorations in this regard, particularly Shigeru Ban's efforts in developing and building post-tsunami and post-earthquake housing. Yet, in many other parts of the world, the majority of critical decisions tend to be 'resolved' without design intention, often placing ad-hoc provisions ahead of design quality. Think, for example, of the 145,000 FEMA trailers that were deployed after Hurricane Katrina in 2005, a $2.7 billion plan that was later deemed an "official policy of premeditated ignorance" due to the high level of formaldehyde present in the trailers.[22] Perhaps a more fertile territory for architecture to address is one that has a sense of urgency, but not the truncated timeframe that follows emergencies or disasters. The previously discussed example of Kunlé Adeyemi's Makoko Floating School in Lagos stands as a poignant example. The settlement of Makoko suffers from chronic flooding, which affords the government an 'excuse' to displace its inhabitants. The pace, budget, and aims of Adeyemi's project can still be classified as 'urgent;' yet there was enough time for the architect to conduct research, engage partners and sponsors, and develop a well-considered and thoughtful design agenda. We see a similar approach in the work of Lateral Office, a Toronto-based firm headed by Lola Sheppard and Mason White, whose work is featured in this section. In their Arctic Food Network project, Lateral Office confronts the complex web of social and environmental issues in the northern territories of Canada, where many problems stem from the lack of infrastructure and connectivity in Arctic regions. They put forward strategies for initiating a food-based network to serve communities there. While this began as a research project that was instigated by social concerns, Sheppard and White have received a number of significant grants to support this work, and are exploring ways to implement their propositions.

What might these types of practices, such as Lateral Office, suggest? How do we identify and address situations of 'urgency' in measured ways? Many of these projects emerge through 'detective work' conducted in various geographic locations, and quite often involve working in territories outside of one's immediate context. From these examples, we can understand the challenges of exporting knowledge and techniques into other regions. These practices also grapple with the sensitive questions of how to translate to 'home' the specific advocacy-based strategies that are developed in foreign contexts. As we have discussed, construction of many socially-conscious projects has relied on community participation in gathering local materials and fabricating building components. How might we explore ways to export these kinds of hands-on practices to more knowledge-based or industrial economies?

3. Empathy

One might argue that architects, by the nature of the profession, must possess the ability to empathize; that is, to see and feel the world through the embodiment of another. How else would an architect be able to understand the needs and desires of clients, after all? Still, the issue of empathy is perhaps not as centrally located in contemporary architectural discourse as it should be, except perhaps in the area of 'inclusive design.' Even in those instances, one often finds the discussion gravitating toward metrics and performance, for example, assessing whether an environment is suitable for those with certain disabilities. I would like to suggest that the notion of empathy must play a more culturally profound—and even provocative—role in design processes that shape advocacy-based architecture.

In the work of Diébédo Francis Kéré, it is not difficult to sense the high level of empathy that he feels toward the people who inhabit his projects, as Kéré himself was raised in Gando. While he maintains a practice in Berlin, he spends much of the year in Burkina Faso, fundraising through a nonprofit foundation that he founded, Building Blocks for Gando. Since finishing architecture school in 2004, he has been tirelessly "build[ing] schools, health clinics, and other civic-minded projects."[23] His passion for helping those in his community can be felt. As Jenna McKnight writes in *Architectural Record*, "During his rousing lectures, it's not uncommon for the exuberant architect to jump off the stage or pound on the floor to illustrate a point. His talks typically draw standing ovations."[24]

The word "empathic" is underscored by Marika Shiori-Clark, who is currently the Principal of SOSHL Studio, and is one of the founders of MASS Design Group, "an architectural nonprofit dedicated to designing well-built environments that aid in the reduction of global poverty."[25] In her 2011 talk titled "Empathic Architecture,"[26] she discussed the trajectory of working with Partners in Health (a Boston-based NGO), along with the Clinton Foundation, the Ministry of Health and other local officials, to design, develop and build the Butaro Hospital in Rwanda. While she and her colleagues initially worked on the project while they were based in Cambridge, Massachusetts, as students at the Harvard Graduate School of Design, the turning point came when they traveled to Rwanda and decided to live at the hospital site. Shiori-Clark recounts:

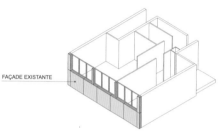

FAÇADE EXISTANTE

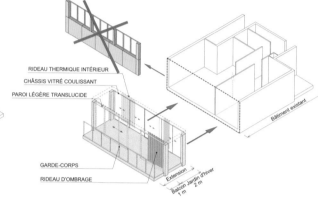

RIDEAU THERMIQUE INTÉRIEUR

CHÂSSIS VITRÉ COULISSANT

PAROI LÉGÈRE TRANSLUCIDE

Bâtiment existant

GARDE-CORPS

RIDEAU D'OMBRAGE

Extension

Balcon Jardin d'hiver
1 m   2 m

APPARTEMENT T2 EXISTANT

APPARTEMENT T2 + EXTENSION (JARDIN D'HIVER 15 m2 + BALCON 7,5 m2)

Architect as Advocate

Opposite Page

Top Left: Tour Bois le
Prêtre, before renovation

Top Right: Tour Bois le
Prêtre, under construction

Middle: Tour Bois le Prêtre,
balcony module axonometric

Bottom: Tour Bois le
Prêtre, after renovation

Top: METI Handmade
School, interior

Bottom: METI Handmade School

Joyce Hwang

We show up in Rwanda all of a sudden, wet behind the ears, knowing nothing, architecture students who have never designed a thing in their lives. Pretty much out of desperation and not knowing any better, we decided to set up an office in Rwanda, as a way to try to understand the community. That initial decision, I think, has actually shaped the way we end up running our organization over these last five years… This idea that we really do try to embed ourselves in the community and literally live there on site… we were living on the actual hospital site with the patients, the doctors, and the nurses…trying to, through osmosis, to learn about how people were living on the site.[27]

This is a case in which an initial sense of sympathy shifted toward empathy as a consequence of the design process. At first, the architects—like many socially conscious others—wanted to use their skills to 'do good' by helping a nonprofit organization. After living at length in Rwanda, however, they were able to foster empathy by more deeply experiencing the day-to-day existence of their project's users.

One could argue that Shiori-Clark's account of developing empathy tells perhaps the most straightforward way of doing so: to put oneself as close as possible to experiencing the world through the eyes and body of another. At the same time, the perceptual embodiment of another is perhaps one of the most challenging facets of contending with architecture as an advocate for underrepresented, underserved populations. To understand the lives of others outside of one's own culture and comfort zone requires a nuanced and patient approach, one which grapples not only with tangible experiences, but also with issues of identity, such as culture, ethnicity, race and class. Architects are increasingly confronting these sociopolitical factors as part of their research agendas. The work of Yolande Daniels, for example—whose current practice Studio SUMO was formed with her partner Sunil Bald—specifically examines the spatial and political landscapes of African-American identity and memory, through processes of revealing nuances of repression in underrepresented populations. In some of her built projects, such as the Museum of Contemporary African Diasporan Art, she directly addresses issues of cultivating identity by bringing a dignified and highly visible presence to a particular cultural institution.

To answer the questions of how one can more intimately understand the complexities that shape identity, and how that understanding can translate to the design process and the designed environment, is not a straightforward path. Ultimately, this is one of the greatest challenges that face architects as advocates. General questions that address issues of advocacy include: How can one truly empathize with and understand the cultural values of others? How can one serve their needs while pushing forward agendas of space and aesthetics? Beyond these general questions, specific questions of identity pertaining to ethnicity, race, gender, and other cultural factors eventually emerge in either overt or nuanced ways. For example, how might an architect's ethnic identity influence the design of a building's aesthetic and experiential qualities? Or, how might an architect's cultural bias shape the formation of project leaders and teams, who, of course, directly impact a project's development? Indeed, taking on the role of the Architect-Advocate does not simply rest on intentions of 'doing good.' Rather, it demands the cultivation of genuine empathy and skill in considering the identities of oneself and others in a world that is driven by commerce and consumption, and sensitivity in a practice that is otherwise driven by the 'bottom line.'

Architect as Advocate

How might we now understand the role of advocacy in architecture today, and its potential for the future? Several effective practice models have already been set in motion, and continue to evolve. Yet, I will argue that the Architect as Advocate must progress beyond the task of innovating a practice model, and also begin to navigate the complex milieu of time, labor, risk, urgency, and empathy, to develop concrete agendas, strategies, and modes of production. Thus, architects can indeed become agents of societal change. As we see in the work of Lateral Office, Studio SUMO, and many others, Architects as Advocates are actively establishing larger social, political, and economic agendas in their work. As such, they are changing the status quo in practice and reshaping the construction of identity and power in the field.

Butaro Hospital, under construction.

NOTES

1. Architecture for Humanity, http://architectureforhumanity.org/about/what-we-do

2. This description (or a slight variation of it) is listed in several websites that describe Architecture for Humanity's mission, including:

    Archinect, http://archinect.com/architecture-for-humanity (accessed June 7, 2014);

    Indiegogo, http://www.indiegogo.com/partners/arch (accessed June 7, 2014);

    Clinton Bush Haiti Fund: http://www.clintonbushhaitifund.org/programs/entry/architecture-for-humanity/ (accessed June 7, 2014).

3. The 1% Program of Public Architecture, http://www.theonepercent.org/About/Overview.htm (accessed June 7, 2014).

4. Public Architecture, http://publicarchitecture.org/the_1/ (accessed June 7, 2014).

5. Cannon Design Open Hand Studio, http://www.cannondesign.com/practice/community/open-hand-studio/ (accessed June 8, 2014).

6. Cannon Design is a large firm that generated $202,260,000 in revenues worldwide, notably ranking 3rd in revenue-generation in a list of U.S. firms, only after HKS, Inc. and RTKL Associates Inc. Design Intelligence Almanac of Architecture and Design 2014, http://www.di.net/almanac/firms/?firm_revenue_world=100000000-300000000 (accessed June 9, 2014).

7. Look, for example, at the amount of time that is pledged by firms in the 1% for Public Architecture Program. A few examples among firms of various sizes include Beyer Blinder Belle Architects and Planners LLC with a staff of 155 who have pledged 20 hours annually (7.75 hours per person per year), and Gensler with a staff of 2000 who have pledged 43680 hours annually (21.84 hours per person per year).

    Public Architecture, http://www.theonepercent.org/About/Participants.htm (accessed June 7, 2014).

8. See the checklist of "Service Offerings" that are provided to non-profit organizations to identify. They include: Facilities Needs Assessment, Capital Campaign Materials, Building & Space Identification, Interior Design & Brand Integration, Accessibility & Code Compliance, Healthy & Sustainable Environments, Facilities Renovation. Public Architecture, http://www.theonepercent.org/Nonprofit/Service_Offerings.htm (accessed June 8, 2014).

9. "Destroying Makoko: Nigeria's commercial capital," The Economist, August 18, 2012, 46, http://www.economist.com/node/21560615 (accessed June 7, 2014).

10. Michael Kimmelman, "School at Sea," New York Times Magazine, May 24 2013, http://www.nytimes.com/interactive/2013/05/26/magazine/26look-lagos.html?_r=0 (accessed June 8, 2014).

11. Ben Schiller, "A Floating School that Won't Flood," Fast Company, February 8, 2013, http://www.fastcoexist.com/1681346/a-floating-school-that-wont-flood (accessed June 8, 2014).

12. Richard W. Hayes, The Yale Building Project: The First 40 Years (New Haven: Yale School of Architecture and Yale University Press, 2007).

13. Rural Studio, Auburn University, http://www.ruralstudio.org/about/purpose-history (accessed June 12, 2014).

NOTES (Continued)

14. W. Geoff Gjertson, "A House Divided: Challenges for Design/Build Programs in Architecture Schools," Association of Collegiate Schools of Architecture (ACSA), Februrary 10, 2012, http://www.acsa-arch.org/acsa-news/read/read-more/acsa-news/2012/02/10/a-house-divided-challenges-for-design-build-programs-in-architecture-schools (accessed June 8, 2014).

15. Amanda Kolson Hurley, "Schools That Excel in Design/Build," *Architect Magazine*, December 2009, posted online April 8, 2010, http://www.architectmagazine.com/education/design-build.aspx (accessed June 8, 2014),

16. Studio 804, http://studio804.com/about%20us/mission/studio/studio.html (accessed June 8, 2014).

17. URBANbuild: a program of the Tulane School of Architecture, http://www.tulaneurbanbuild.com/index2.php#/rtext_2/2/ (accessed June 8, 2014).

18. Look, for example, at the United States' national representation at the 13th International Venice Architecture Biennale in 2012. Titled "Spontaneous Interventions: design actions for the common good," the exhibition in the U.S. Pavilion featured 182 tactical urban 'interventions.' The project description states: "In recent years, there has been a nascent movement of designers acting on their own initiative to solve problematic urban situations, creating new opportunities and amenities for the public. Provisional, improvisational, guerrilla, unsolicited, tactical, temporary, informal, DIY, unplanned, participatory, opensource—these are just a few of the words that have been used to describe this growing body of work." Spontaneous Interventions, http://www.spontaneousinterventions.org/about (accessed June 8, 2014).

19. In the design world, the The Museum of Modern Art (MoMA) has canonized a number of these projects in its 2010 exhibition "Small Scale Big Change: New Architectures of Social Engagement." Museum of Modern Art, http://www.moma.org/interactives/exhibitions/2010/smallscalebigchange/ (accessed June 1, 2014).

20. Museum of Modern Art, "Primary School" in "Small Scale Big Change: New Architectures of Social Engagement," http://www.moma.org/interactives/exhibitions/2010/smallscalebigchange/projects/primary_school (accessed June 8, 2014).

21. Museum of Modern Art, "METI—Handmade School" in "Small Scale Big Change: New Architectures of Social Engagement," http://www.moma.org/interactives/exhibitions/2010/smallscalebigchange/projects/meti_handmade_school (accessed June 8, 2014).

22. Spencer S. Hsu, "FEMA's sale of Katrina trailers sparks criticism," *The Washington Post,* March 13, 2010, http://www.washingtonpost.com/wp-dyn/content/article/2010/03/12/AR2010031202213.html?sid=ST2010031700841 (accessed June 8, 2014).

23. Jenna McKnight, "Bringing It All Back Home," *Architectural Record,* June 2014, http://archrecord.construction.com/features/2014/1406-Bringing-It-All-Back-Home.asp (accessed June 13, 2014).

24. Ibid.

25. This description (or a slight variation of it) is listed in several websites that describe MASS Design Group's mission, including: IDEO, http://www.ideo.org/fellows/marika-shioiri-clark (accessed June 8, 2014), Cleveland Urban Design Collaborative, Kent State University, http://www.cudc.kent.edu/blog/lecture-marika-shioiri-clark-on-dignifying-design/ (accessed June 8, 2014).

26. Marika Shiori-Clark, "Empathic Architecture" (lecture, TEDxStellenbosch, Stellenbosch, South Africa, July 29, 2011), https://www.youtube.com/watch?v=KTXqJ2fZ0gA and http://www.tedxstellenbosch.org/videos/ (accessed June 8, 2014).

27. Ibid.

PROJECT CREDITS

Makoko Floating School, Makoko, Lagos, Nigeria, 2013
NLÉ (Kunlé Adeyemi, Lisa Anderson, Thijs Bouman, Leslie Ebony, Marije Nederveen, Segun Omodele, Adekunle Olusola, Chryso Onisiforou, Martin Oreoluwa, Berend Strijland, Monica Velasco), with Makoko Community Building Team, BKVV Architects, Dykstra Naval Architects, Pieters Bouwtechniek, SPCIT, Roel Bosch Architecten, Ikeyi & Arifayan, Matrix Designs, Solarmate Engineering Nig ltd.

Elevator B, Hive City Habitat Design Competition Winner, Silo City, Buffalo, NY, USA, 2012
University at Buffalo School of Architecture and Planning (Design Team: Courtney Creenan, Kyle Mastalinski, Daniel Nead, Scott Selin, Lisa Stern; Competition Organizers and Project Advisors: Martha Bohm, Joyce Hwang, Christopher Romano)

Painted Topography, Silo City, Buffalo, NY, USA, 2012
Holes of Matter (Sergio López-Piñeiro, Sandra Berdick)

2XmT, Silo City, Buffalo, NY, USA, 2013
University at Buffalo School of Architecture and Planning (Christopher Romano, Nicholas Bruscia)

Tour Bois-le-Prêtre, Paris, France, 2011
Frédéric Druot, and Lacaton &Vassal (Anne Lacaton, and Jean-Philippe Vassal)

Primary School, Gando, Burkina Faso, 2001
Diébédo Francis Kéré

METI-Handmade School, Rudrapur, Bangladesh, 2006
Anna Heringer and Eike Roswag

Butaro Hospital, Burera District, Rwanda, 2011
MASS Design Group

Navigating Territories of Engagement

Lola Sheppard

The landscape of architectural practice is changing. The territory in which it operates is transforming. New terms of engagement will be required if the profession is to evolve and be able not only to respond to rapidly changing conditions, but indeed anticipate and innovate in the face of them. There is recognition that the current structure of the profession is relatively narrow in scope, one in which architects deliver a prescribed set of services or tasks. There appears, on the one hand, to be ever more specialization within the profession—curtain wall and building envelope architecture, interior architecture, healthcare architecture, airport architecture, sport architecture, project management firms, and sustainability experts, among others—leaving the actual scope and role of the profession in question. On the other hand, architects are increasingly embracing expanded scopes of practice. Small firms often take on a range of tasks, from branding, graphic, product, and furniture design to interiors and small buildings, while larger firms offer services ranging from the complete design of buildings to the production of construction documents, master planning, and project management. A century ago, Gropius tasked the architect, in *The Scope of Total Architecture* (1943), to understand design and fabrication processes, in order to combine "the qualities of an artist, a technician and a businessman"[1] able to design a fork, chair, building, or city. Gropius called upon architects to avoid subjugation to purely technical imperatives, and he advocated against specialization. He argued that "good architecture should be a project of life itself and that implies an intimate knowledge of biological, social, technical, and artistic problems."[2]

With a renewed interest in landscape, urbanism, ecology, infrastructure, technology, and fabrication, many architects continue this ambition of a return to a total or expanded scope. Yet some might question whether the attempt to hybridize or enlarge the scope of practice leaves the architect in a tenuous disciplinary position: a jack of all trades, but master of none. For Gropius, the architect is artist; with a Bauhausian ambition to design at all scales comprehensively, whether it be object, building or city. Yet as our physical environments become ever more complex and the information available about them increases algorithmically, the ambition to design it all, and with similar design methodologies, comes into question. The issue, therefore, is less one of expanding scopes but rather of recognizing that this broader scope requires expanded working methods and approaches; that design at different scales must accommodate different degrees of contingency and indeterminacy.

Perhaps, then, the first task is to consider possible models for this 21st century architect. The Webster dictionary defines an architect as: (1) a person who designs buildings and in many cases also supervises their construction, (2) a person who is responsible for inventing or realizing a particular idea or project. However, it includes "related words": builder, maker, producer; captain, commander, director, handler, leader, manager, quarterback; contriver, designer, formulator, originator, spawner; arranger, hatcher, organizer, planner, plotter, schemer; finagler, machinator, maneuverer; developer, generator, inaugurator, initiator, inspirer, instituter, pioneer.

These related and rarely considered words seem far more productive in defining a possible ambition for the profession today. They suggest an anticipatory role, one that is strategic and opportunistic. It repositions the profession from one *that 'invents' buildings and spaces* to one that conceives of ideas, schemes, and relationships, of which buildings, environments, and structures are parts. In these scenarios, the outcomes are less clearly defined, yet perhaps more full of potential. They offer an alternative to the conventional view of the architect as creator and implementer. What models might exist for this expanded model of practice?

THE ARCHITECT AS ORIGINATOR AND COMPREHENSIVE THINKER

Inventor and engineer Buckminster Fuller embodied perhaps most clearly a model of comprehensive thinker and experimenter. He was also a somewhat maligned character, frequently discounted as a dilettante. He argued that, in an age of over-specialization, architecture is "almost the only profession that is trained to put things together and to think comprehensively."[3] Fuller lamented that "architects, engineers and scientists are all what I call slave professions. They don't go to work unless they have a patron... When you're an architect, the patron tells you where he's going to build and just what he wants to do. ... The architect is really just a tasteful purchasing agent."[4] Instead, Fuller advocated, in his actions and writing, for architects to think expansively and across scales; to consider the global systems and resources impacting our built environment, while simultaneously addressing the challenges of design at the scale of manufacturing and domestic materials. Fuller developed the notion of "Design Science", a problem-solving approach in which he believed the solutions came not from the introduction of technological wizardry but, rather, from a systematic study of the ordering of components in the environment relative to a given project. He also developed the idea of "Synergetics", the empirical study of systems in transformation; effectively, the study of spatial complexity with emphasis on total system behavior unpredicted by the behavior of any isolated components, including humanity's role. Many critics have discounted these "disciplines" as pseudo-science, but what is striking is Fuller's anticipation that a new discipline, with new tools, was necessary to address the scope of issues he deemed within the architect's and engineer's purview. Furthermore, Fuller's emphasis on establishing the question as the first act of design, rather than the solution, seems critical. He argued, "The specialist in comprehensive design is an emerging synthesis of artist, inventor, mechanic, objective economist and evolutionary strategist."[5]

THE ARCHITECT AS ORGANIZER

If Fuller privileged technology, engineering, and fabrication as the set of tools which might allow the architect to expand his and her sphere of influence, American forester, planner, and conservationist Benton MacKaye advocated thinking synthetically at multiple scales. He helped pioneer the idea of land preservation for recreation and conservation purposes, and was a strong advocate of balancing human needs and those of nature, developing the term "Geotechnics" as an approach. His celebrated Appalachian Trail proposal embodied this comprehensive approach, encompassing recreational trails, rail infrastructure, and the incorporation of local economic centres in an integrated spatial framework. MacKaye argued, "We should say that planning is discovery and not invention. It is a new type of exploration. Its essence is visualization—a charting of the potential now existing in the actual."[6] He argued that planning ought to consider not simply an area of land, but also the movement and activity—whether human, ecological or infrastructural—happening within the area, effectively recognizing the site and forces within it as dynamic, shifting, and extensive.

If MacKaye offered design as a framework of organization, Greek architect and planner Constantinos Doxiadis understood design as a method of systematic analysis of human settlements. Doxiadis defined two terrains of architectural investigation:

> The first comprises the problems which require an understanding of local environmental situations and the role of architecture as the consolidating and coordinating discipline. The second category consists of the problems which are not connected with the environment and require action at a much higher level. The problems here are those which architecture faces in relation to industry, art, government, and the other forces of modern expanding society. It is our task to define the role of architecture in both these fields.[6]

Doxiadis further defined five principles for understanding human settlement: (1) maximization of man's potential contacts with the elements of nature; (2) minimization of the effort required for the achievement of such contacts; (3) optimization of man's protective space; (4) optimization of the quality of man's relationship to his environment by means of buildings and networks; and, finally, (5) settlement understood as the means of optimizing the first four principles. Doxiadis' methods analyzed existing systems of mobility, economy, energy, and built form. He called his comprehensive approach to understanding cities, "Ekistics", or a science of human settlement, and he outlined its scope, aims, and intellectual framework.

A significant impetus behind the development of this new science—and indeed he conceived of it as a science—was the emergence of increasingly large and complex settlements, often operating as regional conurbations and even as global cities. Doxiadis had a relatively clear vision of the priorities urbanism should address. As a result, his analytic tools, while broad in the scope of analysis, maintain a clear methodology, at the risk of over systematizing research.

What is striking, however, about the work and approach of Gropius, Fuller, Doxiadis, and MacKaye, is that each sought to establish a set of methodologies or priorities for approaching design; some broader, some more prescriptive. What new strategies and approaches might enable architects to respond to and address today's complex entanglements of ecology, urbanism, infrastructure, global economics, and logistics?[7]

THE ARCHITECT AS SCHEMER

In her book *Enduring Innocence,* architect Keller Easterling suggests that the contemporary architect might well learn from the cunning of global economies and geo-political operations, not least in understanding their data, logistics, and spatial products. The architect, in Easterling's view, has remained a bystander in the evolution of these spatial "formats," both in understanding them, and intervening upon these complex spatial, political, and economic manoeuverings. "Architects often treat them ('spatial products') as banal or unresponsive to recognized systems of architectural language, and, indeed, architecture is, for these formats, often only a by-product of data and logistics."[8]

As evidence of their proliferation, Easterling tracks a series of spatial products—greenhouses in southern Spain, cruise ships in North Korea, golf courses in China—to uncover their geopolitical and economic logics. In each case, these places—often expansive in size and in their cultural and economic impact—have come into being with no architect involved. In *Organization Space,* she similarly reveals the protocols that dominate the landscapes of North America—suburban tract housing, roads, and regional landscapes. Fundamentally, Easterling acts as decoder and detective, revealing the invisible logics that inform the DNA of our constructed environments.

THE ARCHITECT AS DETECTIVE

I would therefore offer up another identity for the architect working in an expanded model of practice—that of detective. In the detective story, the answers and outcomes are less interesting than *the process* and *procedures* of detective work. Significantly, the

detective must approach each investigation with its own set of questions, adapted to the conditions, place, and events involved. While detective work has certain established procedures, the methods must respond to specificity of each case. Furthermore, detective work requires a shifting of scales—focusing on the details of an event or a series of very specific facts; and stepping back to understand a much broader set of spatial, temporal, and human relationships.

Each of these methods and practices are vehicles for design thinking, and for questioning and repositioning the role of the architect within our physical and cultural environment. Part of this repositioning involves destabilizing many of the givens within which architecture has traditionally operated. To this end, I would offer five strategies for an expanded territory of engagement.

(1) **Scale:** Architecture, landscape, and urban design, regardless of the scales of their specific sites, must embrace their larger contexts of geography, economics, and ecology. These design fields should recognize the fluidity or elasticity of boundaries, and the multiple forces and demands operating within a site. Architecture can only engage the larger forces which affect it if it operates at the scale which these forces are operating at. This does not necessarily mean building bigger buildings, but rather, thinking about an expanded territory of engagement.

(2) **Stakeholders:** Architecture needs to engage a larger set of stakeholders, not simply humans but species, ecologies, and environments. Stakeholders may have competing interests which may be brought together symbiotically to productively leverage each other. Equally, clients for projects may not exist at the outset of a project, but, rather, may only emerge as the stakeholders of the project become clear, bringing new advocates into the fray.

(3) **Tools:** If architecture is to engage more complex environments and issues, it must find new and adapted tools of analysis and visualization to document and understand existing conditions and put forward proposals. How can spatial, temporal, and social complexity be documented? Research in this context cannot be understood as an alibi for a project, but indeed, the first act of design, asking *unanticipated* questions and revealing opportunities and challenges.

(4) Entrepreneurialism: Architecture, landscape architecture, and urbanism must rethink its current understandings of sustainability, beyond simply environmental 'performance,' to embrace notions of economic, ecologic, and social sustainability. Infrastructures should be entrepreneurial, generating new economies and new public realms; embracing life-cycles and larger networks of flows.

(5) Contingency: Contingency is an anticipatory act and is often devised as a response to an unpredictable eventuality. The role of contingency in architecture permits opportunism at the moment when architecture interacts with the complexity of its wider environment.

ARCHITECT AS QUARTERBACK

One might argue that the pursuit of architecture today is a process that is increasingly immersed in states of contention. Working in such culturally and geo-politically complex contexts raises the question: to what degree can the architect propose ideas or solutions, particularly when working in unfamiliar environments? Places such as the Canadian Arctic challenge the architect to think, observe, and operate differently—to look at the context entirely anew—leveraging existing spatial practices, social practices, and economic structures, among others, as agents in design. Both the challenge and opportunities of such contexts is that the rules—of what architecture, urbanism, or public realm tuned to the unique climate and culture of the place might be—have yet to be imagined.

Because the built environment in the North has largely failed technically and culturally, work in that context demands wholesale engagement and knowledge of it, and equally demands that architects re-evaluate the fundamental questions that architecture needs to pose. Arctic Food Network and Next North envision an architecture that is adaptable, responsive, and temporal, rooted in this unique climate, geography, and culture. Rather than import Southern or universal models, or imagine vast emptiness, the Arctic Food Network proposes to rewire existing systems and harness local knowledge. The project posits the critical role that architecture and infrastructure can play in shaping identity—not simply in imagining new Northern vernaculars that bridge traditional and contemporary practices, but more significantly, in imagining new roles and programs for social infrastructure—adapted to the unique geography and culture of the Arctic region.

ARCHITECT AS PIONEER AND FORECASTER

Given the ever more complex circumstances of architecture today, the changing nature of the profession, and the shifting territories of engagement, the architect can no longer only be an implementer of designs, but will need to take on more anticipatory roles. Projects such as the Arctic Food Network seek to position the architect as originator and forecaster of project potentials rather than simply implementer of designs. It argues that part of the architect's role is to be anticipatory—revealing opportunities for design in contexts were architecture may have been overlooked or undervalued. The first role of the architect is to pose questions—to frame the challenges and opportunities of inhabiting such a climatically and culturally complex region. In order to uncover hidden possibilities, the architect must embrace the roles for which Fuller, MacKaye, Doxiadis, Easterling, and others advocated; the architect as comprehensive thinker, organizer, schemer, detective, and then as formulator. If each of these thinkers proposed new disciplines—Synergetics, Geotechnics, Ekistics—what new discipline might be needed to confront the challenges of the 21st century?

Such practice will find architects delving into phenomena far outside their own discipline—from anthropology to science to environmental issues. Such practice does not diffuse or compromise the role of the architect, but, indeed, strengthens it, for such forays into other disciplines do not side-step design, but advocate for architecture's broader engagement in society, culture, and environment. In so doing, it hopes to return cultural, technical, and economic relevance to practice, and to promote new scopes for architecture's reach.

....

NOTES

1. Walter Gropius, *The Scope of Total Architecture* (New York: Collier Books, 1943), 23.

2. Ibid, 18.

3. Buckminster Fuller, in Hays, Michael ed., *Buckminster Fuller: Starting with the Universe* (New York: Whitney Museum of Art, 2008), 197.

4. Calvin Tomkins, Profiles, "In the Outlaw Area," *The New Yorker*, January 8, 1966, p. 35.

5. Buckminster Fuller, *Ideas and Integrities* (Englewood Cliffs, New Jersey: Prentice Hall, 1963).

6. Benton MacKaye, "Regional Planning and Ecology," *Ecological Monographs*, Vol. 10, No. 3 (Jul., 1940) 349-353, http://www.jstor.org/stable/1948509 (accessed August 24, 2010).

7. Constantinos Doxiadis, *Architecture in Transition* (New York: Oxford University Press, 1985), 88.

8. Keller Easterling, *Enduring Innocence: Global Architecture and its Political Masquerades* (Cambridge: The MIT Press, 2007).

INVESTIGATIONS IN A REMOTE TERRITORY

NEXT NORTH

The Canadian North has provided a fertile territory in which to test these assertions and speculations. Indeed, in many regards it demands new models of research and practice. Long overlooked by architects, the Canadian North's unique combination of climate, culture, and geography has produced complicated infrastructures, settlements, and socio-political negotiations. Questions of how to document the scale and complexity of the region and how to envision futures that reconcile development with traditional living patterns and fragile ecosystems are key challenges for the design profession in the coming decades.

How then to chart the 3.5-million-square-kilometer context of the Canadian North — and with what tools and methods? The initial research was organized into six themes: *settlements, culture, transport, monitoring, resources,* and *ecology* — systems that seemed central to the development and evolution of the North. The intention of the research was to seek out potential cross-overs — where phenomena overlapped or intersected in some way — in order to leverage and test latent or overlooked opportunities.

Immersing oneself in this context, if only remotely at first, became crucial. The office's homepage was set to the Nunavut daily news-paper, *Nunatsiaq News,* and we began checking the regional broadcaster *CBC North* regularly. Developing methods for organizing information also proved to be critical in our work processes. As one example, we began a rigorous bookmark tagging system by which to save, organize,

Above: On the trails of the Canadian North

This page: Collection of cards used to track and sort various data being researched on the Canadian North. Cards were classified by color into six themes: Ecology, Mobility, Resources, Monitoring, Culture, and Settlements.

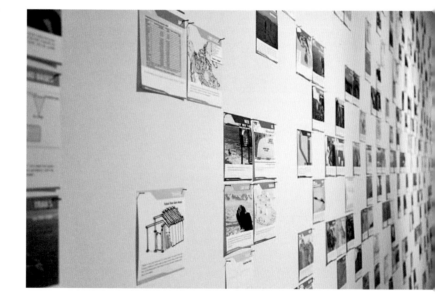

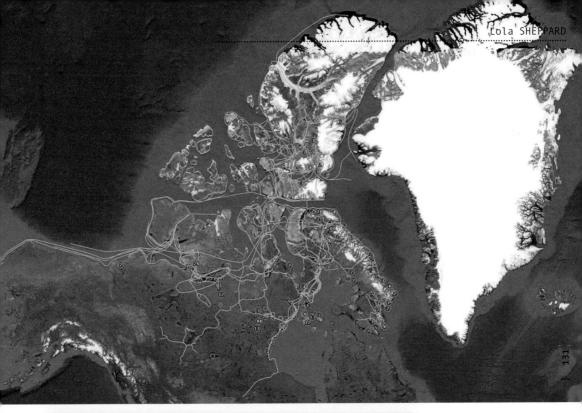

Top: Anthropologist Claudio Aporta has been mapping the traditional Inuit trails in Baffin Island using GPS and interviews of local hunters.

Center and Bottom: Iqaluit, the capital city of Nunavut

132

Top: Rankin Inlet, Nunavut
Bottom: Portrait of Inuit youth

and classify any online information we came across. The bookmark system, shared by all the team members, became a digital library of all information regarding the Arctic which we encountered over the course of the first two years of research. We also created an ongoing catalog of 'data' cards, which we used to classify information from other sources such as newspaper articles and scholarly journals.

The process of discovery and organization revealed that, most often, our research had little to do with architecture *per se*, but rather, extended into a range of other questions: economics, employment, food security, social challenges, anthropology, science, and technology, amongst other things. This was not to *avoid* architecture, but rather, to approach the role of architecture in this environment with a new set of relevant questions. In a region so little studied and documented — in terms of spatial practices, built environment, infrastructure, and architecture — part of our role in this context was to help visualize spatial information, document patterns of use, and identify overlooked design opportunities.

Both the challenge and opportunity of looking at the Canadian North is that few precedents exist for design thinking. Until the 1950s the Inuit were a semi-nomadic culture, with no permanent communities. In fact, the very idea of permanence and settlement was entirely foreign to the Inuit. In many instances, settlement and relocation were imposed upon them by the Canadian government in order to better provide health and education services, and to assert sovereignty, but often yielded unfortunate social results. It was Inuit mobility and flexibility that allowed them to adapt to climate, food, and geography in a lifestyle that was as dynamic as the land to which they were tied.

Most building types and infrastructures built in the North today serve singular uses and are typically imported from regions of southern Canada, with over-engineered adaptations. Many buildings and infrastructures are failing both from a technical standpoint and a social one. This lack of architectural and planning legacy amplified the motivation to understand the broader context of the region's physical environment.

Amplifying the dearth of research, very few successful built or unbuilt precedents for distinctly "Northern urbanism" exist. Ralph Erskine's work in Northern Sweden and Canada in the 1970s, in which he evolved the notion of the urban wind-screen as a way to define a sense of place while mitigating the impacts of climate, remain significant as built examples, although his plan for Resolute Bay, partially completed in 1973, failed to address the social realities of Inuit culture, preferring a southern social model. Some unbuilt and "utopian" visions from the 1970s did little to address pressing social or environmental realities in the North. Part of their failure lay in the lack of holistic research into the unique social, cultural, and environmental issues Northern communities face, and also in their attempts to design a community wholesale. In contrast, Next North argues for an adapted, incremental, scalable system of growth; for community architecture, infrastructure, and an integrated northern public realm. As with most development in the North, these earlier visions imposed southern models of housing and urban form, with little adaptation to local conditions. Next North seeks to respond to these challenges and root itself in traditional and current practices.

133

NEXT NORTH

A series of proposals centered on an ecologic and social empowerment of Canada's unique Far North and its attendant networks.

This page: Next North

....

Opposite: A calendar of access to local foods was created, which identified how a series of structures might augment access

Next North consists of six speculative design projects: Caribou Pivot Station, Liquid Commons Unit, Ice Road Truck Stop, Health Hangar, Arctic Food Network, Iceberg Rigging, and, most recently, Knowledge Clouds. These projects have examined, respectively, the role of research stations; the potential of education and cultural networks; an augmented role for the ice roads of the Northwest territories; the potential for a decentralized and networked health system; the notion of a network of food harvesting hubs; the link of tourism and military; and the potential for a mobile distributed higher educa- tion network. The projects, while rooted in the tangible realities of the North, do not overtly seek out solutions *per se*, but rather, position themselves as a series of questions, or speculations on a set of ideas and conditions. Collectively, however, they attempt to put forward a position and approach to thinking about design in the North, and a manifesto about the role of architecture, infrastruc- ture, and public realm in remote northern communities.

ARCTIC FOOD NETWORKS: NEW STRATEGIES

The Arctic Food Network became a testing ground for many of these ideas about alternative ways of conceiving of and mobilizing a design project. The project began with the observation that the role of hunting and fishing, as well as food storage and preparation, in the North has been central to collective life, because of the constant challenges of traditionally sourcing food. In a region of low employ- ment, where all materials, goods, and even services are imported, food security is an ongoing challenge among Inuit families.

As a nomadic population, the Inuit would historically move season- ally to hunt, fish, and collect berries. Even today, the tradition of going out into the land to hunt continues (as partial subsistence living), and many Northerners have cabins 'out on the land'. There is also a strong tradition of sharing food amongst families, and even amongst communities, in times of need. As a consequence, food is deeply embedded in the Inuit people's relationship to the land, to mobility, and culture. However, these traditions are on the decline as the Inuit experience dramatic cultural and climatic transformations in the space of one or two generations. There is, for instance, an elaborate network of seasonal trails across the region that have been passed down for generations; however, this knowledge transfer is currently under threat.

In response to these conditions, the project proposes to address the threats of poor health, poverty, and decline of traditional culture through the integration of communities with a unique infrastructure system.

A regional study on mobility, food security, and health in the region led to the pursuit of a network of small structures that acknowledge the Inuit tradition of temporary enclosure in a cold climate. Conceived of as an Arctic snow highway with rest stop cabins, the Arctic Food Network is a system of trail hubs that re-enforce the use of the trails by strategically deploying a regional network of hunting cabins, arctic farms, and camp hubs encircling Foxe Basin in

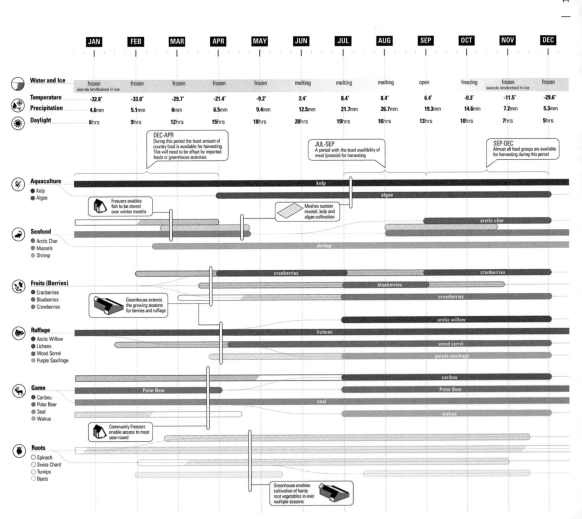

	JAN	FEB	MAR	APR	MAY	JUN	JUL	AUG	SEP	OCT	NOV	DEC
Water and Ice	frozen islands landlocked in ice	frozen	frozen	frozen	frozen	melting	melting	melting	open	freezing	frozen islands landlocked in ice	frozen
Temperature	-32.8°	-33.0°	-29.7°	-21.4°	-9.2°	2.4°	8.4°	8.4°	6.4°	-0.3°	-11.5°	-29.6°
Precipitation	4.6mm	5.1mm	6mm	6.5mm	9.4mm	12.5mm	21.7mm	26.7mm	19.3mm	14.6mm	7.2mm	5.3mm
Daylight	6hrs	9hrs	12hrs	15hrs	18hrs	20hrs	19hrs	16hrs	13hrs	10hrs	7hrs	5hrs

DEC-APR During this period the least amount of country food is available for harvesting This will need to be offset by imported foods or greenhouse activities

JUL-SEP A period with the least availibility of meat (protein) for harvesting

SEP-DEC Almost all food groups are available for harvesting during this period

Aquaculture
● Kelp
● Algae

kelp

algae

Freezers enables fish to be stored over winter months

Meshes sustain mussel, kelp and algae cultivation

Seafood
● Arctic Char
● Mussels
● Shrimp

arctic char

shrimp

Fruits (Berries)
● Cranberries
● Blueberries
● Crowberries

cranberries

cranberries

blueberries

crowberries

Greenhouse extends the growing seasons for berries and ruffage

Ruffage
● Arctic Willow
● Lichens
● Wood Sorrel
● Purple Saxifrage

arctic willow

lichens

wood sorrel

purple saxifrage

Game
● Caribou
● Polar Bear
● Seal
● Walrus

caribou

Polar Bear

Polar Bear

seal

walrus

Community Freezers enable access to meat year-round

Roots
○ Spinach
○ Swiss Chard
○ Turnips
○ Beets

Greenhouse enables cultivation of hardy root vegetables in over multiple seasons

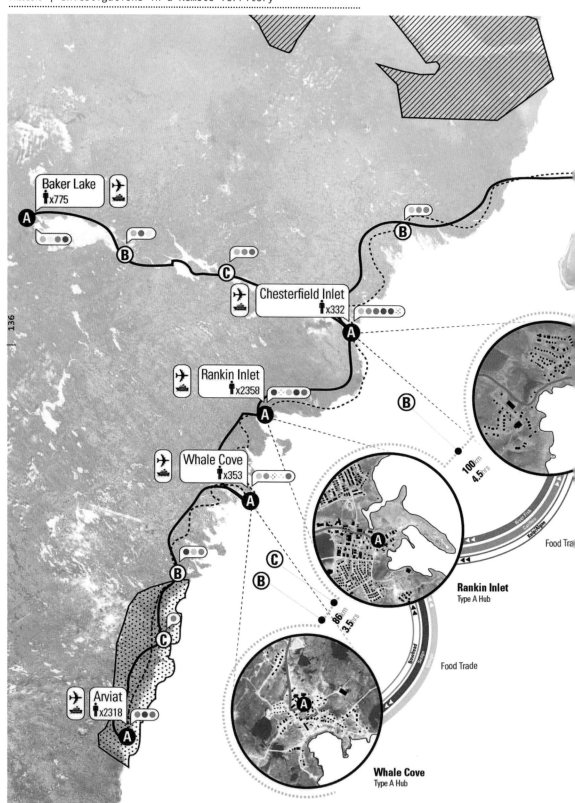

Baker Lake
†x775

A

B

C

Chesterfield Inlet
†x332

A

B

Rankin Inlet
†x2358

A

Whale Cove
†x353

A

B

C

B

100km
4.5hrs

Rankin Inlet
Type A Hub

86km
3.5hrs

Food Trade

Arviat
†x2318

B

C

A

Whale Cove
Type A Hub

Food Trade

River Fish

Kelp/Algae

Bowhead

136

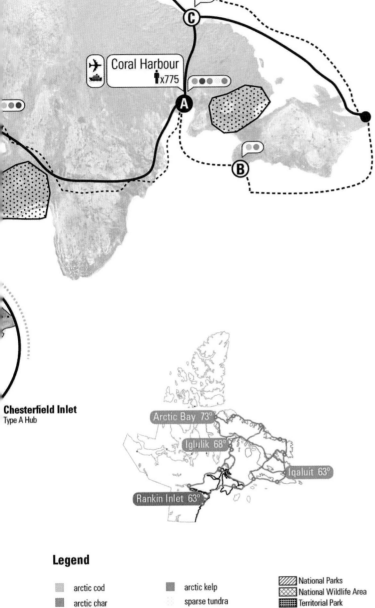

Coral Harbour
♀x775

AFN Kivalliq Network Map

The AFN is conceived as a network of distributed structures located at the intersection of communities, access to food sources and proximity to traditional trails.

Chesterfield Inlet
Type A Hub

Arctic Bay 73°

Igloolik 68°

Iqaluit 63°

Rankin Inlet 63°

Legend

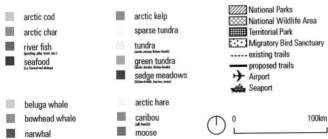

arctic cod	arctic kelp	National Parks
arctic char	sparse tundra	National Wildlife Area
river fish (grayling, pike, trout, etc.)	tundra (arctic stoney lichen-heath)	Territorial Park
seafood (i.e. bowed red shrimp)	green tundra (arctic shrubs, lichen-heath)	Migratory Bird Sanctuary
	sedge meadows (lichen-heath, berries, roses)	existing trails
		proposed trails
beluga whale	arctic hare	Airport
bowhead whale	caribou (all herds)	Seaport
narwhal	moose	
ringed seal	musk-ox	
bearded/harbour seal		

0   100km

Nunavut. The AFN also taps into contemporary socio-economic conditions, encouraging cultural sustainability through the recovery of
traditional building methods, merged with contemporary technologies.
Responding to the Inuits' mixed economy — one that combines both
employment, through activities such as carving or guiding tourists,
and the active pursuit of hunting as a way of life — the project is
equal parts regional agriculture, seasonal camps, data transmission
centers, and ecological management stations. Hubs along the snowmobile trails might be just one shelter or several, depending on the
needs of the adjacent communities, and intensity of use. In addition,
they provide a secure food and travel network.

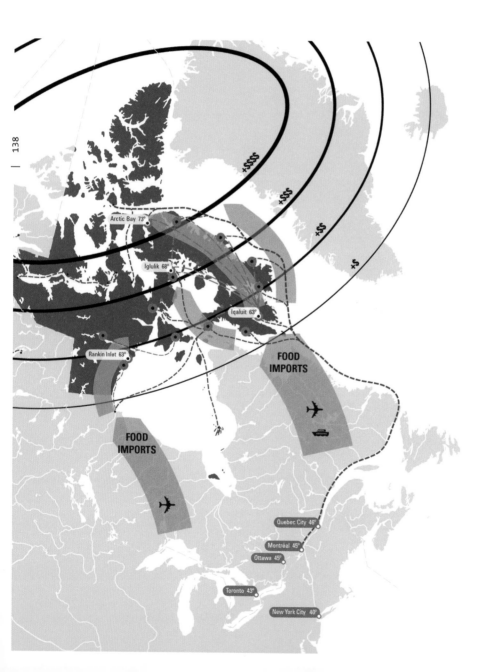

At a tactical and regional level, the Arctic Food Network seeks to enhance the production and exchange of local food, to create small-scale local trade and sharing of food resources. In framing a larger question, the project attempts to rethink its current understandings of sustainability, beyond simply environmental 'performance', to embrace notions of economic, ecologic, and social sustainability. Infrastructures should be entrepreneurial, generating new economies and new public realms, while embracing issues of life-cycles and sharing networks, and building local capacity and larger networks.

Opposite: Currently low quality food is flown in from the south of Canada at great expense, resulting in high levels of food insecurity.

Left: AFN argues for augmenting the local network for sharing and trading country food in order to increase local food sustainability and encourage local micro-economies.

TYPOLOGY OF STRUCTURES

The project is conceived of as a kit of parts, intended to be adaptable, deployed incrementally, and cost-efficient. Each of the eleven participating communities can develop hubs based upon local ecology or cultural activities. Cabins consist of ice fishing shacks, smoking shacks, food preparation space, and overnight cabins for hunters. Sheds consist of seasonal greenhouses, root vegetable vaults, and underground freezers. Meshes laid horizontally can grow kelp and seaweed for harvesting. Laid vertically, they can be used for drying

Stacks

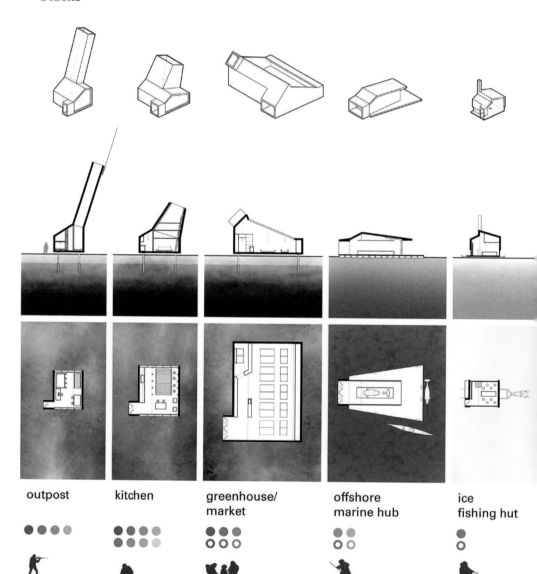

| outpost | kitchen | greenhouse/
market | offshore
marine hub | ice
fishing hut |

fish and meat. Poles are used for way-finding, either as lighting in the winter darkness or as telecommunications towers. The components of the project build upon existing traditions of hunting, storing, and sharing food. Indeed in many ways, many of these typologies already exist within the North — although always treated as equipment rather than places of social and cultural integration, nor conceived in relation to each other.

Each of the hubs is strategically located along the trails in relation to existing food sources and proximity to communities. The

The project is conceived of as a kit of parts allowing customization by participating communities, to identify structures and programs which would best address local needs.

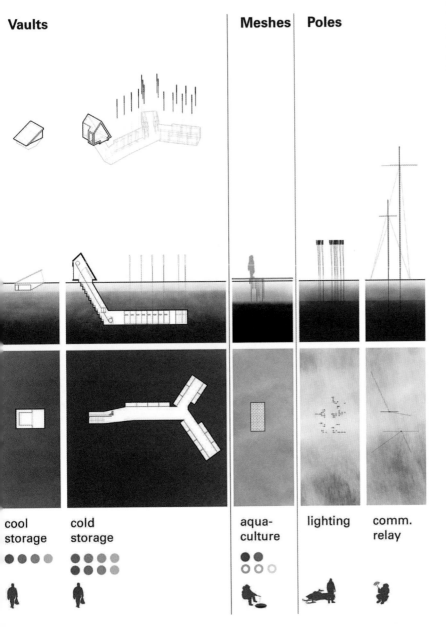

Vaults   Meshes | Poles

cool storage   cold storage   aqua-culture   lighting   comm. relay

142

Top: View of a cluster of overnight cabins out in the land.

Left: Interior view of community kitchen for smoking meats, showing tied wooden structure

Right: Community consultation kits were created to enable community members to offer feedback on which structures might work best, and in what arrangement.

hubs are spaced at intervals that can be reasonably travelled by snowmobile. There are three hub types: (a) located in towns; (b) located 30-60km from town; and (c) located out in the land, between communities. Each hub is imagined to aggregate different structures and types, centered on the Inuit way of life through emphasizing country food and making a unique place for food, communication, and mobility. This allows communities to customize sites to ecology and availability of country food, and also to different forms of food sharing, knowledge exchange between elders and youth, and community building.

HYBRIDIZED TECHNOLOGIES

Contemporary building science suggests that buildings shield and defend against the elements, yet in the construction of vernacular building types, particularly in the North, the Inuit have developed innovative ways to adapt architecture and assembly with climate and environment. One of the ambitions of the project is not only to address hybridity and cross-over at a cultural level, but equally at a tectonic level. Design explorations of the material and construction of the cabins seek to imagine hybridizations of traditional building methods from the North with contemporary building systems of the South.

The cabins' structural frames employ readymade as well as prefabricated CNC-milled joinery. The frames are tied together using a method similar to Qamutik construction (traditional Inuit sled) and Umiak construction (large Inuit canoe). Similarly for the building enclosure, one orientation is made of copper with integrated flexible PV cells, to enable the cabins to be off-grid part of the year, while the two end walls of the cabin are left as optional closures. They are an open frame system dimensioned to a typical snow block, as found in traditional igloo structures. This allows the option for the cabin to be porous in the warmer sunny months. A significant challenge to construction in remote regions of the North involves designing units that can be transported and built out in the land, given the absence of roads. All the structures are conceived as kits of parts that can be transported by traditional Qamutik and erected by four people on-site easily. Beyond the potential for tectonic innovations, the project offers the opportunity for local capacity building. AFN seeks to merge new technologies with traditional cultural practices to support an emergent twenty-first century Northern future.

Given the fraught role that architecture has played in the Canadian North, virtually any project situated there demands community consultations to establish dialogues and exchanges. To this end, a set of innovative design tools was developed to enable community members to visualize the components within the kit of parts, test how they might aggregate, debate where they might be located within a community, and give feedback on how construction might work. A set of game pieces enable discussion about massing and location, while a demountable structural model encourages feedback on construction, buildability, local capacity, and other relevant issues. In such a process, the architect takes on a significant role as quarterback — advocating for its importance, identifying potential stakeholders, seeking funding, and reaching new audiences.

PROJECT CREDITS

Next North, Cambridge Galleries, Cambridge, ON, Canada 2011.
Lateral Office / InfraNet Lab with Finn O'Hara and Hemming House Pictures (Mason White, Lola Sheppard, Fionn Byrne, Nikole Bouchard, Maya Przybylski, Neeraj Bhatia, Suzy Harris-Brandts, Marianna de Cola, Kyle Elderhorst, Zack Glennon)

Arctic Food Network, Baffin Island region, Nunavut, Canada, 2012
Lateral Office (Mason White, Lola Sheppard, Ali Fard, Matthew Spremulli, Fionn Byrne, Nikole Bouchard)

A conversation with

Lola
SHEPPARD

by
Kim DAI

//

Kim Dai:

In your talk you discuss approaching a site as having strata of information. How would you sort through this to determine which information is relevant to the project and which can be filtered out?

Lola Sheppard:

What interests us is the difference in how we understand site versus territory. I think architects have, as a profession, looked at site as a fairly literal thing with a specific boundary. One might look at surrounding buildings or the immediate context as something to inform a project. But I would argue that a site or territory might have many things that contribute to its 'context': there might be environmental conditions, a geopolitical context; or different socio-demographic groups that imprint onto the site.

There are also ecological factors, such as hydrology or geological strata or conditions in the air. I am interested in the idea that the site is three dimensional, that it has a thickness above and below ground. These systems have variable boundaries: where species migrate may be entirely different from the boundary of human occupation for instance. The idea that there are many sites within the site and multiple boundaries is provocative when thinking about a project.

KD: So it's not exactly visible or tangible.

LS: Exactly. I think the question "What is the site?" is very interesting. When you look at the products of globalization, such as Walmart stores, and view them as a site, there's the literal site of the store. But there are also all of the distribution networks, transfer buildings, and highway networks, which are all integral to the actual site. So how do you define the 'site' of a Walmart?

Equally, if one is looking at environmental questions in relation to a site, such as toxicity, how does one define the limit of that site? Does one go all the way to the source of the toxicity, which might be remote from the site itself? I'm interested in the idea that there are things happening outside of the immediate limits of the site that may be impacting it.

KD: Do you think the information you look at to define the site is more relevant to the project's program or to the site's geographic location?

LS: In a sense, it depends on what you're looking at and what you're looking for. I think that some form of cartography becomes integral as a way of deciding what to include, and what are the limits of what you're looking at. Part of how one manages that information is the act of visualizing it, because that is the point at which one decides what gets included, what gets prioritized, and what gets put in relation to other things. Bateson, in his book *Steps to an Ecology of Mind*, talks about the idea of the impossibility of knowing the territory. At one point, he says, "A map will never get at it all." You're never getting at the truth, in a sense, because no map is truthful, but he talks about the idea that the map is instrumental, as a kind of structuring device.

The visualization tools — whether they're maps, calendars or diagrams — become the DNA of the design project because they become a way of organizing information and prioritizing it. They become a structure for understanding the site in which you're going to work. This becomes very useful when one is dealing with so much information and trying to figure out how to establish priorities.

KD: In the work you do, especially the work that you talked about in the lecture, it's interesting that you collect information before being aware of your site and then create your site afterwards. In your project, Arctic Food Network, you work with specialists from other disciplines such as economics, ecology, and energy. How do you see your role and their roles in the collaboration? How is information exchanged between the architect and the non-architect — the specialist — that you work with?

LS: We talk a lot about this idea of specialists and generalists, and the architect maybe being a kind of hybrid between these. I think that one of the things that architects, landscape architects, or urban designers bring to the table is a capacity for synthetic thinking. We are not necessarily deeply knowledgeable about the technicalities of other disciplines. However, architects can read 'context' in complex ways - in social, technological, spatial and environmental terms. We have an ability to see where things can come into relationship, or be leveraged, or have synergies. And I think that this, in a way, is the role of the architect in complex contexts.

145 |

Rankin Inlet, Nunavut, epitomizes the suburban model of housing
and planning that were brought up to the Canadian North

So, in the context of Arctic Food Network, we will never know that much about mobility trails because there are anthropologists who are spending decades of their life tracking this. But we bring an ability to think, "Ah these trails intersect with these other things and here's an opportunity to intervene," for instance. I think that is really the role of the architect. In traditional practice, the architect is choreographer, somehow bringing into line various consultants: environmental, mechanical, structural, cladding specialists. I don't think in our case it's an argument about the 'orchestrator' as much as someone who can synthesize the deep knowledge of many disciplines and seek opportunities to see where things can be put into relationships in spatial ways.

KD: Is there any instance where the architect becomes the specialist?

LS: That's an interesting question. In a way, the ability to think spatially is a specialization. Ecologists, for instance, will think about things spatially but in a very specific sense relative to the species they're looking at. However, they may not ask how existing physical constructions could be designed to be enablers. Many disciplines are very strong at analysis, but less at projection. So I think that ability to synthesize spatial information, to visualize and to project forward possibilities is unique to the design disciplines.

KD: So, the 'action' or the 'expertise' is in processing information, rather than collecting knowledge?

LS: Yes, and I think that, in the end, an act of designing requires a certain knowledge base - whether it's architecture or landscape or infrastructure. It takes an ability to both synthesize cultural context, and to have knowledge about environmental conditions, and technical exigencies. The ability to think about relationships and opportunities between disciplines is hugely valuable and powerful.

KD: In your practice, Lateral Office, you work at an infrastructural level and you've mentioned your interest in the territorial scale. Can you talk about the restraints and constraints in working at a large infrastructural scale?

LS: One of the things that interests us is how architecture can have an impact beyond its immediate site. Certainly if one builds a building in a community, the immediate site and the immediate community will benefit from it. But particularly in the context of northern Canada — where resources are scarce and communities are dispersed — the need to think about buildings and infrastructures as a network, or as mobile, or as able to share social or cultural resources, is key. These challenges present interesting possibilities because suddenly an intervention may have benefit for several communities or a larger territory.

It raises the question, "Can one have an impact on a larger territory without literally building larger structures?" A highway, for instance, has impact on a territorial scale but it's also literally built at the scale of the territory. In contrast, in a project such as the Arctic Food Network, the ambition was to develop a strategy is territorial, yet the structures are very small. What is important is how they can perform as a network and how they connect to mobility routes and create potential for trade and sharing of food, to allow them to have an impact at a large scale.

Differentiating between 'having an impact on a large site' versus 'building a bigger piece of infrastructure' is important because I think a question as an architect is always, "What is *the least* you can do?" not "What is the most you can do?" especially in contexts where resources are scarce. The challenge is to know what is a reasonable territory and scale and sphere of influence for a project. We're also interested in the idea of geographically scalable projects — to imagine a project that might start small, and then be able to grow, such that the scale of impact could expand over time.

KD: Retrofitting current infrastructure or repurposing land to accommodate new functions may enable communities in new ways, but a large-scale shift can also play a role in gentrification. How do you see the role of architects in this discussion?

LS: I think that retrofitting infrastructure doesn't necessarily lead to gentrification, but it happens in specific contexts. So you need an urban density, and you need a demand. However, I think the idea that infrastructure could be a catalyst for small scale economies, and in support of the public realm is crucial, given how much we spend on infrastructure. Infrastructure has tended to be seen as a piece of engineering that's fairly mono-functional, but can it take on more roles and become a kind of catalyst for new things, at timescales that one may not be able to anticipate? These questions make sense both from an economic perspective and also in terms of defining new public realms that we haven't anticipated to date. The way that we understand cities, particularly in North America, is changing so radically. The traditional building blocks of urbanism have been challenged for decades. The idea that there might be new formats of public realm that are tied to infrastructure seems to open up interesting design discussions.

KD: The Arctic Food Network project has the potential to change a lot of social patterns in northern Canada. Considering this change, how do you see your role as an architect? What might be a way of thinking about what the architect provides?

LS: I think that in almost all our projects, and especially in the Arctic Food Network, the hope is to offer a small tweak to the system. This is why we privilege research so much in our projects — to understand what is already there, whether it is in terms of cultural values, social networks, mobility networks, etc. The aim is never to introduce something entirely new but to identify things that already exist. So, the hope is that the project doesn't radically transform things but just allows subtle shifts

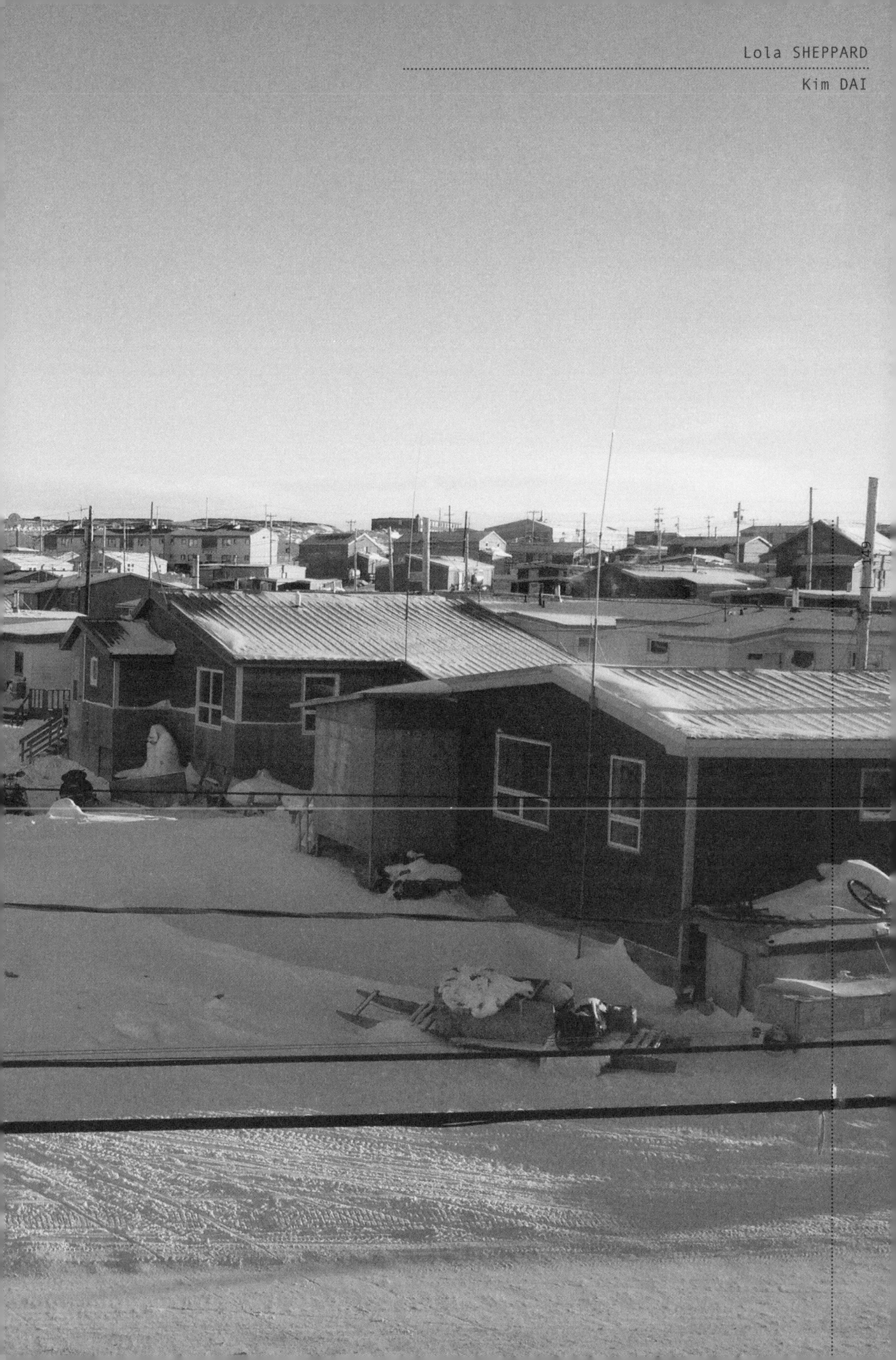

to happen. We like the idea of inverting, turning up the volume, or slightly shifting things that exist already, to create new potentials.

But you're right, the nature of any built project is that it will transform the landscape of the built environment it is in. You can only predict that to a certain degree, and I think that it's a risk worth taking, especially if one knows that certain things aren't working in a given environment. This said, in the context of the north, gentrification is not going to happen any time soon.

KD: As social infrastructure is constantly changing, how does architecture keep up with it?

LS: Certainly, the Arctic Food Network and many of our earlier projects such as the Salton Sea project or some of our public space projects are interested in the idea of designing a catalog or kit of parts, so that different communities could decide what is best suited to their needs. So, it is less the architect declaring the best answer for a particular community, but rather offering a range of components that can contribute programmatically and spatially.

In the case of the Arctic Food Network there is a food storage and food preparation component, there is a space for harvesting, a market, and so forth. The project serves as a question to the community, to ask what is needed, and what combination of infrastructures would best suit a community now? But also to speculate what elements could be added over time, or how could a structure shift uses. If the argument is to work at the scale of the territory, one has to accept that there is much more contingency. Even in more normative conditions, many buildings will go through five uses in their lifetime. But the more complex the set of questions one is asking, the more unpredictability there is. So, one needs to think about design in a fluid or adaptable way such that it can respond to changing needs.

KD: You had mentioned that architects already work, in a sense, like "detectives." Your practice intensifies this tradition, or form of architectural research. What is your approach to research and how does it influence your design process? And do you see detective work as the first step in all design processes?

LS: In almost all our projects, we begin with research, not least because it becomes a way to undermine preconceptions. It can be very easy to approach a design problem with a previous project or precedent in mind, and attempt to rework that on the site. However, research blows open preconceptions because it reveals things one hadn't considered, whether they are challenges or opportunities, and this in turn encourages a level of innovation. One can never account for all the research you do; there are certainly a lot of dead ends. Things look interesting, and then one might realize there is no 'project' within a specific line of research. So it's certainly not always a time-efficient process, but the upside is that one uncovers unexpected possibilities.

KD: It seems that the design process that you've discussed here — with all of its dead ends — resonates with the kind of work that is "beyond patronage." There are weeks that you pour into a specific task that may not yield results. Would it be difficult to approach a 'regular' project with deadlines in this way?

LS: One of the things we're interested in trying to do is to reverse the role of the architect, or shift the moment when the architect comes on board in the process. Current models of practice start with a client finding a site, establishing the stakeholders, the program, and then selecting an architect to give shape and form. But I hope that this process might change if the architect could come onboard much earlier. If architects become the ones to identify a potential opportunity, they could come in at the very forefront of a project and seek out the client, writing the brief for a set of opportunities, finding economic partners, and so forth. It is another form of creativity and potentially empowers the architect to claim larger authorship on a project beyond merely what the building looks like. In those moments, there's an ability to reshape how we think about buildings, cities, public space.

KD: You said in your lecture that one of the most challenging things to do is to advocate for architecture itself, to allow people to see that architecture has a role beyond what is commonly perceived. So, how do you begin to alter the common perception of the field of architecture into an expanded field? What have you been doing to jump start that process?

LS: I think if one is realistic, all work requires streams of funding – and this really ties into the Beyond Patronage conference. Architects need to be resourceful about finding funds and partners – not just money but also partners that would support alternative forms of practice, so that there are opportunities to be creative in the actual design phases. Part of the detective work may come even before a project begins. In our practice, we will have a hunch about a specific project and then we try to find the government partners or the private sector partners that might have a vested interest in the project and might support it. Part of the idea of the expanded practice is that you have to be creative about how you define clients, how you imagine funding structures and fee structures and so forth.

KD: In your work, how do you transition from detective work to being an 'architect as advocate?' What are the adjustments that you need to make? Is there a process or method that you use to filter out information in advocating versus when you are collecting information as a detective? You mentioned that when you were advocating for the Arctic northern communities, you had to speak with the local government, and speaking with them was a different process on its own. Could you talk about this a little more?

LS: Certainly we're in an early phase on a couple of different projects, in terms of advocating and dealing with politicians and

| 151

community leaders. However, what remains consistent is an advocacy
for the role of design — less in how it *looks*, but rather how it
could perform socially, environmentally, economically. One consistent message, regardless of whom we are speaking to — architects,
government officials, community leaders — is how can architecture be instrumental in a much broader sense? I think politicians
and community leaders and clients often tend to see the building
of appearance, square footage and cost. But the question is,
"What can it do for a community or a neighborhood and what can it
produce beyond itself?" In the case of the Arctic Food Network, we
are partly trying to build an economic argument by saying, "If we
implement this system, there will be less reliance on transporting
food from the south which is very expensive. You might actually
produce, and you could actually export and sell."

KD: You talked about some of the resistance you experienced toward
       the Arctic Food Network project. In that case, in advocating
       for it, is there a planned strategy to target or convince local
       populations?

LS: We're still quite new to working in the North, compared to some
       firms that have been building there for decades. You learn to be
       very humble operating in the context of the North. You cannot
       go there and purport to have 'answers'. We are outsiders to the
       culture and context. When we present a project such as the Arctic
       Food Network, it is a way of asking questions, in order to under-
       stand how the project could become instrumental. It becomes a
       platform for discussion rather than a suggestion that we have "an
       answer to a problem." In an ideal world, the project would keep
       evolving based on community and government feedback without losing
       any design integrity. Further community consultation will enable
       better feedback on how components might be used, how a design
       could perform, and how it might be built by a local community or
       local tradespeople. The project is really about asking how archi-
       tecture can engage in a complex cultural and geographic context
       and work outside of the traditional boundaries of what it does as
       a practice.

Yolande Daniels

Blindspots

The projects compiled here explore the boundaries of architectural subjects and forms while also seeking to redefine the limits of social advocacy in architecture. In these projects—each an investigtion of the social narratives embedded in architectural forms—I have discovered blindspots. These absences emerge in the often imperceptible connections between present and past that shape the built environment. Very often the history of racialized subjects in the United States has not been recorded; nor are its artifacts built of durable materials or considered worth saving. For this reason, the lack of material effects and the revaluing of materials are central interests of this work. To make this relationship between narrative and material artifact more tenable, I have by necessity explored ways to define new descriptive terms and forms in architecture and the built environment.

Each of the projects included is the result of an independent speculative architectural practice within the framework of the collaborative architectural design practice, studioSUMO, which I co-founded with Sunil Bald as partner in 1995. The projects are characterized by a mix of scholarship and exploration as informed by architecture, art, and the play of forms across media. In the pursuit of expression of an idea,

media is a variable. Relationships between the solo and collaborative works consist of continued conceptual, formal, and ideological investments, as well as productive overlaps resulting from collaborative and interdisciplinary work.

These projects were completed over a ten year period and are presented in chronological order. This essay introduces six projects—Silent Witness, Intimate Landscapes (of the Shotgun House), de Facto/de Jure: by Custom/by Law, black city^2: the miscegenation game, MoCADA, and Mitan—and provides insight into my working process. In this group, several of the installations were exhibited in invited group shows of African-American architects and academics. The last two projects illustrate how my interests and sensibilities are given form when the primary directive is client-driven. Although defined by the client's program, both projects resulted from prior research that not only answered but also expanded the mandate of the program. As with the independently initiated projects, this expansion was enabled by the support of our practice and collaboration, as well as academic and institutional fellowships and grants, thereby exceeding the bounds of the standard architectural contract.

SILENT WITNESS: REMNANTS OF SLAVE SPACES IN BRAZIL

Silent Witness is an installation of corner projections completed in tandem with the essay, "Silent Witness: Remnants of Slave Spaces in Brazil," during my second year at the Independent Study Program of the Whitney Museum of Art as a Helena Rubenstein Critical Studies Research Fellow. The project was funded in part by a travel grant from the New York Chapter of the American Institute for Architects. Although both the installation and essay explored the collisions of past and present spaces across time, in the essay I sought to theorize a concept of "negative monumentalization" for absent histories and monuments that counter official acts of historicization, formalization and monumentalization, or lack physical presence.

The region studied was the northeast of Brazil; specifically, three coastal cities where once-bustling slave ports exist in varying degrees of decline and preservation: Salvador in Bahia; Alcantara in Sao Luis, Maranhao; and Ouro Preto in Minas Gerais. The subject of the installation is Casa Dos Contos, a former tax house and historic monument in Minas Gerais that contains a space in the cellar where goods, including slaves, were kept. Although this space physically exists, it is not officially documented. In the corner projections, I sought to convey subjective qualities of embodiment and absence that the space triggered.

On line at the center of the radial paving stones, adjacent to the courtyard where the whipping post was located, as one passes through the great hall, a small stair is sighted. It is a stair with a landing seat, now a board painted blue or green. It has a hole to remind us that this was once the location of a primitive toilet.

Through the hole, a vertical chase is visible below. Rough-hewn out of the stone wall, the chase travels down. It once carried a trailing stench. Below and behind the stair, the privy trough empties at an opening in the black rock walls. One-inch thick vertical iron bars define the view. A view outside, of a stream with wildflowers over-shadowing broken rocks. Broken rocks, black like the rock walls. Through this opening adjacent to sewer and stream a deeper space becomes present.

A space of fiction, a space of history, a habitable and liminal space. In it, the past and present meet and circulate in exchange about my body. The space registers as layers of blackness, through which begin to appear rough-hewn stone walls, floor, and a ledge.

The ledge, near five feet in height, comes forward and recedes in the darkness. The only light is from barred openings. The rock edge is worn soft. The curved surfaces, once perpendicular, contain two carved out indents. With a foot in each, it might be possible to hoist oneself up. I am unable to.

A space of fiction, a space of history, a habitable and liminal spaces. In it the past and present meet and they circulate in exchange in space of history, a habitable and liminal space. In it the past and present meet and they circulate in exchange about my body.

A space of fiction, a space of history, a habitable and liminal space. In it the past and present meet and they circulate in exchange about my body.

A space of fiction, a space of history, a habitable and liminal space: In it the past and present meet and they circulate in exchange about my body.

Project: Silent Witness
Type: Installation
Media: Corner Projections
Location: University of Colorado, Boulder, CO
Date: 2000

| 155

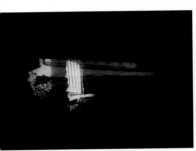

INTIMATE LANDSCAPES (OF THE SHOTGUN HOUSE)

The installation Intimate Landscapes (of the Shotgun House) took place within the Project Rowhouses Public Art program in the Third Ward of Houston, Texas, at the invitation of Professors William Williams and David Brown, with funding from Rice University.

The installation engaged the physical shotgun house in the play between the metaphoric and material states of knowledge, reflection, light, and dark. Seen as more than singular instances, these material and metaphoric 'states' modified each other as they re-mapped the shotgun house to reveal within it a landscape of intimacy and connectivity. Although the installation house was whitewashed, it was neither isolated nor empty; the doors, windows, rooms, and porches of the adjacent houses aligned, creating connective paths, as the sun instigated a play of light and shade in and around the houses. These material qualities served to bind the house to the community network of the block. Materials, light, shadow, and reflection were used to evoke slippages between physical presence and metaphoric projection, and were the media through which domestic relationships were mapped.

The shotgun house type is often associated with poor communities in the rural South. Despite the modest size and generic quality, it is embedded with provocative narratives, beginning with a name derived from the alignment of openings from the front door to the back of the house as a path for shotgun bullets. In independent analyses of southern plantation architecture, historians Rhys Isaac and Jon Vlach construct a typological genealogy that links the shotgun house back to slave dwellings, and further back to traditional wood dwellings of Western Africa. They further revealed that slaves set up secret paths in the countryside and woods surrounding plantations, forming alternate circulation systems between plantations in fields, marshes, woods, and waterways, thereby building clandestine and loosely struc-tured networks that crossed property lines.

Drawing from this historical work, the installation interior was zoned as a plantation network that contained spaces of agency of the enslaved at three scales that traced signs of domesticity: the collective or field, the family or hearth, and the individual or self. To describe the internal and external reaches of domestic space, firsthand accounts of former slaves that characterized traces

Project: Intimate Landscapes (of the Shotgun House)

Group Show: Row: Trajectories of the Shortgun House

Type: Installation

Media: Mixed

Location: Project Row Houses, Houston, TX

Date: 2002

of domesticity and intimacy were selected from narratives published
in *To Be a Slave*, by Julius Lester. These were collected by the
Works Progress Administration to convey the discovery that the will,
thoughts, and feelings of the enslaved were not wholly subjugated.
Narratives that described thoughts about self-determination were
located at the breezeway; those toward family and loving commitment
were located at the hearth; and those reflecting community and coming
together outside the auspices of plantation laws were located in the
field.

As a shawdowy substance mapped within the shotgun house, their words
evoked a previously unrecognized interior landscape that recounts the
self-determination that existed, despite repression. The installation
was a vehicle to consider an expansion of domesticity, and by infer-
ence, civility, to include the private life of the enslaved. It was
an intimate space that revealed the determination of the enslaved to
inhabit a private domestic space and entertain a private self.

DE FACTO/DE JURE

The installation de Facto/de Jure was a response to the invitation
of Professor William Williams to participate in the Dresser Trunk
Project. The project called for the design of a travel valise that
opened to reveal aspects of African-American culture in states along
the (Southern) Crescent train line, a former primary route for the
migration of African-Americans out of the rural South, prior to
passage of the Civil Rights Act of 1964.

de Facto/de Jure (by Custom/by Law) represents and replays the
relationship between legal and spatial fields in the thirteen states
in which the Southern Crescent line stopped, from North to South:
New York, New Jersey, Pennsylvania, Delaware, Maryland, Washington
D.C., Virginia, North Carolina, South Carolina, Georgia, Alabama,
Mississippi, and Louisiana.

Although train travel and the space on board trains was governed
by federal laws, train stations and the cities in which they were
situated were governed by state laws. In researching public accommodation laws — those that govern the use of public space — de Facto/
de Jure relates the effect of differing state laws on passengers
travelling across state lines by train during the era of segregation.
Enacted as law in 1866, the first Federal Civil Rights Act declared
all US-born persons citizens, regardless of race, color, or previous
condition (including slavery or involuntary servitude). This federal
statute was largely circumvented by Slave Codes, Black Codes and Jim
Crow Laws that legalized discrimination at the state level in public
spaces in states south of the Mason Dixon line before passage of the
second Civil Rights Act of 1964.

Moving from station to station, through cities and states, the rules
in the space of the train car are constant. Trains not only traverse
physical landscapes, they also move through culturally determined
and legally demarcated territories. Departing the train, an array of
public services provides or denies visitors entry to cities, as they
shift from public to increasingly private realms. In the segregated
terrain of the 20th Century, where blacks often lived 'across the
tracks,' or on the outskirts of towns, trains became metaphorical
and literal conduits of conditional freedom. Trains not only cross
boundaries, while moving from city to city, they also shift through

158

Project: de Facto/de Jure

Group Show: Dresser
Trunk Project

Type: Installation

Media: Mixed (Plexi plates,
Vinyl graphics, Wood trunk
per AMTRAK dresser-
trunk specifications)

Location: Extension for
Architecture Gallery, Chicago,
IL; University of Virginia, VA;
University of Pennsylvania, PA

Date: 2006-8

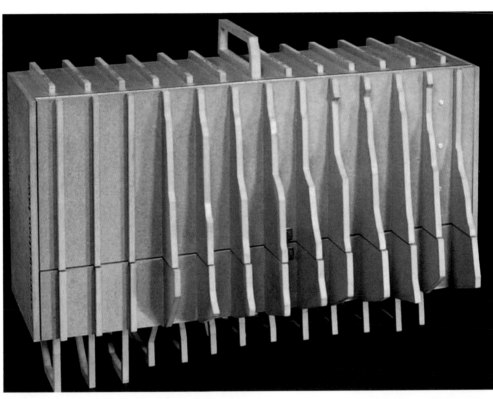

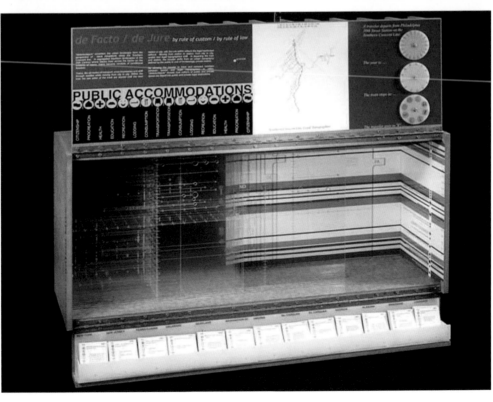

realities. Although the two sides of the track blur until the next station or city, the rules aboard reflect the legal conditions outside of it. Moving between stations and cities, spatial and legal topographies shift. Depending on the year or city, a traveler may have been asked to change seats, or suffer a penalty. The repetition of laws affecting specific public accommodations at the state level suggests that citizens continued to bend or break laws until the 1964 federal law was passed.

The de Facto/de Jure valise operates as an atlas that spatially maps the legal terrains within state lines, while it transports a contemporary traveler to the era before integration. The process of representing the interplay between values, laws, and space involved legal, social, and formal research. Public accommodation laws passed between 1866 and 1964 were grouped along a public-to-private matrix: Transportation, Consumption, Lodging, Recreation, Education, Health, Procreation, and Citizenship. With the train station as the origin of the public-to-private matrix in each city, public accommodations were mapped from the most public station to the most private home. The spatial fields for the matrices of federal and state public accommodation laws regulating use of space were layered and organized along axes that valued integration positively. Train and track terminology and dynamics (switch, merge, split, buffer, loop, interlock, separate, cross) influenced the forms of the legal and spatial indices, as they offered a way to describe and analyze the impact of legal actions and possible spatial effects.

Examining the legal right to public accommodation reveals spatial topographies defined by laws that affect the occupation of public (and private) space. de Facto/de Jure makes explicit the states of suspension and risk experienced by travelers as they passed through changing restrictive legal topographies of each location. Whether de facto (by fact) or de jure (by law), the laws reflect contests over public interaction and the use of public space.

Upon selecting a state, or time, or public accommodation, de Facto/ de Jure gives to a contemporary train traveler a sense of segregated America, and recalls the "Green Book," an instructional guide for African Americans who wanted to enjoy automotive travel without incident. By inviting the public to consider the legal history of access to public accommodation, de Facto/de Jure provides a narrative of the continuing struggle of integrationist and segregationist values in the United States, and of their spatial and formal effects.

BLACK CITY[2]: THE MISCEGENATION GAME

black city[2]: the miscegenation game, is an installation that was initiated by the invitation of the curator and director Thelma Golden to exhibit work exploring the gentrification of Harlem at the Studio Museum. It was given direction by questions and provocations introduced earlier in my essay, "Black Bodies, Black Space: a-Waiting Spectacle." Both projects explore what happens when metaphors and symbols become embedded in lived conditions and are reproduced as reality. The essay explores the myths and relationships between stratified — and often polarized — representational and urban forms.

black city[2]: the miscegenation game, moves beyond the limitations of the discourse of representations and forms of blackness as defined by surface images and appearances. The foundation of the installation is an analysis of the formation of segregated 'black' ghettoes in twentieth century American cities. black city[2] sought to project urban strategies beyond the segregation and ghettoization that stratification generates. To accomplish this, the first objective was to illustrate the hidden dynamics between the concepts, policies, and forms that produced the racially stratified 'black city.' The second objective was to generate tactics to subvert segregation, and develop altenative strategies to redefine the city.

The 'black city' is outlined in policies, statistics, concepts, and forms that produce specific dynamics. It is shaped by implicit and explicit policy, and is represented in statistics at three scales (neighborhood-to-city, city-to-nation, nation-to-world), in urban forms that occur at the national level in cities (e.g. Chicago, Detroit, Los Angeles, Miami, New Orleans, New York, ...) as affected by larger global flows (e.g. war, capital, time, ...), and indexed locally in spatial tropes and forms (e.g. street, ghetto, pen, projects, ...), yielding concepts (e.g. race, minority, color-line, black belt, white flight, poverty line, upward mobility, glass ceiling, ...) that effect polarizing dynamics (e.g. deplete/amass, densify/isolate, migrate/segregate, police/display, reproduce/ riot). In black city[2]: the miscegenation game, play is introduced using subversive techniques and values to yield new forms for these concepts.

The periods after the First and Second World Wars saw floods of African-Americans migrating from Southern states to urban and industrial centers in Northern states with greater opportunities. Their migration was simultaneoulsly heralded as the era of "the new Negro" from which new cultural forms and a growing elite were produced, and as the northward spread of the "Negro Problem" and growing poverty.

As a racialized group, African-Americans have been analyzed in statistics and epitomized in pathologies that continue to be reproduced in policies and forms, even when proven false. Statistics from census data and social surveys represent the structures of the concepts of 'blackness' that have been mapped in urban contexts. As such, they are a key formal element in black city[2]. In the game, organic and inorganic physical bodies are represented as numbers and given form using Geographical Information System software. Although the data is didactic, the mappings reveal how representations and data alike produce visceral effects, thus demonstrating the potential to transform preconceptions through representational tactics.

The term 'black' comes with negative metaphoric associations that are often collapsed onto the entities to which the term is applied. "Black cities" and "black ghettoes" have been characterized as separate, in and of themselves; this has contributed to characterizations of ghettoes and their inhabitants as realms of malignancy. De facto segregation was prescribed in residential covenants, codes, and practices. With the post-World War II disinvestment of urban centers, many whites and those with economic means relocated to suburban enclaves. The notion of the 'blackened' city expanded beyond just the areas in which African-Americans settled, to characterize the entirety of the city itself.

black city[2]: the miscegenation game, promotes diversification (over segregation), and miscegenation (over homogenization) as ideal urban models. In the playing field of the twentieth century's 'black city', value is produced at the surface; the field is universalizing,

161

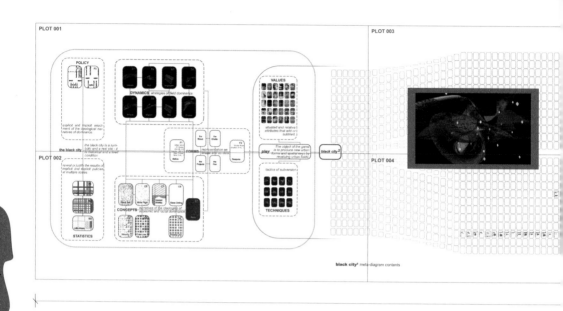

black city² meta-diagram contents

162

Project: black city²: the
miscegenation game

Group Show: Metropolis
as Metaphor

Type: Installation

Media: Video Projection

Location: The Studio
Museum in Harlem, NY

Date: 2003/4

centrist, and discernibly limitless. black city² encourages operations of appropriation, production of multiples, and shifting centers
and peripheries to counteract centrist strategies and the extrusion
of value from surfaces.

In black city²: the miscegenation game, this is encapsulated in
a meta-diagram that forms the basis of the playing field. The
abstraction of the playing field to a matrix accommodates varia-
tions of the 'black city' that occur across America. Play, in the
game, is modeled after the example of patois, signifying Southern
inflected African-American language and music. Drawing from Henry

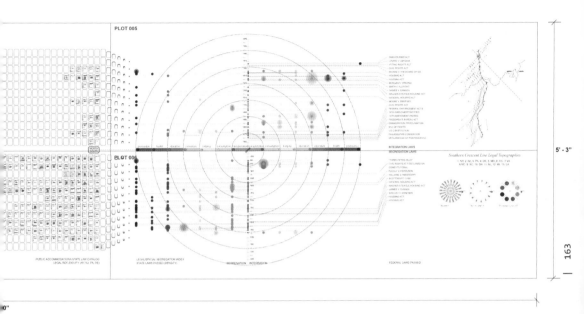

Louis Gates, Jr.'s analysis of a lineage of a "black rhetoric," such signifying techniques (e.g. association, appropriation, reflection, inflection, reorientation, resonance, slippage, disruption, refraction, juxtaposition, displacement, paralleling, etc.) are employed to generate inter-textual three-dimensional forms in response to specific behaviors in the 'black city'. In this project, the forms are reinterpreted and reworked to model new possibilities for urban conditions that address the complexities of assessing 'value' in gentrifying cities.

MUSEUM OF CONTEMPORARY AFRICAN DIASPORIC ART/ MOCADA

The Museum of Contemporary African Diasporic Art (MoCADA) is sited in a historic black neighborhood on the ground floor of the 80 Arts Building, a complex of non-profit art organizations, and is the first public art institution to open in the new Brooklyn Academy of Music (BAM) Cultural District. The project was funded by the NYC Department of Cultural Affairs and the BAM Local Development Corporation.

Our response to the client brief for a small museum was informed by research on the African Diaspora, and by the client's request to display a map of Africa. These guided the formal studies and resulted in a spatialized diaspora map in MoCADA's reception area. The play between two-dimensional and three-dimensional fields is formalized in the abstracted global map, which sites migrations of the African Diaspora.

To enhance the presence of the museum, the window wall of the building is utilized to project the museum's institutional identity to the street. The long narrow space opens onto a street corner that is the point of entry into the reception area. In there, the African Diaspora is mapped within by city, to emphasize the role of global migrations over the boundaries of states. The cities are mapped according to post-emancipation migrations, transatlantic and sub-Saharan slave trade migrations, military base migrations, and migrations due to drought and famine. The museum map privileges migratory flows over political boundaries to project a narrative of displacement and connection. While the reception area installation operates as a literal map in two dimensions, the third dimension is used to address various programmatic needs of the reception area, such as desk, display shelves, and a screen. Through this space one passes into the gallery and offices. Reconfigurable from one large space to six smaller spaces, using a series of pocketed pivoting walls, the gallery is illuminated by a floating light plane that screens the mechanical system above and provides even, diffuse light.

MITAN

In working on Mitan, a block of luxury-affordable housing in the Little Haiti district of Miami, we found similar forms in Haitian housing types to shotgun houses and villas. We revisited the housing typology research we began on the shotgun in Intimate Landscapes, and this led to the specific formal configurations in the design of Mitan. Ours was the winning entry in a competition instituted by Professor Nathaniel Belcher of Florida International University, with funding from the NEA and the Little Haiti Housing Corporation.

Mitan translates as "core" or "heart" in Haitian dialect. Intended to serve as a model for culturally specific, environmentally responsive, and economical developments in a rapidly gentrifying district, Mitan incorporates aspects of traditional Creole housing types, passive solar design, and contextual color and texture. The shotgun and manor units adapt precedents through interior spatial organization, cross-ventilation tactics, communal space, and exterior connections. The design modifies the typical Miami housing block model of three floors of units above parking, by mirroring it in two bars across the site, forming a green core open to prevailing cross-breezes. The design of the housing bars is informed by narrow Creole "shotgun" units and wide Creole "manor" units.

Project: Museum of
Contemporary African
Diasporic Art / MoCADA

Location: Brooklyn, NY

Date: 2004-6

Each bar is comprised of two prototypical units, with several configurations used, for a total of five variants. The units are distinguished by flexible open plans, alcove kitchens, private patios with translucent patio walls, a spa bathroom, a master bedroom suite, and, for the manor units, up to two additional bedrooms and a private 'backyard' patio. At varying scales, walkways, patios, and green spaces enhance the complex and provide fitness opportunities, such as a parcourse that traverses public spaces to promote healthy living and social interaction.

Several tactics were used for optimal passive design: the patio over-hangs of the manor units and the courts of the shotgun units create pockets of shaded, cooled air; cross-ventilation of the courtyard and all units by prevailing southeast summer winds and northeast winter winds is facilitated by the building's orientation; and units are oriented so that bedrooms will be illuminated by morning light and living rooms will be illuminated by evening light.

In the planning process, we were warned of the difficulty of selling the idea of apartments for purchase to the Haitian community, and were advised to focus on amenities. Miami was experiencing a housing boom at the time, and the concept of luxury-affordable housing was being entertained. However, this was set aside when the economy failed in 2006, and all housing in Miami effectively became afford-able housing.

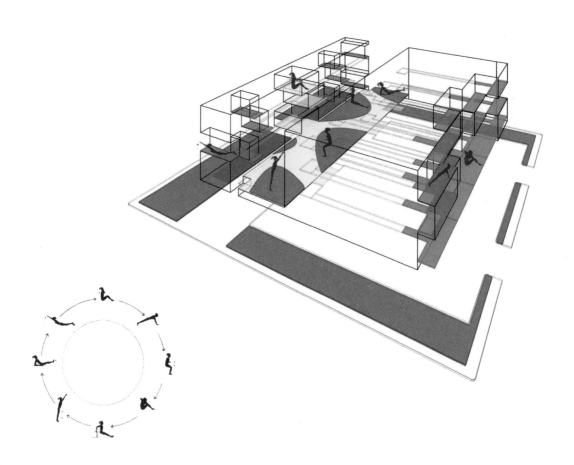

Project: Mitan Housing, Little Haiti Housing Corporation

Location: Miami, FL

Date: 2005-6

Size: 21,000sf

Competition awarded studioSUMO: Yolande Daniels, Sunil Bald, David Huang, Brad McCoy

This collection of work redefines activism in the framework of the architectural project, where architecture-as-advocacy borrows from art and research practices to put forward ideas of subjectivity and engagement. While the African-American community remains central in the audience, the projects seek to address communities as multilayered, hybrid, and diverse conglomerates. Furthermore, city agencies as central institutional mediators have been replaced by private practices, universities, arts institutions, and granting bodies.

Whether speculative, client-driven or somewhere in between, these works share a desire to illuminate historic facts through an aestheticized lens and within an architectural framework. This shift to the formal does not render the work less political; while the context is architectural, the content of this work acknowledges architecture and the built environment as cultural constructions that, like the subjects inhabiting them, are susceptible to much broader social conditions. While the works are initiated within the field of architecture, they also speak to communities beyond disciplinary boundaries. This work examines and deploys architecture as a medium for social work or advocacy, and simultaneously politicizes the landscape of architectural practice. In this sense, we can enact a more meaningful form of architectural activism.

PROJECT CREDITS

Silent Witness: Casa dos Contos, Ouro Preto, Brazil, Installation at University of Colorado, Boulder, CO, USA, 2000
studioSUMO (Yolande Daniels)

Intimate Landscapes (of the Shotgun House), Installation in group show: Trajectories of the Shotgun House, at Project Row Houses, Houston, TX, USA, 2002
studioSUMO (Yolande Daniels, Sunil Bald)

de Facto/de Jure, Installation in group show: Dresser Trunk Project, at Extension for Architecture Gallery, Chicago, IL, USA, University of Virginia, VA, USA, and University of Pennsylvania, PA, USA, 2006-2008. studioSUMO (Yolande Daniels, Laura Lee, Brad McCoy, David Huang)

black city^2: the miscegenation game, Installation in group show: Metropolis as Metaphor, at The Studio Museum in Harlem, New York, NY, USA, 2003-2004
studioSUMO (Yolande Daniels, Jeffrey Dee, Lloyd Aragon, Vivian WenLi Lin, Seth Spielman, Mitch McEwen, Sarah Williams)

Museum of Contemporary African Diasporic Art/ MoCADA, Brooklyn, NY, USA, 2004-2006
studioSUMO (Yolande Daniels, Sunil Bald, David Huang, Shai Turner, Laura Lee, Brad McCoy)

Mitan Housing, Little Haiti Housing Corporation, Miami, FL, USA, 2005-2006
studioSUMO (Yolande Daniels, Sunil Bald, David Huang, Brad McCoy)

A conversation with

Yolande
DANIELS

by
Joseph SWERDLIN

///

Joseph Swerdlin:

Much of your research is focused on the invisibility of underrepresented people. Are you interested in increasing the visibility
of these populations in actual communities, or would you say that
your work is more speculative, more about generating critical
discourse?

Yolande Daniels:

Yes to both. It's both speculative and intentional that I'm
addressing underrepresented communities. There are certain things
that are not really visible because they are underrepresented, and
so a lot of the work is just trying to make them visible; however,
I operate more in the academic and artistic realms than in the
grassroots realm. One of the criticisms of the work is that the
images are beautiful but they're somewhat abstract. So, if part
of my intention is to communicate things that are not easily seen,
but the process that I use is a personal abstract language, then
the work might not be easily accessible to everyone. That's something that I struggle with in my work. I think, in some projects,
I try to make things immediately visible to all, and in others
just operate more speculatively, exploring aesthetics and the
languages of representation in architecture and art.

JS:

Can you talk about your aesthetic agenda to shed light on under-
represented populations and how something thus is revealed or
communicated to the public via design?

YD:

I'm adamant that, even though I'm addressing social issues, the
work also has high aesthetic values. It's important to me that
architecture is as aesthetically high-minded as it is socially

high-minded. I think some people believe that if work is socially motivated, it couldn't possibly concern itself with aesthetics. And so the aesthetics suffer, and I am really against that. I want both.

JS: In your studio practice, SUMO, you have been taking on larger projects, such as the Josai School of Management and the Mizuta Museum of Art in Japan. You mentioned in your presentation that you had used some of the research on shotgun housing in your project for the Mitan Affordable Housing Competition. Are there are other instances where your research influences your practice, whether in direct or indirect ways?

YD: In the case of Mitan, it's a direct connection. In the project, we developed a series of residential prototype studies in Haiti to ground our approach to housing immigrant Haitian populations in Miami. There were two housing types, a manor or villa type, and a shotgun type that is a lot like an urban railroad apartment. If you just remove some of the walls and increase the scale a little bit, a railroad or shotgun is basically like a loft. We were playing with the fluidity between the types, just tweaking them slightly. So, that's very direct.

But then there are projects that are indirectly connected. For example, I very much see an aesthetic connection between the project, Intimate Landscapes, that was an installation in a gutted row house in Project Row Houses Public Art program in Texas, and the Mizuta Museum. In Intimate Landscapes, one of the ideas we explored to reveal histories of the house was to design strips of light to see traces of where partitions had once been. We flush mounted light boxes to define a trace of the old partitions. That kind of aesthetic sensibility is similar to our design for the façade of the Mizuta Museum. In that, there are cutouts in the façade that act as light strips. Formally, they are like the cutouts in Intimate Landscapes. In the Mizuta Museum, the

strips are more like the absence of material, allowing light to go through, allowing you to see through. It's a different take on the same formal tactic.

JS: Have you found that your interest in exploring cultural identities has transferred into your practice as well? How has it informed your professional design work?

YD: Just thinking in terms of the types of clients that we've worked with, it's weird to use the word "minority" because it really depends on where you are. A lot of our clients have been what are considered ethnic minorities in the United States, and our projects have also tended to be cultural as well as institutional projects.

JS: Do you then approach these projects in terms of cultural identity, or does that not factor into the way you work through design?

YD: I think yes and no. My partner Sunil and I are very curious. We're both educators and we're really interested in ideas. The clients don't usually hire us for that, but we're interested in cultural ideas and we do think they inform the projects. So, for every project, even client-driven ones, we do a certain amount of background research on social and cultural conditions. But then we also have our own aesthetic investment as a practice that we bring to any project.

JS: Going back to your talk, each project that you presented worked with different architectural media, from a photography exhibition to an experimental installation, from typology research to interactive games, and finally a gallery design. In each of these projects, you spatialize research and ideas into experiential environments. Could you talk about your interest in deploying different methods for representing and presenting your work?

YD: The different methods stem from a way of working in the practice where the medium is in service to the ideas. It's an important thing, because finding the best way to represent ideas is usually how a project will develop. With the game, for example, I wanted to do something that would directly engage the public. I also wanted to develop something that would educate people, without them knowing that they're being educated. So, combining those two motives led to the medium of the game.

Lori Brown

The Beyond Patronage symposium was a thought-provoking day with a series of all-woman panels comprised of an array of design research and creative practices demonstrating what beyond patronage architectural practices look like. And that the day's events only included women is critically important and must be acknowledged. The theme of the symposium and, by extension, the book is such a timely topic. Publicly discussing what *beyond patronage* means, in order for the profession to evolve and be more responsive to our contemporary society, is of utmost importance today.

When I began to think about what moving beyond patronage means, I could not help but think about the connection between gender and architecture. In my mind, when patronage and architecture are spoken about together, gender is inextricably a part of this relationship. I do not believe we can speak about moving beyond patronage without acknowledging and addressing issues of gender and architecture too.

When considering ways the Beyond Patronage symposium intersects with my own work, I came across an essay by two men entitled, "What About the Men? Why Our Gender System Sucks for Men, Too." One issue they discussed was the idea of privilege, and that it is invisible for those who have it.[1] As I begin this essay, I would like to ask you, the reader, to think about what this word represents; about ways privilege is touted or even camouflaged, politically and culturally. So often these two terms—privilege and patronage—are interchangeable and quite interconnected. What forms do your own patronage and privilege take?

Where are you from? What color is your skin?

Where are or were you educated?

What do your parents do? Your grandparents?

How do you begin to recognize your own patronage and privilege and all the associations and connections these include?

Architect as

Philip Johnson Group, 90th Birthday Celebration at Four Seasons Restaurant, July 9, 1996

The image I begin with is of Philip Johnson's 90th Birthday Celebration at the Four Seasons Restaurant in New York on July 9, 1996. Philip Johnson could be considered the grandfather of 20th century architectural patronage, connecting rising and risen stars with astounding clients and commissions. You will notice all of the 'star' architects of the day. Seated on the floor are Peter Eisenman and Jacquelin Robertson; in the first row are Michael Graves, Arata Isozaki, Philip Johnson, Phyllis Bronfman Lambert, and Richard Meier; in the second row are Zaha Hadid, Robert A.M. Stern, Hans Hollein, Stanley Tigerman, Henry Cobb,

and Kevin Roche; and in the third row are Charles Gwathmey, Terrence Riley, David Childs, Frank O. Gehry, and Rem Koolhaas.

The woman seated directly to Johnson's left is Phyllis Bronfman Lambert of the Bronfman family fortune that includes the Seagram distillery business. She is a patroness in her own right. Formally trained as an architect at the Illinois Institute of Technology, she was instrumental in inviting Mies van der Rohe to become architect and collaborator with Philip Johnson for the design of the Seagram Building, the headquarters for the Canadian distiller, Seagram's, where her father was CEO.[2] She also founded the Canadian Centre for Architecture in Montreal, Canada, in 1979. As their website mentions, "The CCA was conceived as a new form of cultural institution to build public awareness of the role of architecture in society, to promote scholarly research in the field, and to stimulate innovation in design practice…and is devoted to interdisciplinary research in all aspects of architectural thought and practice."[3]

What does *beyond patronage* mean for architecture? How can this be a new model for the future of our profession? I saw this symposium—and now book— as an extension to the larger discussion regarding the ramifications of what moving beyond patronage is actually asking; questioning the construct of how we teach, how we learn, and how we practice architecture; a model that has had very little change for well over a century. *Beyond Patronage* is a critique of this system and the ongoing status quo of architecture. This book provides critical alternatives to the system of patronage that architecture has relied on since its founding, ideas about how to seek work that people are committed to and truly invested in pursuing, and insights into possibilities of accessing new client bases and publics for engagement.

Architectural patronage

This essay will first highlight two obvious forms of patronage practices in architecture; next, zoom out in scale to position the ideas inherent within the book in a larger social, political, and economic context; and then conclude by speaking more directly to our profession, positing ideas of moving beyond patronage.

The first form of patronage I would like to highlight is the Pritzker Architectural Prize. The prize gets its name from the Pritzker family, whose international business includes Hyatt Hotels. Based upon the Nobel Prize, Pritzker laureates receive a $100,000 grant, a certificate of citation, and, since 1987, a bronze medallion.[4] As their website states, "The prize is awarded irrespective of nationality, race, creed, or ideology."[5] The nominating process "actively solicits nominations from past laureates, architects, academics, critics, politicians, professionals involved in cultural endeavors and with expertise and interest in the field of architecture… Nominations are accepted internationally from people in diverse fields who have a knowledge of and interest in advancing great architecture… Additionally, any licensed architect may submit a nomination for consideration."[6]

Since 1979, the Pritzker Prize has been awarded to 39 architects. Two years have included firms: Herzog and De Meuron in 2001, and SANAA (with Sejima and Nishizawa) in 2010.[7] Of these, only two have been women—a mere 5% of all architects awarded. If we expand this to actually include Denise Scott Brown of Venturi Scott Brown and Lu Wenyu, the partner with Wang Shu of Amateur Architecture Studio, the 2012 laureate, we would double women's awards. The fact that these women were not included, and that there have not been more women and people of color awarded the Pritzker Prize, is a clear reflection of patronage and privilege at work. Since the Beyond Patronage symposium in October 2012, there has been much publicity on this issue, including a Change.org petition by Women in Design, a student organization of Harvard's Graduate School of Design, asking the Pritzker committee to retroactively recognize Denise Scott Brown with her partner and husband Robert Venturi, as he was solely awarded the prize in 1991. Although the petition garnered over 19,000 signatures, the Pritzker Committee declined to give Scott Brown the recognition she so clearly deserves.[8]

The second example is the American Institute of Architects Fellow award. The FAIA "was developed to elevate those architects who have made a significant contribution to architecture and society, and who have achieved a standard of excellence in the profession. Election to fellowship not only recognizes the achievements of architects as individuals, but also their significant contribution to architecture and society on a national level… Out of a total AIA membership of over 80,000, there are over 3,000 members distinguished with this honor."[9] Of the 105 AIA members who became fellows in 2012, only 19 were women, roughly 18%, or slightly three times more than those awarded Pritzker Prizes. Of the 105 fellows, three were African American men, 2%, compared to only one African American woman, or just 0.9% awarded. Clearly, this is inadequate recognition for women or people of color in our profession. Although representation is higher than 50 years ago, explicit patronage is alive and well in both our discipline and our professional organizations.

Contextualizing 2012

Whether serendipitous or not, the timing of Beyond Patronage could not have been more in sync with current events. There is a movement afoot with a critical mass, beginning to speak louder and louder, gaining traction across a broad spectrum of issues concerning equity and social justice. I think this is important because a critical mass has more power to effect and force change. I would like to highlight two events that I believe reflect a cultural pulse that contextualizes the broader issues this symposium and book raise and serve as important parallels to Beyond Patronage.

In January of 2012, the Obama administration mandated, "most health insurance plans must cover contraceptives for women free of charge," refusing the Roman Catholic Church's proposed religious exemption.[10] Not even one month later, after receiving strong backlash from religious groups, the administration announced a compromise requiring the "insurer—rather than the employer—to provide contraceptive coverage."[11] This announcement precipitated a House of Representatives Oversight and Government Reform committee hearing. One of the most distressing and outrageous aspects of the first hearing was that the coterie of witnesses included only five men of various religious and academic affiliations. Women in support of contraceptive coverage were not allowed to testify.[12] As committee chairman, Representative Darrell Issa tried to argue, "The hearing is not about reproductive rights and contraception, but instead about the Administration's actions as they related to freedom of religion and conscience."[13] Committee member Representative Carolyn Maloney (D-NY) asked, "What I want to know is, where are the women? ... I look at this panel [of witnesses], and I don't see one single individual representing the tens of millions of women across the country who want and need insurance coverage for basic preventive health care services, including family planning."[14] In objection, Representatives Maloney (D-NY) and Eleanor Holmes Norton (D-DC) walked out.[15]

Jumping to the summer of 2012, probably the most widely read article that year that precipitated an avalanche in both print and online journalism was Anne-Marie Slaughter's essay in the July/August issue of The Atlantic, "Why Women Still Can't Have it All."[16] Slaughter was the first woman director of policy planning at the State Department, under former Secretary of State Hillary Clinton from 2009-2011, and was dean of Princeton University's Woodrow Wilson School of International Relations. She is currently the Bert G. Kerstetter '66 University Professor Emerita of Politics and International Affairs at Princeton University. Her article stems from her own experience juggling an incredibly successful career in academia and government along with immense personal difficulties she experienced while at the State Department, when issues arose with one of her teenage sons at home. She wrote the article because, as she states, "When many members of the younger generation have stopped listening, on the grounds that glibly repeating, 'You can have it all,' is simply airbrushing reality, it is time to talk." She continues, "I still strongly believe that women can 'have it all'...But not today, not with the way America's economy and society are currently structured. My experiences over the past three years ... forced me to confront a number of uncomfortable facts that need to be widely acknowledged—and quickly changed."[17] She quotes authors Kerry Rubin and Lia Macko of Midlife Crisis at 30. Their research found, "while the empowerment part of the equation has been loudly celebrated, there has been very little honest discussions among women of our age about the real barriers and flaws that still exist in the system, despite the opportunities we inherited."[18]

Slaughter argues that "[t]he best hope for improving the lot of all women, and for closing ... a 'new gender gap'—measured by well-being rather than wages—is to close the leadership gap: to elect a woman president and 50 women senators; to ensure

House of Representatives Oversight and Government Reform Committee Hearing, Lines Crossed: Separation of Church and State. Has the Obama Administration Trampled on Freedom of Religion and Freedom of Conscience?

THE IDEAS ISSUE: 23½ BIG IDEAS
OUR ANNUAL LIST

the Atlantic

WHY WOMEN STILL CAN'T HAVE IT ALL
By Anne-Marie Slaughter

Chris Christie &
Bruce Springsteen:
A Love Story
By Jeffrey Goldberg

The Surprising
Comeback of the
Family Farm
By Chrystia Freeland

| 177

PLUS
The World's Most
Self-Aware Man
By Mark Bowden
My Romance
With JFK
By Caitlin Flanagan

Ice Man:
A Short Story
By Elmore
Leonard

JULY/AUGUST 2012
THEATLANTIC.COM

The Atlantic cover for July / August 2012

Lori Brown

that women are equally represented in the ranks of corporate executives and judicial leaders. Only when women wield power in sufficient numbers will we create a society that genuinely works for all women. That will be a society that works for everyone."[19] Slaughter advocates that, in order for better balance to exist, several key factors must change. The three ideas I find most relevant for architecture are the following:

1. Changing the culture of face time — One that we in architecture can clearly identify with.

"The culture of 'time macho'—a relentless competition to work harder, stay later, pull more all-nighters, travel around the world, and bill the extra hours that the international date line affords—remains astonishingly prevalent among professionals today."[20] As she writes, in professions where total hours spent on the job are not "explicitly reward[ed]... the pressure to arrive early, stay late, and be available, always,"[20] even on weekends, can exert great pressure. Options that redefine the time and place of work—working from home and employing technologies for telecommuting—are available to all, changing how we manage work and personal time. Clearly, this is quite a serious concern for the cultures of both architectural education and the profession of architecture. If we teach students to value their time (the equal benefit of all classes, not just design studio) and to value the quality of their life, there would be a dramatic shift in the types of jobs students will seek in the profession at large.

In the fall of 2013, I tested a design studio work contract in the hope of changing studio culture and putting some of my ideas into practice. The negotiated contract, eventually agreed upon and signed by every student, created parameters that all students would follow. These included such things as a nightly departure time, implementation of a work ethic during studio class hours—foregoing emailing, video watching, or socializing—and the biggest one of all: pulling no all-nighters. Did this work? Overall, yes. We had sporadic check-ins and the students were honest when they fell short. Some of these rules were broken near project deadlines, but the contract did begin to influence and change their work patterns. Two former students mentioned to me in passing the following semester, that they are continuing to follow our contract. This demonstrates the potential of working with students to help them change their work habits and realize what better work–life balance feels like.

2. Redefining the arc of a successful career

I would add redefining what a 'successful' career even looks like for an architect. As Slaughter

has written, "[t]he American definition of a successful professional is someone who can climb the ladder the furthest in the shortest time, generally peaking between ages 45 and 55. It is a definition well suited to the mid-20th century, an era when people had kids in their 20s, stayed in one job, retired at 67, and were dead, on average, by age 71."[22]

One example she provides that resonates with architecture communities is the tenure track process. This example demonstrates how an institution can create policies that support all faculty.

[I]n 1970, Princeton established a tenure-extension policy that allowed female assistant professors expecting a child to request a one-year extension on their tenure clocks. This policy was later extended to men, and broadened to include adoptions. In the early 2000s, two reports...discovered that only about 3 percent of assistant professors requested tenure extensions in a given year...[a]nd women were much more likely than men to think that a tenure extension would be detrimental to an assistant professor's career. [I]n 2005, under President Shirley Tilghman, Princeton changed the default rule...announc[ing]...all assistant professors, female and male, who had a new child would automatically receive a one-year extension...with no opt-outs allowed. Instead, assistant professors could request early consideration for tenure if they wished. The number of assistant professors who receive a tenure extension has tripled since th[is] change.[23]

3. Innovation nation

Slaughter mentions Deborah Epstein, the president of Flex-Time Lawyers, a national consulting company committed to increasing retention rates of female attorneys, and formerly a big-firm litigator. Epstein describes, in her book *Law and Reorder:*

... a legal profession "where the billable hour no longer works"; where attorneys, judges, recruiters, and academics all agree that this system of compensation has perverted the industry, leading to brutal work hours, massive inefficiency, and highly inflated costs. [Does this sound familiar?] The answer—already being deployed in different corners of the industry—is a combination of alternative fee structures, virtual firms, women-owned firms, and the outsourcing of discrete legal jobs to other jurisdictions. Women, and Generation X and Y lawyers more generally, are pushing for these changes on the supply side; clients determined to reduce legal fees and increase flexible service

are pulling on the demand side. Slowly, change is happening.[24]

It is important to note that both law and medicine have been more successful in retaining and promoting women into their upper ranks. Clearly, this rethinking of law's professional structure will make even more positive changes in the practice of Law. Architects must take note that change is happening in other historically male-dominated professions.

Slaughter concludes by writing "[i]f women are ever to achieve real equality as leaders, then we have to stop accepting male behavior and male choices as the default and the ideal. We must insist on changing social policies and bending career tracks to accommodate *our* choices, too. We'll create a better society in the process."[25]

Although there has been much warranted critique of Slaughter's essay, including numerous articles, op-eds, blog posts, and TV and radio discussions,[26] I believe the national conversation is critical. People are now talking about these issues more broadly and are receiving much more exposure and airtime. However, I find the article does not accurately reflect the generations of us, both men and women, who are younger than she is. Although Slaughter acknowledged her position of privilege (including a tenured husband also teaching at Princeton), what is not being discussed is the critical point, that all those who fall outside of the elite world she is writing about, such as single people,[27] the working poor, and middle class families struggling to make ends meet, have very little power to demand such things as flex time from work, equal pay, or even paid sick leave. On the most basic level they would just like to remain employed. These are people that patronage and privilege excludes.

To a certain degree, Slaughter's article tries to challenge, albeit unsuccessfully, reliance on simplistic stereotypes based on gendered social definitions, such as 'women nurture more,' 'women choose family over career more often,' 'men are socialized to be the breadwinner while women are socialized to be the caregiver.'[28] These are just beyond passé. As philosopher Linda Hirshman writes in regards to Slaughter's article, "[these stereotypes are] destructive because she legitimates a lot of behaviors and attitudes that make the gender claim a self-fulfilling prophecy…. But most destructive of all is that the problem she's identified—the staggering speedup of jobs at the top—is not a woman's problem. It's the predictable and unavoidable result of the increasing inequality of the American economy. The chasm between the 1 percent and the rest is so deep and so life-defining that people will do anything to stay in the 1 percent."[29]

Another issue that Slaughter's article provoked me to consider is the general acceptance of architecture's professional structure, a structure that our students are socialized into accepting from beginning design studios, onwards. Rare is it to hear about either an academic setting or a design firm that calls out for radical rethinking of how work *works*. A few examples that call into question these structures are highlighted below.

At Transform in May, 2013, in Melbourne, Australia, an event hosted by Parlour, an Australian women's architecture group invested in women, equity, and architecture, one session asked, "Do architectural workplace cultures need to change?"[30] I was so encouraged to find an array of small to large firms speaking about their different approaches to how time is structured and managed. For example, Dunn & Hillam Architects, the Sydney-based award-winning design firm, spoke about how all employees, including the partners, only work part time.

In conversations since the event, Lee Dunn confided to me that even before her architectural education—during primary school that included students from 5 to 12 year olds in the same classroom—her teacher would give to the different age levels their work to accomplish for the week. It was up to each student to figure out when to do her work: you could finish all your work early in the week and then have the rest of the time to play, or do some work every day. This clearly influenced her experience and, while an architecture student, she thought it just did not make sense to work all the time. The lessons of these educational experiences were further reinforced while working for Richard LePlastrier, prior to opening her office. She discussed with me how this work experience influenced how she and her partner created their own life-work structure. LePlasterier lives a nuanced balance of how work fits into his life, and demonstrates how an organized life with no strict hours for work can produce excellent design.

Dunn & Hillam have structured their firm to encourage their employees to have lives outside of the office. Because everyone works part time, there is a great need for flexibility from both employers and employees. If work is slow they let people know so if opportunities arise, their staff can teach or take on a side job, for example. They also ask other firms to temporarily hire some of their staff during slow times. However, when there is a lot of work, they still manage to work part time. In fact, they have a kill switch for the power, and if people are working past 6 p.m., they threaten to use it. They are insistent that people do not work late. She believes part of their success is being

Top: Mattapan Mobile Farm
Stand;,Studio Luz and BR+A+CE

Middle: Holding Pattern for
MOMA PS1, Interboro Partners:
Jacob Riis neighborhood
settlement and their new foosball
table, Kids of LIC Kids and
their new rock climbing wall

Bottom: Fast Trash
Website, Juliette Spertus
with Project Projects

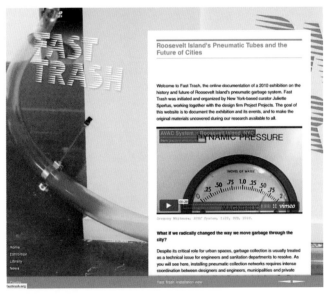

able to effectively manage workflow, and not overload their employees.

Financially, they pay their staff for every hour they work, so they do make less profit than other firms. They are completely open with their staff about their business practices, and all four employees are knowingly paid the same amount. More broadly, they believe architecture is not about sitting behind a screen all day long, but living out in the world. For, how else are you supposed to design for life if you yourself do not have one?[31]

Beyond Patronage participant Hansy Better Barraza, with Studio Luz and BR+A+CE, works to socially reform and entrepreneurially innovate our discipline in ways that specifically engage constituencies historically ignored. Through crowd-sourcing websites and micro-grants, raising their own money to enable projects such as the Mattapan Mobile Farm Stand and the Big Hammock, Barraza and her partners are proving that small-scale micro-infrastructural public installations can work to slowly subvert and overturn the layers of patronage in architecture. No longer financially reliant upon a person or company to actualize these small-scale projects, this process democratizes architecture and can provide more opportunities for communities to become involved in shaping their built environment.

Another example challenging how, for whom, and what gets architecturally produced is by Georgeen Theodore, with Interboro Partner's Holding Pattern for MoMA PS1. The firm's rethinking of the architect–client relationship and the products that result from it moves beyond fixation on the 'precious object' to relationships in which utility and adaptability are essential in engaging contemporary conditions. The fact that the project has more than 50 afterlives demonstrates how architectural strategy can impact a far greater cohort of people and varied demographics. Radically repositioning the architect as community advocate and community planner, and expanding that role to consider PS1's neighbors, is a clear way to educate the public about the value of design while simultaneously improving the lives of those in the neighborhood.[32]

Patronage + Architecture

So, where does this leave us, thinking about the role of patronage and *moving beyond patronage* - looking at other ways to 'do architecture'? I believe Hirshman's connection to the 1% is quite important because patronage typically perpetuates and guards against any change—especially economic and social relations in which alternatives may be problematic for those administering patronage, as well as for those benefitting from it. This is an area I have been

interested in and committed to for many years in order to advance and evolve our profession. This interest led to a travelling exhibition and subsequent book, *Feminist Practices: Interdisciplinary Approaches to Women in Architecture,* focusing on various forms of architectural investigations that employ a range of feminist methods of design research and practice by women designers, architects, and architectural historians. Two primary goals of the project are: to raise awareness for those both within and outside of the profession about the influences, diversities, and impacts of the feminist design practices happening now, and to expand how architecture is being defined today.[33]

I must dispel the belief that feminism is only about women—or for that matter that moving *beyond patronage* is strictly a woman's concern. Although the feminist movement began with a vested interest in women's rights and equality, that movement has expanded far beyond to encompass broader issues of social justice and equality for all under-privileged and under-represented people. In *Feminist Practices,* I define feminism by two particular positions. First, "as both feminist geographers Heidi Gottfried and Pamela Moss argue, feminist practices are political acts that seek to challenge the status quo and identified relationships of power. One of the many potentials these geographers see in using a feminist methodology is that of 'an open and dynamic knowledge community.'"[34] The second position is that, "there are those who work to improve and better the lives and spaces of others, concerned with larger social justice efforts, but may never call themselves feminist. As feminist activist bell hooks writes, there are those who "may practice theorizing without ever knowing/possessing the term, just as we can live and act in feminist resistance without ever using the word 'feminism.'"[35] I seek a feminism that encompasses a wide array of social justice issues in order to create a more equitable world for all.

I am interested in how one can more broadly define architecture, and what relationships can be made between feminist methodologies and their various approaches to design. "If feminism," as hooks posits, "defined in such a way call[ing] attention to the diversity of women's social and political reality, ... compelled [us] to examine systems of domination and our role in their maintenance and perpetuation,"[36] then we as designers must begin by questioning normative design relations and their expected outcomes,[37] such as systems of patronage that exclude us.

Another project presented in the symposium, by Juliette Spertus, "From Fast Trash to NYC Tubes," demonstrates how Spertus and her collaborative team seeks alternative approaches for waste management in New York. Beginning with an exhibit in a community-run art space that she describes as "part infrastructure portrait, part urban history, and part site-specific installation," her project creatively engages various approaches to bring information to the public, from walking tours, a symposium, and an online exhibit, to a video about invisible garbage. The use of cultural programming as a way to educate the public about the serious issues of garbage enabled not only greater public awareness around waste but also the engagement of city officials. This was a smart approach. It demonstrates imaginative possibilities for a way to move *beyond patronage* and raise awareness of the value of design.

If not patronage, then what?

I led a series of roundtable discussions at the Van Alen Bookstore in New York, in March, 2012, with various female architectural practitioners and academics discussing some of the themes of my book. It became clear that there is still a great need for support and mentoring for women and minorities in our profession. Many people who attended spoke out about many of their concerns. I began an ongoing conversation about these issues with a person I met at the last Van Alan event, Nina Freedman, Director of Projects for Shigeru Ban. We began to strategize about ways to build upon the momentum and energy of the events, and the need to start something that would address what we had been feeling as a real crisis in the profession. In September, 2012, we launched a group for women in New York, with about 30 people attending—creating networking and mentoring across a wide age range of women. We successfully completed an online fundraising campaign to create ArchiteXX with our online presence and ongoing programming efforts.[38]

Clearly, all these concerns are not new. Is it déjà vu? Is it a rehashing of the 1970s? I would argue no, but a building upon those who have come before us. An important article, published in September, 2012, in *The Design Observer Places,* by Gabrielle Esperdy, "The Incredible True Adventures of the Architectress in America," speaks to this, where she provides an historical analysis of the 1970s, when women were, as she writes, "redefining architecture itself; women were bringing feminist voices to existing systems and institutions and challenging the architectural establishment; women were forming new feminist alliances and addressing their own professional needs."[39] The term "architectress," re-coined by Joseph Hudnut, a former dean of Harvard's Graduate School of Design, was the title of a two-part article that he wrote in 1951 in support of women in the profession of architecture.[40]

As the Beyond Patronage symposium confronted the idea of moving *beyond patronage*, it inadvertently and cleverly challenged the long legacy of struggle for change within our still-very-male profession. This built upon a history of others who enabled all of us to be here today. As Esperdy's article questions:

> [Is] sexism in the architecture profession in the middle of the last century rendered safe for consumption at the beginning of this century… now that women have designed important buildings, won Pritzkers, made partner, become deans, gotten tenure and, in the United States, represent approximately 20 percent of practicing architects[?] No one would question women's considerable advances in the six decades since "The Architectress." But those advances didn't happen overnight and they didn't happen without effort, organizing and activism.[41]

But from where I sit, there are still many critical issues needing far greater movement, for ongoing and significant change to occur.

Whether or not the f-word, dare I say, 'feminism' in architecture is one embraced by many any longer, there is clearly a resurgence of its need. To think of different and even more radical approaches to practice, moving *beyond patronage* requires that all possibilities be on the table for consideration. I have noticed in my 13 years of teaching that there is a real distancing from feminist associations by students and even some faculty. But it was interesting to note that, although younger students and recent graduates may not self-identify as feminist, they turned out to the Van Alen events in search of something that is integral to feminist principles and social justice movements working for greater diversity and inclusion.[42] As one younger woman commented in the last roundtable discussion, "People are looking for this [referring to the discussion of the state of the profession]. These conversations are not happening in the schools. People are freaking out."[43] Another woman, who mentioned that she was a sole practitioner, said that there is no real support and exchange of work and opportunities. She is finding the profession to be a very isolating environment. If you are trying to juggle everything, you are very alone, regardless of gender.[44]

It is only obvious to connect the Beyond Patronage symposium with the Peter Reyner Banham Fellowship at the University at Buffalo. As the fellowship website mentions, "[t]he Banham Fellowship in Architecture is intended to support design work that situates architecture within the general field of socio-cultural and material critique."[45] Banham's essay, "A Black Box," criticizes architecture for its entrenchment within itself and the solipsism that the discipline instills and perpetuates from the very beginning of architectural education, especially within design studio pedagogy and culture. The discipline, as he argues, operates on a very narrow value system with "unspoken—or unspeakable—assumptions on which it rests." Architecture, no longer acknowledged as the "dominant mode of rational design," is seen as the "exercise of an arcane and privileged aesthetic code." He goes even further, lambasting architecture as too proud and too accepting of a "parochial rule book [that] can only seem a crippling limitation on building's power to serve humanity." However, he ends the essay with a glimmer of hope, that if architecture would allow itself to be "opened up to the understandings of the profane and the vulgar, at the risk of destroying itself as an art in the process,"[46] then architecture may find an active and engaged existence in the world.[47]

It is precisely this existence and participation in the profession that Beyond Patronage seeks. It is a practice where, to quote the editors of *Architecture and Participation,* "participation is not always regarded as the guarantee of sustainability within a project, but as an approach that assumes risks and uncertainty."[48] These uncertainties and places of potential conflict "forc[e] it to engage with issues that in the long term will make architecture more responsive and responsible." This results in an "alternative means of production ... [that] leads to alternative aesthetics and spatialities." Moving *beyond patronage* suggests an "expanded field for architectural practice; it is a means of reinvigorating architecture, bringing benefit to users and architects alike."[49]

Conclusion

Returning to Linda Hirschman's earlier critique, I would like to borrow and extend her argument connecting to the issues that the symposium raises around patronage and privilege. They are actually about the 1% and the ways our entrenched systems of practice and teaching, including pedagogy and curriculum, perpetuate and even promote inequalities. This space *beyond patronage* is where agency and true empowerment is located. The symposium and this book are evidence of just such possibilities. Every participant, in various ways through her own practice, demonstrates what *beyond patronage* looks like.

For example, Natalie Jeremijenko, designer, artist, innovator, and inventor, among other titles, seeks to capitalize on new technologies for social change. Through public experimentation, folly and science, and relying upon participatory research, "she is interested in the production of knowledge, and information, and the political and social possibilities (and limitations) of information and emerging technologies."[50] One of her projects, the Environmental Health Clinic, requires the public to be engaged and work to change environmental health issues that one is concerned with. Rather than passively waiting for a doctor to diagnose and prescribe, the 'patient's' prescription is to go out and

183

Environmental Health Clinic / Natalie Jeremijenko

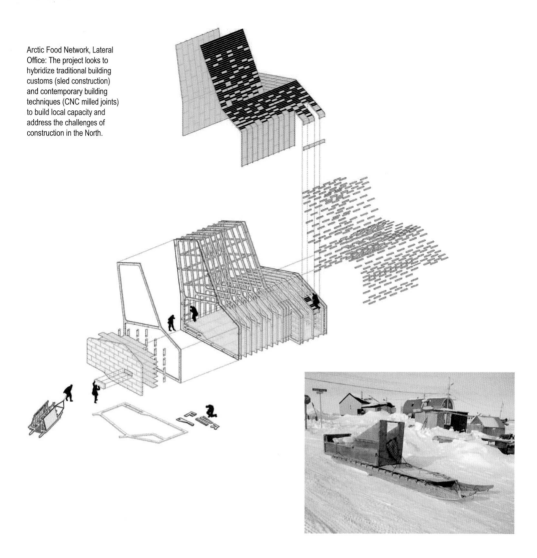

Arctic Food Network, Lateral Office: The project looks to hybridize traditional building customs (sled construction) and contemporary building techniques (CNC milled joints) to build local capacity and address the challenges of construction in the North.

take action! As Jeremijenko states, "I try to under-score the fact that we are complicit and responsible for our technology, to dispel the notion that it is a foreign object...We're not being passively impacted by these technologies. Rather, we are actively designing them, and we can use sociotechnical analyses in generating new designs."[51]

Lola Sheppard and Lateral Office seek possibilities beyond the normative idea of site by engaging environmental data, economic forces, and ecologies as elements to be researched and mined for their spatial agency. Within the conceptual framing of Arctic Food Network, the project proposes a new system for northern Canadian populations to access and further develop local food traditions and as possible sources of revenue streams for themselves. Design in this project is not as concerned with creating spaces for inhabitation, which it does, but also, more importantly,

with creating knowledge exchange and education, social connection, and cultural and historical recla-mation. As design takes on these significant issues it moves beyond preoccupation with form to issues that are integral to the sustainability of civilization.

This is the future of architecture and, using the symposium organizers' own words, "is central and critical to the survival of our profession."[52]

Another important area to consider in moving *beyond patronage* is holding architectural practices more accountable to fair and inclusive work policies. At the last Van Alen roundtable, Yale University architec-ture professor Peggy Deamer mentioned that, one day when she was walking through the Yale Law School, she noticed the "Top Ten Family Friendly Law Firms" advertised for upcoming graduates. Her immediate response was that you would never see this in architec-ture schools. She was shocked by her own response, asking "What is the difference, why not in architecture?" Digging a bit deeper on the Yale Law Women's website, I realized this is a student organization that has been putting pressure on law firms to change for over 8 years. Yale Law Women are interested in firms that are deconstructing gender stereotypes of "breadwinner" and "care-giver" by creating "family friendly options to attorneys of both genders on equal terms." They highlight part-time/flex-time and family care policies as well as leadership and promotion rates as a way to promote those firms who have fairer practices. Quoting from their site: "Yale Law Women produces its annual Top Ten Family Firms report to raise awareness of gender disparities within the legal profession as well as to highlight progress and innovative solutions. We believe that the legal industry is capable of making major strides to improve the experiences of women and men attorneys alike. That improvement hinges on careful attention to utilization in addition to availability of family-friendly policies."[53] Students are such a critical piece in moving *beyond patronage.* As English Professor Gayle Greene writes in "Putting Principle into Practice":

How can we use our educational apparatuses and institutions to make social change—how we can reinvigorate "our capacity as agents to act as well as to know otherwise, to intervene in the world as well as the academy, to have an effect."[54]

Yale Law Women are doing just that.

As educators, we all have a responsibility to question and think beyond the models we were educated under. Architecture is always one of the last professions to embrace current intellectual movements, be those theoretical, technological, or sustainable. It remains far behind in diversifying our ranks. According to the 2011 National Architectural Accrediting Board report:

79% of full professors are men and 85% are white

73% of associate professors are men and 79% are white

68% of assistant professors are men and 72% are white

70% of instructors are men and 75% are white[55]

Architectural curricula still embody the legacies of "dead white men" and communicate that the "best" architects you should emulate "are white and male."[56] Furthermore, a school's public events roster is also quite telling. Those who are invited speakers for lectures and symposia remain predominately male, with students having far fewer opportunities to be exposed to female architects and designers.[57] For the fall and spring semesters of the 2012-2013 academic year, my research assistants found that, of the 73 schools where information was easily accessed, almost **62%** had between either no women or only one woman invited as a public lecturer. Additionally, over **1/3 or 34.3% of these schools had no women as part of their public programming at all.** This is a disturbing statistic. As Stratigakos has noted:

Jeremy Till, head of the London art and design college Central Saint Martin's, has pledged to refuse to participate in lecture series with less than 30 percent female representation. His position, he writes, "is more than just a numbers game. It is often said that knowledge is power. These male-dominated platforms are the means for the perpetuation of male models of knowledge, and with them the perpetuation of male systems of power.... I am increasingly intemperate of male-dominated discourse and the values it represents: the architect as thrusting hero, the endless 'show and tells' with the architect at the centre, the clubbiness of the whole scene with women excluded from those all important informal networks.

As demonstrated by the Yale Law Women, students can also put pressure on schools and the discipline at large to force change. What would happen if architecture students across North America began to put pressure and demand more diverse lecture series? Or more diverse faculties?

Beyond patronage = radical rethinking

Where I find such great potential in moving *beyond patronage* is how these strategies are creating new ways of defining what architectural practice is. I believe agency comes from the desire, the actual necessity to figure out how we can stake our claim within a still very homogeneous profession. *Beyond Patronage* reconfigures and rethinks both academia and practice.

Another participant from the symposium included Linda Taalman. Her interest in challenging the iconic idea of "architect as sole creator" has shaped her entire career thus far. Willing to relinquish some aspects of design control and venture into the unknown, she and her collaborators have sought different ways to work and fully participate in the process of design. This takes real courage and confidence where one is willing, as Banham suggests, to allow one's work to be "opened up to the understandings of the profane and the vulgar, at the risk of destroying itself as an art in

This page: IT House,
Taalman Koch

Opposite Top: Silent
Witness: Remnants of Slave
Spaces, Yolande Daniels

Opposite bottom: black
city², Yolande Daniels

Moving Beyond Patronage

Silent Witness: *Remnants of Slave Spaces*
Casa dos Contos Corner Projections, Ouro Preto, Brazil

On line at the center of the radial paving stones, adjacent to the courtyard where the whipping post was located, as one passes through the great hall, a small stair is sighted.

Policy
  P1 Implicit
  P2 Explicit

Statistics
  S1 Neighborhood-City
  S2 City--Nation
  S3 Nation--World

Forms
  F1 Native—Urban sites (Chicago, Detroit, Los
     Angeles, Miami, New Orleans, New York,...)
  F1.1 Spatial keys (street, ghetto, pen, projects...)
  F2 Diasporic--Global flows (capital, time...)

Concepts
  C1 Race
  C2 Minority
  C3 Color line
  C4 Black belt
  C5 White flight
  C6 Poverty line
  C7 Upward mobility
  C8 Glass ceiling

Dynamics
  D1 Migrate
  D2 Riot
  D3 Mix/Segregate
  D4 Police
  D5 Display

Play
  T1-12 Techniques
  V1-∞ Values

Production
  BC1-∞ Hybrid

black city² meta-diagram contents

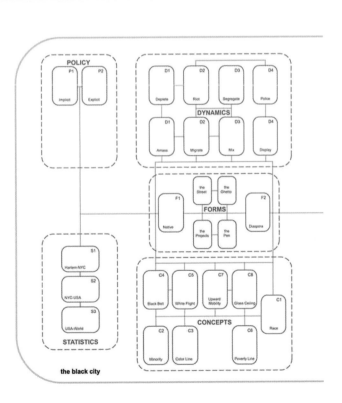

Lori Brown

the process."[59] The IT House system and its ongoing development exemplify this potential. By designing adaptable systems, both spatially and environmentally, this project is able to engage a much wider audience with ongoing iterations, both domestically and commercially. It is also interesting to note that the use of social media has greatly expanded future client potentials and communication strategies with 'fans' and clients alike.

Yolande Daniels' projects presented at the symposium investigate and critique complex social and political issues, specifically those pertaining to race. Seeking to both reveal and speculate upon this often-sidelined area in architecture, her work presents new possibilities for the role of design thinking. Through mapping space's invisible structures, be those of history, text, census data, or policy, she mines this data for new potentials and futures of such spaces.

All of the projects included in this anthology and that were presented at the symposium confront real social and economic problems overlooked by our government and social structures, and provide creative design solutions to improve community members' lives in the process. In their own ways, each envisions and practices a different way to 'think and practice' architecture. Part

grassroots and part community activists, if we architects and designers are going to change the world, I argue it is from the ground up that it is going to happen. We can no longer, as Better Barraza argued at the symposium, play the 'waiting for opportunities' game, but are now required to be architect, entrepreneur, and community activist. Moving beyond mere form-maker, we must recognize and acknowledge the complexities inherent in our world—be those economic, social, political, environmental—and capitalize on their potential as agents of change.

We must enable more women and people of color into our ranks, at all levels. We must create successful networking and mentoring programs. Yes, it is important to discover ways to change from within these structures, but I also think we must be far more radical in ways to work outside of them—*moving beyond patronage, privilege, and the 1%*. We have to begin to take this on because the future of our profession, and design in general depends on us doing so.

NOTES

1. Noah Brand and Ozy Frantz, "What About the Men? Why Our Gender System Sucks for Men, Too," AlterNet, July 10, 2012, http://www.alternet.org/story/156194/what_about_the_men_why_our_gender_system_sucks_for_men% 2C_too?akid=9055.133917.-pE7RY&rd=1&t=5&paging=off (accessed October 6, 2012).

2. Susan Wagg, "Phyllis Lambert," The Canadian Encyclopedia, http://www.thecanadianencyclopedia.com/articles/phyllis-lambert (accessed July 15, 2013); Michael Brown, "Phyllis Lambert," Jewish Women's Archive Jewish Women Encyclopedia, http://jwa.org/encyclopedia/article/lambert-phyllis (accessed July 15, 2013).

3. Canadian Centre for Architecture, Institutional Overview, http://www.cca.qc.ca/en/collection/294-institutional-overview (accessed October 15, 2012).

4. "History," The Pritzker Architecture Prize, accessed October 7, 2012, http://www.pritzkerprize.com/about/history.

5. "Nomination Process," The Pritzker Architecture Prize, http://www.pritzkerprize.com/about/nomination (accessed October 7, 2012).

6. Ibid.

7. For further information please see "Laureates By Year," The Pritzker Architecture Prize, http://www.pritzkerprize.com/laureates/year (accessed January 20, 2013).

8. For more on this see: Cat Garcia Menocal, "Denise Scott Brown calls for inclusion in Pritzker recognition," Designboom.com, April 18, 2013, http://www.designboom.com/architecture/denise-scott-brown-calls-for-inclusion-in-pritzker-recognition/?utm_campaign=daily&utm_medium=e-mail&utm_source=subscribers (accessed February 12, 2014); Women In Design, "Petitioning Martha Thorne, Executive Director," Change.org, https://www.change.org/petitions/the-pritzker-architecture-prize-committee-recognize-denise-scott-brown-for-her-work-in-robert-venturi-s-1991-prize (accessed February 12, 2014); Gareth Cook, "What about Denise?," Culture Desk of The New York Times, April 15, 2013, http://www.newyorker.com/online/blogs/culture/2013/04/what-about-denise.html (accessed February 12, 2014); Carolina A. Miranda, "Pritzker Architecture Prize Committee Denies Honors for Denise Scott Brown," Architectmagazine.com, June 14, 2014, http://www.architectmagazine.com/design/pritzker-architecture-prize-committee-refuses-to-honor-denise-scott-brown.aspx (accessed February 12, 2014); AD Editorial Team, "Twitterverse responds to Pritzker's Rejection of Denise Scott Brown Petition" June 16, 2013, ArchDaily, http://www.archdaily.com/?p=389103 (accessed February 12, 2014); Despina Stratigakos, "Unforgetting Women Architects: From the Pritzker to Wikipedia," *The Design Observer Places,* http://places.designobserver.com/feature/unforgetting-women-architects-from-pritzker-to-wikipedia/37912/ (accessed February 12, 2014). For a critical analysis of the Pritzker award see the article by Hilde Heynen, "Genius, Gender and Architecture: The Star System as Exemplified in the Pritzker Prize," *Architectural Theory Review,* 17: 2-3, 2012, 331-345.

9. 2012 FAIA Announcement, The American Institute of Architects, http://www.aia.org/practicing/awards/2012/fellows/index.htm (accessed October 7, 2012).

10. Robert Pear, "Obama Reaffirms Insurers Must Cover Contraception," *New York Times,* January 20, 2012, http://www.nytimes.com/2012/01/21/health/policy/administration-rules-insurers-must-cover-contraceptives.html?scp=5&sq=health%20care%20mandate%20and%20contraception%20coverage&st=cse (accessed March 14, 2012).

11. Laura Bassett, "Obama Birth Control Compromise Announced [UPDATE], *Huffington Post,* February 10, 2012, http://www.huffingtonpost.com/2012/02/10/obama-birth-control_n_1267677.html (accessed May 16, 2012).

12. Robert Pear, "Passions Flare as House Debates Birth Control Rule," *New York Times,* February 17, 2012, http://www.nytimes.com/2012/02/17/us/politics/birth-control-coverage-rule-debated-at-house-hearing.html?scp=3&sq=congressional%20hearing%20on%20contraception&st=cse (accessed May 16, 2012).

13. Jen Doll, "Why Are Men Dominating the Debate About Birth Control for Women?" *The Atlantic Wire,* February 16, 2012, www.theatlanticwire.com/national/2012/02/why-are-men-dominating-debate-about-birth-control-women/48809/ (accessed May 16, 2012).

14. J. Lester Feder, "Carolyn Maloney, Eleanor Holmes Norton walk out of contraception hearing," *Politico Pro,* February 16, 2012, http://www.politico.com/news/stories/0212/72971.html (accessed May 16, 2012).

15. Doll 2012.

16. Anne-Marie Slaughter, "Why Women Still Can't Have It All," *The Atlantic* July/August 2012, http://www.theatlantic.com/magazine/archive/2012/07/why-women-still-cant-have-it-all/309020/ (accessed October 6, 2012).

17. Ibid.

18. Ibid.

19. Ibid.

20. Ibid.

21. Ibid.

22. Ibid.

23. Ibid.

24. Ibid.

25. Ibid.

26. Anne-Marie Slaughter, "The 'Having It All' Debate Convinced me to Stop Saying 'Having It All," *The Atlantic* July 2, 2012, http://www.theatlantic.com/business/archive/2012/07/the-having-it-all-debate-convinced-me-to-stop-saying-having-it-all/259284/# (accessed October 6, 2012); Anne-Marie Slaughter, interview by Katie Couric, "Can Women have it All?," Aspen Ideas Festival, 2012, http://www.aspenideas.org/session/can-women-have-it-all (accessed October 6, 2012).

27. Kate Bolick, "Single People Deserve Work-Life Balance, Too," *The Atlantic* June 28, 2012, accessed October 6, 2012, http://www.theatlantic.com/business/archive/2012/06/single-people-deserve-work-life-balance-too/259071/.

28. Slaughter "Why Women Still Can't Have It All" 2012.

29. Linda Hirschman, "The 'Having-It-All' Crisis Isn't About Women, It's About the 1%", *The Atlantic,* June 27, 2012, http://www.theatlantic.com/business/archive/2012/06/the-having-it-all-crisis-isnt-about-women-its-about-the-1/258894/ (accessed October 6, 2012).

30. For more including access to online videos of the speakers please see http://www.archiparlour.org/transform-a-quick-recap-with-pictures/.

31. For an overview of Dunn & Hillam Architects, please go to http://dunnhillam.com.au/.

32. Holding Pattern for MoMA PS1: Interboro Partners, "Holding Pattern Competition Entry," 2011, http://www.interboropartners.net/2011/holding-pattern/ (accessed October 10, 2012); "Holding Pattern by Interboro Partners," MoMA PS1 Young Architects Program, 2011, http://momaps1.org/yap/view/14 (accessed February 12, 2014).

33. Lori A. Brown, "Introduction," *Feminist Practices: Interdisciplinary Approaches to Women in Architecture* (Surrey, England: Ashgate Publishing Limited, 2011).

34. Lori A. Brown, "Conclusion," *Feminist Practices: Interdisciplinary Approaches to Women in Architecture* (Surrey, England: Ashgate Publishing Limited, 2011), 367.

35. Ibid, 368.

36. Brown, "Introduction," 4.

37. Ibid.

38. Please see www.architeXX.org for more information.

39. Gabrielle Esperdy, "The Incredible True Adventures of the Architectress in America," September 10, 2012, *The Design Observer Places,* http://places.designobserver.com/feature/incredible-true-adventures-of-the-architectress-in-america/35578/ (accessed October 8, 2012).

40. Ibid.

41. Ibid.

42. Despina Stratigakos, "Why Architects Need Feminism," *The Design Observer Places* September 12, 2012, http://places.designobserver.com/feature/why-architects-need-feminism/35448/ (accessed October 8, 2012).

43. "Feminist Practices: Pedagogy" roundtable discussion, Van Alen Institute Bookstore, March 21, 2012, New York, NY.

44. Ibid.

45. Peter Reyner Banham Fellow, UB School of Architecture and Planning, http://ap.buffalo.edu/People/faculty/facultyfellows/banham-fellow.html (accessed December 23, 2013).

46. Reyner Banham, "A Black Box The Secret Profession of Architecture," *A Critic Writes* (Berkeley: University of California Press, 1999), 294, 297–99.

47. Lori A. Brown, *Contested Spaces: Abortion Clinics, Women's Shelters and Hospitals* (Surrey, England: Ashgate Publishing, 2013), chapter 1.

48. Peter Blundell Jones, Doina Petrescu and Jeremy Hill, "Introduction," in *Architecture and Participation,* eds. Peter Blundell Jones, Doina Petrescu and Jeremy Hill (London: Spon Press, 2005), "Introduction," xiv.

49. Jones et al. 2005: "Introduction": xv, xvi.

50. Faculty Profile NYU Steinhardt School of Culture, Education and Human Development, http://steinhardt.nyu.edu/faculty_bios/view/Natalie_Jeremijenko (accessed October 13, 2012).

51. David Case, "An Engineer for the Avant Garde," *Yale Alumni Magazine* March/April 2004, 2012, http://www.yalealumnimagazine.com/issues/2004_03/jeremijenko.html (accessed October 13).

52. "Beyond Patronage" symposium abstract February 2012.

53. Yale Law Women 2012 Top Ten Family Friendly Firms, http://www.law.yale.edu/stuorgs/topten.htm (accessed October 9, 2012).

54. Heidi Gottfried, "Introduction Engaging Women's Communities: Dilemmas and Contradictions in Feminist Research," *Feminism and Social Change: Bridging Theory and Practice,* ed. Heidi Gottfried (Urbana: University of Illinois Press, 1996), 14.

55. "2011 Report on Accreditation in Architecture Education," The National Architectural Accrediting Board, Inc. (March 2012), 28-30.

56. Despina Stratigakos, "Why Architects Need Feminism," *The Design Observer Places,* September 12, 2012, http://places.designobserver.com/feature/why-architects-need-feminism/35448/ (accessed October 8, 2012).

57. Ibid.

58. Ibid.

59. Reyner Banham, "A Black Box The Secret Profession of Architecture," *A Critic Writes* (Berkeley: University of California Press, 1999), 294, 297–99.

A conversation with

Lori
BROWN

by

Gabrielle Printz

///

Gabrielle Printz:

> Lori, I have to say that I was incredibly impacted by your
> talk that concluded the symposium. I remember coming away from
> it thinking, "Yes, exactly!" You had explicitly and thought-
> fully articulated the issues that were for us implicit in the
> structure of the symposium — that is, getting a bunch of women
> architects in a room to talk about different ways they were
> operating in practice. You really made explicit this funda-
> mental statement that gender — and more broadly, privilege —
> and architecture are *still* inextricable. This really resounded
> with me, having been the only woman in a graduate design
> studio, but also because I'm struck by how quickly people
> are willing to assert that gender is no longer a factor,
> that equity has been achieved and we shouldn't talk about it
> anymore. So, in light of this reticence to even acknowledge
> gender, I wonder if you could first talk about what it means
> to vocalize this problem? What does it mean to invoke feminism
> (a word that few are willing to use) in architecture? Is it a
> conversation that necessarily precipitates action? Or is it a
> matter of awareness, of acknowledging that an issue persists?

Lori Brown:

> I believe I would begin with awareness. For me, just bringing
> awareness is the first step forward. People may think this is
> the norm, or that it only happens to me, or see it as only a
> woman's issue. But we know, and it has been proven over and
> over again, that women's issues are everyone's issues. If we
> improve the lives of women and bring more equity to women, it
> raises the bar for everyone. If we do not state it, say it out
> loud, people can continue to ignore it and pretend it does not
> exist. I then hope action will follow from the vocalizing.

GP:

> What about for women architects who see their gender as irrel-
> evant to their practice? How do we initiate a conversation
> about women in architecture when some of them don't want to
> take part in that conversation?

LB:

> I would say they are kidding themselves on so many levels.
> It is not about talent or ability - in this, women are just
> as capable and daring as men. But the discipline has been a
> man's discipline for centuries with very little tolerance,

support, or mentoring for those who are not male. The mantra
for so many successful women who I have heard speak is that I
worked hard, sacrificed, and made my way to the top. But it is
just so naïve not to acknowledge institutional privilege and
patronage that has participated in peoples' successes. It is
more difficult for women both in offices and out on job sites. I
think Hilda Heynen's essay "Genius, Gender and Architecture:
the Star System as Exemplified in the Pritkzer Prize" (in
Architectural Theory Review 17: 2-3, 331-345) articulates this
very well. Those women who do make it to the pinnacle of
architecture rarely acknowledge these difficulties because they
do not want to seem different from their male peers. But I
argue that is exactly what we need to do. We must have these
conversations publicly and call out difficulties and inequities. How else is the discipline, both out in practice and
within the academy, going to change?

How do we address this issue, both in academia and practice?
As someone who straddles that divide, I wonder what approaches
you find are required for these different architectural communities? Especially because this symposium, the product of an
academic cohort and context, attempted to bridge academia
and practice together by acknowledging new work of women
practitioners for a primarily academic audience, I wonder
if you think there is transference between the way we move
beyond patronage, beyond gender-bias, in schools and in the
profession?

Well, I certainly hope so! I actually think it is critical
to have transference between the two. I know for decades the
academy and practice have seen themselves as two very distinct
and different realms. I was educated under that model. The
longer I teach and continue to have a practice, the more it
becomes clear that we must collaborate and work together.
Intellectually, I understand why the distinctions have
existed, but I really think they are at cross-purposes in the

Jackson Women's Health Organization
Jackson, MS

longer run, for the discipline of architecture. It is important to think about this in phases. If I educate my students
within different and more diverse pedagogical approaches
and definitions of what architectural spatial practices can
be, this will begin to have a trickle-up effect. In turn,
publicity and acknowledgement come to those whose practices
are challenging the status quo of architecture. There has to
be change from the middle. Architecture will further distance
itself from real world problems and solutions if it continues
to be something that only the elite and wealthy can afford.
I also believe that large corporate offices need to be held
accountable. How many women partners and principals are in
these firms? Why haven't they been more proactive in promoting
women into positions of leadership? And in turn, what support
mechanisms are in place for all to have families and better
work/life balance?

GP: I wonder, as a practitioner oriented toward advocacy, how you
see yourself as a political actor, and how you situate that
activism? It seems that this takes place for you both outside
the profession (thinking about redefining landscapes of access
to women's health services) and within it, with efforts like
the Women in Architecture campaign. The focus of your research
and the topic of your new book is "Contested Spaces," and it
seems that the field in which you operate is itself a contested
space. Would you agree?

LB: Yes, very much so, although I do not want the immediate
assumption to be one of antagonism - sometimes it is and sometimes it is not. I think the more invested I have become in
researching and working for and within these politicized and
contested realms — to bring architecture into contact and
engagement with quotidian space — the more responsible as a
political actor I have become. My research and my intellectual location stem from asking myself: how can I just sit
on the sidelines and not be more instrumental? At what point
does and can action occur? These relationships have evolved
as my creative practice has evolved. I purposefully seek out
research and design projects that are political and politi-
cizing. For example, with my recent book, the research into
and interviewing of abortion providers led to the idea of
creating a design competition for the only clinic remaining
in Mississippi. They need design services to create a more
secure, private and aesthetically responsible fence around
their building. Architects should be involved in this, and I
realized I need to make this happen because no one else will.
The research led to the design action that will be taking
place in the near future.

So, how do I situate my activism? That is a difficult question
because it is not premeditated but responsive, reactive,
and adaptive. My activism seeks to raise the awareness of
students, the discipline, and the general public about ways
to improve the built environment for everyone. My activism
is inspired by the idea that our built environment is important and that architects and designers must be more critically
engaged in improving it, and that our discipline must be far
more reflective of our societal composition in order to engage
the broadest and most diverse groups as possible — to have the
largest effects possible.

287 MEN PHARMACISTS

175 WOMEN PHARMACISTS

66% MALE PHARMACIST PERCENTAGE THAT DO NOT CARRY PLAN B

34% MALE PHARMACIST PERCENTAGE THAT CARRY PLAN B

55% FEMALE PHARMACIST PERCENTAGE THAT DO NOT CARRY PLAN B

45% FEMALE PHARMACIST PERCENTAGE THAT CARRY PLAN B

62% ♂ | 38% ♀ | 62% | 38% PB | 7%

PHARMACY STATISTICS

Mississippi_Pharmacies

LEGEND   # OF PHARMACIES   DOES NOT STOCK PLAN B   STOCKS PLAN B

"no one working on staff will sell it today"

"we sure don't" 46   24   20

19

"don't know what it is"

"need prescription, can't find non-perscription kind"

14   14   13   10

"have 9 expired pills"

"never had a call for it before"

"we stock but I won't dispense it"

Mississippi Pharmacies: These statistics are based on the results from calling all the pharmacies in the state in 2007. The question was asked "Do you sell emergency contraception? Can I fill my prescription?" At the time of calling, you still needed a prescription to access this medication if younger than 18 years of age.

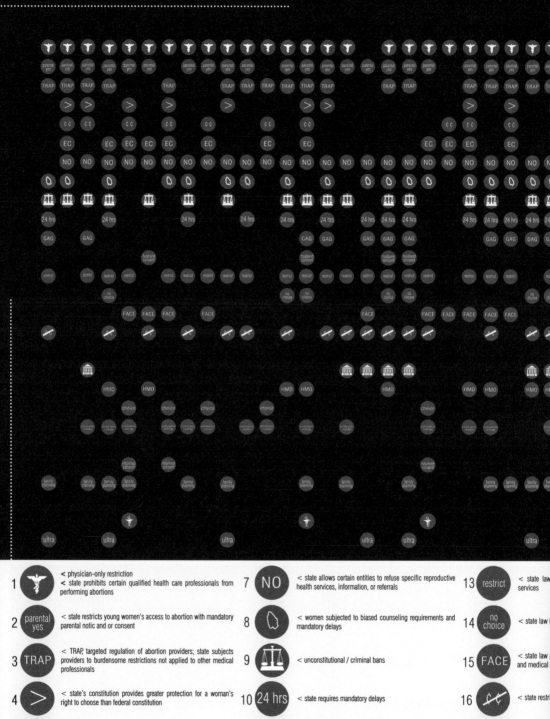

1 < physician-only restriction
< state prohibits certain qualified health care professionals from performing abortions

2 parental yes < state restricts young women's access to abortion with mandatory parental notic and or consent

3 TRAP < TRAP, targeted regulation of abortion providers; state subjects providers to burdensome restrictions not applied to other medical professionals

4 > < state's constitution provides greater protection for a woman's right to choose than federal constitution

5 ¢ ¢ < state provides low-income women access to abortion

6 EC < state allows women greater access to emergency contraception

7 NO < state allows certain entities to refuse specific reproductive health services, information, or referrals

8 < women subjected to biased counseling requirements and mandatory delays

9 < unconstitutional / criminal bans

10 24 hrs < state requires mandatory delays

11 GAG < state prohibits certain state employees or organizations receiving state funds from counseling or referring women for abortion services

12 husband consent < unconstitutional and unenforceable law mandating husband notice and/or consent before married woman may obtain abortion

13 restrict < state law ...
services

14 no choice < state law i...

15 FACE < state law ...
and medical ...

16 ¢ ¢ < state restri...

17 $ < certain sta...
state funds fo...

18 < state proh...
abortions

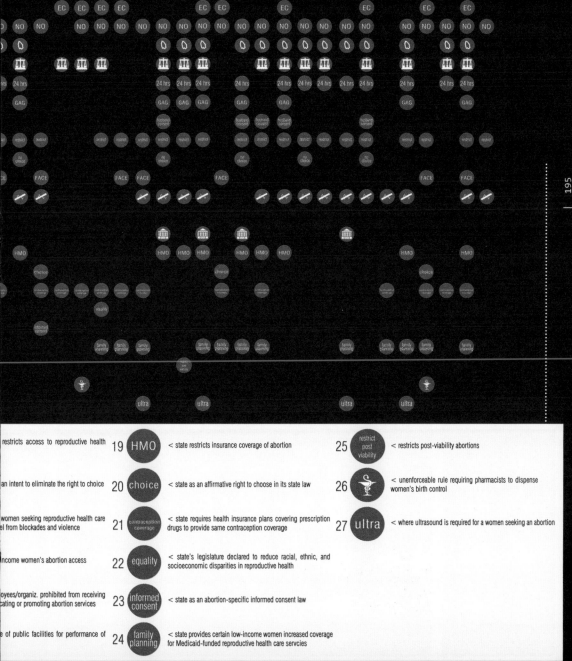

restricts access to reproductive health

19 **HMO** < state restricts insurance coverage of abortion

25 **restrict post viability** < restricts post-viability abortions

an intent to eliminate the right to choice

20 **choice** < state as an affirmative right to choose in its state law

26 < unenforceable rule requiring pharmacists to dispense women's birth control

women seeking reproductive health care el from blockades and violence

21 **contraception coverage** < state requires health insurance plans covering prescription drugs to provide same contraception coverage

27 **ultra** < where ultrasound is required for a women seeking an abortion

ncome women's abortion access

22 **equality** < state's legislature declared to reduce racial, ethnic, and socioeconomic disparities in reproductive health

oyees/organiz. prohibited from receiving cating or promoting abortion services

23 **informed consent** < state as an abortion-specific informed consent law

e of public facilities for performance of

24 **family planning** < state provides certain low-income women increased coverage for Medicaid-funded reproductive health care servcies

GP: Maybe you could talk about the Women in Architecture campaign you've initiated with Nina Freedman, which outlines a set of specific actions to further the interests and agency of women in our field. Now that you've been funded, have you been able to operationalize some of the strategies outlined in your proposal?

LB: We are in the process of doing exactly that. Now that we have our identity and tagline — "ArchiteXX, we ask how, not Y" — we are developing our website. We believe this will be critical as an aggregate for activities, actions, mentoring, reading group literature, and blogging. We are also in the process of helping to establish umbrella Women in Architecture groups in all of the New York State accredited architecture programs. The group will also organize the competition for the Mississippi clinic, as our first design action. Additionally, we are hosting our first workshop with the Wage Project. They will be working with women in New York City, learning more about the wage difference between women and men, how to better determine our value, and how to become better negotiators.

GP: Because the issue continues to make itself relevant, I wonder if you might comment on the petition to seek Pritzker attribution for Denise Scott Brown? What does the (failed) attempt to rectify her non-recognition now mean for current and future architectural attribution, particularly in partnerships like hers or that of last year's Pritzker awardee, Wang Shu, and his partner, Lu Wenyu?

LB: This was really disappointing, on many levels, and revealed the entrenchment of those in power within the architectural establishment. The fact that the Pritzker Prize Committee did not include Lu Wenyu last year further confirms they are not

ArchiteXX wordmark and tagline

interested in being at the forefront of more equitable practices and partnerships in architecture. Sometime either before
or after the failed attempt by Harvard GSD students, Caroline
James and Arielle Assouline-Lichten, on behalf of Denise Scott
Brown, I read that Robert Venturi felt compelled to accept the
Pritzker Prize because of the help the monetary award could
provide their practice at that particular point in time. It is
understandable, as $100K is a lot of money. I believe there
needs to be more public outrage about these types of award
practices, and I think there should be a boycott until the
Pritzker Prize award pool becomes diversified to include women
and people of color.

We might also think about Despina Stratigakos' essay,
"Unforgetting Women: From the Pritzker to Wikipedia," in
Places, about battling the erasure of women architects. How
much of our efforts must be aimed at reconstructing histories
as opposed to creating opportunities for new women practitioners? Does one enable the other?

I actually do not consider these two to be oppositional,
but rather, as you suggest, more mutually beneficial. I think
Despina makes a really important point in her essay about how
we all must take responsibility and participate in writing
our history. This requires diligence and coordinated efforts
- something that needs more attention than I think anyone
realized prior to her article.

Of course, if the history of our profession offers only white
male heroes, it's harder to imagine a future of architecture
that equally represents women and people of color. It seems
we need to make an effort to identify examples for graduates
and young practitioners coming up in this landscape. How do
you see the role of mentorship in seeking gender equity in the
profession?

I believe it is absolutely critical. I led the Women in
Architecture panel last month at the New York State AIA annual
conference, and one of the speakers quoted Marian Wright
Edelman, Founder & President of Children's Defense Fund, "You
can't be what you can't see." This is precisely one of the
problems. How are young women and people of color going to
know that they can be architects if they do not see people
like themselves as role models? I believe this mentoring must
begin in school and continue throughout the profession. One
may be fortunate enough to have a great mentor or mentors, as
I have, but there are far more people without them and this is
reflected by the lack of diversity at the upper reaches of both
academia and practice. For example, there are only 22 female
deans out of 154 accredited professional programs in the US -
a mere 14% of all top leadership is female. We need at least
half of all deans to be women, and for there to be advocacy
for broader diversity in hiring and lecture series. If our
student bodies are essentially half and half, why are our
faculties not reflective of this as well? They sure should be!

Before & Beyond:
Re-articulating Practice
in the Academy

Gabrielle Printz

Beyond Patronage is a provocation. It is the beginning of a conversation in architecture — an increasingly discursive practice — one
that actively engages voices that are typically under-represented
in conventional design practices. The notion of patronage-centered
practice conjures an exchange between two individuals: the architect, the idiosyncratic creative hero and often the sole advocate
for a vision that is irreducibly *his;* and the patron, the bene-
ficiary and enabler of that vision. Beyond Patronage not only
confronts the exclusivity of this exchange, but also suggests how
it — architecture-as-conversation — can be more meaningful in its
delivery.

Each of the roles that we've outlined in this book, the emerging
roles that provided the framework of the symposium, introduces
ways of altering and expanding this conversation. The Architect
as Initiator sets new terms for design delivery by instigating
conversations with unlikely parties. Hansy Better Barazza and
Linda Taalman have made novel partnerships with community groups,
institutions, and fabricators, to create new design opportunities.
In rendering information visible, the Architect as Detective
treats both the subject and the audience of her research much more
expansively. For Juliette Spertus, Georgeen Theodore, and Natalie
Jeremijenko, discovery is the result of a participatory exchange.
The Architect as Advocate actively seeks out often marginalized
voices, those without the privilege to access architectural

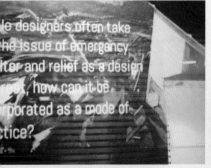

services, and puts forward agendas that aren't typically articulated in architectural projects. Lola Sheppard and Yolande Daniels both pursue projects that attempt to resolve or illuminate much broader social concerns, for remote communities, in Lola's case, and for historically disadvantaged subjects, in Yolande's work.

So, who is doing the talking?

The symposium was, by design, a forum for the work of these exciting women practitioners, a response to the gendered history of architectural patronage, discussed by Lori Brown in her concluding talk at the conference and in the previous chapter. The content of the symposium is not such that it explicitly engages so-called "women's issues" in architecture, but instead acknowledges that women practitioners — who are critically under-recognized — are operating in really exceptional ways, often on the fringe of the mainstream, predominantly male profession.

Although we are talking about practice, this symposium was the product of an academic cohort and context, presented by three professors and a student for both an academic and professional audience. Additionally, the symposium speakers and contributors to this book include practitioners, many of whom are also faculty members at other universities, where much of their work is conducted through teaching and research with students. It is perhaps through such hybridized engagement in the profession and the academy that a designer can more readily develop a reflective practice.

The university offers a liminal enclave of design experimentation, outside of building-making proper, positioned somewhere before and ahead of it. Productive synergies between faculty-practitioners and students are especially well positioned for investigation in this theoretical territory of 'beyond.' The symposium deliberately put these two voices of the discipline in conversation. Consequently, in its consideration of new models of practice, Beyond Patronage also suggests a new model for the way these discussions take place in the academy, namely that students contribute as significantly as faculty in structuring the discourse, as well as in contributing content. It's not often that a student is involved in engineering events — now publications — of this kind. As the student in question, I was particularly invested in promoting a discursive environment at the university that actively included students.

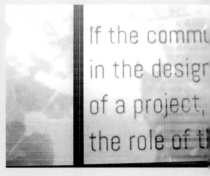

Gabrielle Printz

Student as Instigator was the event that opened the symposium. It was the result of this interest in propagating a more participatory conversation about post-patronage practice, which itself is interested in a more participatory landscape of design practice. Structured as a 'bottom-up' discussion, the Student as Instigator event dispersed the attending crowd into six 'tangents,' where six students presented their work as it coincided with several self-defined practice models. Architect as Organizer, Alleviator, Advocate, Futurologist and Speculator described studio work, thesis research, and independent projects that address design problems by way of redefining how the architect delivers design services. Brijhette Farmer's Architect as Alleviator suggested how architects can work with policymakers to better provide disaster relief. My project with Joseph Wassell positioned the architect as an anti-developer of the high-rise construction of failing corporations, dealing with vacancy as both financial and conceptual speculations. The Architect as Organizer, presented by Joseph Swerdlin, suggested a mode in which the architect not only engages with community stake-holders, but actually assumes the role of community organizer.

In addition to these projects and proposed roles, the students also posed their own questions about changing notions of 'client' and what exactly constitutes architectural services, among other things. Participants in these conversations could respond, ask their own questions, or even scribble notes on the project boards. All of this resulted in a dynamic exchange, wherein the power differential that usually structures lectures or panels — conventional formats for academic discourse — was distributed across a diverse crowd of participants.

As part exhibition, part critique, and part introduction to the "beyond patronage" ethos — all generated by students — the event included students as agents of this transformation of practice. Mutually, in the confluence of academia and practice, the event also demonstrated to students in attendance that there are other ways of operating as architects. "Beyond patronage" is especially meaningful in the academy for this reason. Students who formulate ideas about *practice* — not just the *what* or *why* of architecture, but *how* and *for whom* — can, upon graduation, operationalize values and interests which, for many, do not leave the studio or are squelched by the realities of delivering conventional architectural services.

"Beyond" is as much a temporal descriptor as it is spatial; it not only describes work that reaches outside of the discipline or occupies the fringes of current architectural practice, but dually indicates a future of the way we *might* do architecture and, in fact, the way we *must* do architecture. While the political, economic, ecological and technological climate continues to present new challenges to those entering the profession, it also presents a host of new design opportunities, and new groups and concerns in need of architectural services. As a participant in this conversation, the student as future practitioner is not only subject to, but also implicated in, this critical redefinition of architectural practice. "Beyond patronage" is indeed critical of the history of patronage, of the still-gendered landscape of architectural practice, but it's not simply a response. Rather, "beyond patronage" constitutes a transformative beginning to 21st century architectural practice. In the mutuality of academic and practice-based exploration, we can continue to redefine architectures beyond patronage.

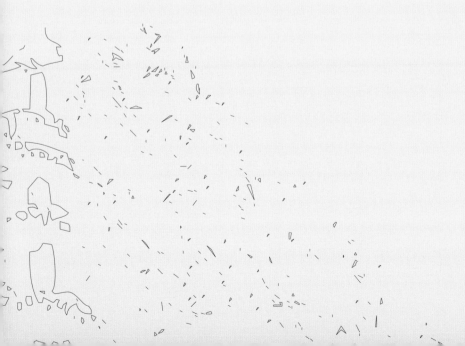

<u>Micaela Barker</u> is pursuing a dual Master of Architecture and Urban Planning degree at the University at Buffalo School of Architecture and Planning. Currently, she is teaching in the first year design studio, and has previously worked as a project manager at the firm architecture+ in Troy, NY.
issuu.com/micaelabarker/

<u>Hansy Better Barraza</u> is an architect and Associate Professor of Architecture at Rhode Island School of Design. From Barranquilla, Colombia, she received a B. Arch. from Cornell University and a M. Arch. in Urban Design from the Harvard Graduate School of Design. She cofounded Studio Luz Architects, with Anthony Piermarini. She also cofounded the nonprofit BR-A-CE in 2011.
studioluz.net/, http://br-a-ce.org/

<u>Martha Bohm</u> is an Assistant Professor in the Department of Architecture at the University at Buffalo. Her research interests include finding ways to integrate analytical tools into design processes in order to better see the unseeable. She earned a Master of Architecture at the University of Oregon and a Bachelor of Arts in Earth and Planetary Sciences from Harvard University.
ap.buffalo.edu/

<u>Lori Brown</u> is an architect whose work lies at the intersections of Architecture, Art, Geography, and Women's Studies. In 2012, she co-launched with Nina Freedman, ArchiteXX, a women and architecture group in New York City. Brown received a Bachelor of Science degree from the Georgia Institute of Technology and the Ecole d'Architecture in Paris, and a Master of Architecture from Princeton University.
www.labpractices.net, www.architexx.org

<u>Kim Dai</u> is a designer with a background in architecture and theatre. Currently a theatre planning and lighting design specialist at Schuler Shook, she received a Bachelor of Science in Architecture and a Bachelor of Arts in Theatrical Design from the University at Buffalo, SUNY.
daixdesign.wordpress.com

<u>Yolande Daniels</u> is co-founding design principal of studioSUMO. She received architecture degrees from Columbia University and City College of New York, and has taught at Massachusetts Institute of Technology, Columbia University, City College, the University of Michigan, and held the Silcott Chair at Howard University. Her work examines architecture and the politics of space.
www.studiosumo.com , www.momonyc.com

<u>Stephanie Davidson</u> studied architecture at Dalhousie University in Halifax, Canada and the Architectural Association in London, England after obtaining a degree in Studio Art from Mount Allison University. She has worked in offices in Montreal, Canada; Vienna, Austria; Cologne and Berlin, Germany, and currently practices with her partner, Georg Rafailidis, as Davidson Rafailidis.
davidsonrafailidis.net

<u>Joyce Hwang</u> is an Associate Professor of Architecture at the University at Buffalo, SUNY, and the Director of Ants of the Prairie, an office of architectural practice and research that focuses on confronting contemporary ecological conditions through creative means. Hwang received a post-professional M.Arch degree from Princeton University and a B.Arch degree from Cornell University.
www.antsoftheprairie.com

<u>Natalie Jerimijenko</u> is an artist, engineer and director of the Environmental Health Clinic at NYU, where she is an Associate Professor in the Visual Art Department and affiliated with the Computer Science Department and Environmental Studies program. Her degrees are in biochemistry, engineering, neuroscience, and History and Philosophy of Science. Her projects have been exhibited internationally.
www.environmentalhealthclinic.net

Jon King is an architectural designer from Cazenovia, New York. He received a Master of Architecture and Bachelor of Science in Architecture from the University at Buffalo, where he also taught a first year studio. He is currently working at Popli Design Group in Rochester, New York.

Gabrielle Printz is a designer from the San Francisco Bay Area. With degrees in Political Science and Art History from Canisius College, she received a Master of Architecture from the University at Buffalo, where she also taught first year design studio. Her work examines spatial-political issues surrounding bodies, gender and technology. She is currently pursuing a Master of Science in Critical, Curatorial and Conceptual Practices in Architecture at Columbia University.
gabrielleprintz.com

Lola Sheppard is an Associate Professor at the University of Waterloo, and is a partner in Lateral Office, based in Toronto, which she co-founded with Mason White. She is a co-editor of the publication series Bracket. She received her Bachelor of Architecture from McGill University and a Master of Architecture from Harvard Graduate School of Design.
lateraloffice.com

Juliette Spertus is an architect focused on improving the urban environment through projects that bypass conventional boundaries between infrastructure planning and urban design. In 2010, she created the exhibit Fast Trash: Roosevelt Island's Pneumatic Tubes and the Future of Cities and the online resource fasttrash.org. She received a BA in Art History from Williams College and a professional architecture degree from l'Ecole d'Architecture des Villes et des Territoires in Marne-la-Vallée, France.
closedloops.net

Despina Stratigakos is an architectural historian with an overarching interest in gender and modernity in European cities, and has published widely on issues of diversity in architecture. Stratigakos received her Ph.D. from Bryn Mawr College and taught at Harvard University and the University of Michigan before joining the faculty at the University of Buffalo's Department of Architecture, where she is currently an Associate Professor.
ap.buffalo.edu

Joseph Swerdlin is an architectural designer, currently working at OFFICE KGDVS in Brussels, Belgium. After graduating from University at Buffalo in 2013, he interned with Ants of the Prairie/Joyce Hwang, Storefront for Art and Architecture, CLOG, and The Morpholio Project. He is co-founder of super•fluous, an illustrated compendium of architectural explorations.
supersuper-fluous.tumblr.com

Linda Taalman currently leads her company IT House Inc., and simultaneously directs her studio Taalman Architecture, formerly Taalman Koch Architecture. She explores architecture collaboratively through investigations into building technologies and systems, integrating sustainability, practicality and ingenuity. Taalman is an Associate Professor of Architecture at Woodbury University. She received a Bachelor of Architecture from the Cooper Union, and cofounded OpenOffice arts + architecture collaborative.
www.taalmankoch.com, www.taalmanarchitecture.com

Georgeen Theodore is an architect, urban designer, and Associate Professor at New Jersey Institute of Technology's College of Architecture and Design, where she is the Director of the Infrastructure Planning program. She received a Bachelor of Architecture from Rice University and a Master of Architecture in Urban Design from Harvard University's Graduate School of Design. Theodore is a founding partner and principal of Interboro, a New York City-based architecture and planning research office.
www.interboropartners.net

Robert Yoos, an M.Arch candidate at the Yale School of Architecture, is from Kings Park, New York and received a Bachelor of Science in Architecture from the University at Buffalo. He is currently working for Handel Architects in New York City and has previously worked for Hollwich Kushner (HWKN) and Ants of the Prairie.

Beyond Patronage editors are Martha Bohm, Joyce Hwang, and Gabrielle Printz.

The book designer is Joel Brenden.

Editorial Assistants are Joseph Swerdlin and Robert Yoos.

Copyeditors of essays and conversations are Gregory Proefrock and Trenton Van Epps.

Conversations and discussions were transcribed by Verbal Ink.

Thank you to the University at Buffalo School of Architecture and Planning and the New York State Council on the Arts (Architecture, Planning and Design Program, Independent Projects Grant), and Storefront for Art and Architecture for making this book possible.

Thank you also to Actar for believing in our project and making this book a reality.

Our work on this book began as a follow-up to the Martell Symposium—Beyond Patronage: Reconsidering Models of Practice, an event hosted by the University at Buffalo, School of Architecture and Planning in October 2012. We would like to thank and recognize the many individuals and organizations that helped support the symposium and launch this project.

The Martell Symposium was made possible with generous sponsorship from Christopher and Sally Martell, the University at Buffalo Gender Institute, the Buffalo School of Architecture and Planning, and the Department of Architecture.

We would like to thank Robert Shibley, Omar Khan, and Kari Winter for their leadership in making Beyond Patronage possible, and additionally for participating as introductory speakers at the event.

Exploration of the symposium's theme initiated in 2011 in a collaborative effort between Joyce Hwang and Shannon Phillips, who also co-organized the event with the editors.

We are also grateful to Denise Juron-Borgese and Bhakti Sharma of the Buffalo Architecture Foundation for organizing a 6Mbs Pro Bono Panel Discussion as part of the day's events. Thank you also to the speakers in this session: Courtney Creenan, Joy Kuebler, and Kathy Callesto.

University at Buffalo faculty and staff were instrumental in supporting our efforts. Thanks especially to: Despina Stratigakos for her enthusiastic support and constant advice; Stephanie Davidson for moderating the Architect-as Initiator panel and starting off the day with a great discussion; and Bill McDonnell for being our go-to person for any and all logistical questions. Also thank you to: Subbiah Manthraram, Rachel Teaman, Doug Mccallum, Maryanne Schultz, Alexandra Maier, Jennifer Oakley, Annette Lecuyer, Nick Bruscia, Mark Shepard, Sergio López-Piñeiro, Jordan Geiger, Barbara Carlson, Debra Eggebrecht, Marion Brush, Susan McDonald, Al Ermanovics, Jim Korta, Bryan Sidorowicz, Pat Donovan, and Jonathon Welch.

Many UB students (and alumni) also actively participated in the symposium. Gabrielle Printz—the symposium's graduate student co-organizer—orchestrated an event, Student as Instigator, that engaged speakers and audience members in series of student-initiated discussion sessions. These groups were led by Printz, Joseph Wassell, Micaela Barker, Brijhette Farmer, Michael Lempert, Jesse Pringle, and Joseph Swerdlin. Additionally, thanks to the following student assistants: Peter Foti, Robert Yoos, Sarah Holtzer, Brian Fentzke, Kim Dai, Danielle Krug, Alex Galante, Vincent Ribeiro, Kevin Schildwaster, Alex Neubauer, Adam Feldman, Dan Vrana, Ariel Resnick, Whitney Vanhouten, Jon King, Christa Trautman, and Bryan Lee.

The symposium was enhanced by a number of outstanding businesses and organizations. We are pleased to recognize the following service providers: Kleinhans Music Hall, Darwin Martin House Restoration Corporation, University at Buffalo Center for the Arts, Talking Leaves Bookshop, Onion Studio, Current Catering, Oliver's Restaurant, Bacchus, Globe Market, Carriage Trade Pastries, and Embassy Suites Hotel in Buffalo.